THE PROCESS
OF COUNSELING
AND THERAPY

D0162136

THE PROCESS OF COUNSELING AND THERAPY

Second Edition

JANET MOURSUND

University of Oregon and
Center for Integrative Therapy
Eugene, Oregon

PRENTICE HALL, Englewood Cliffs, New Jersey 07632

Moursund, Janet.
  The process of counseling and therapy / Janet Moursund.—2nd ed.
    p. cm.
  Bibliography: p.
  Includes index.
  ISBN 0-13-723131-8
  1. Psychotherapy. 2. Counseling.   I. Title.
  [DNLM: 1. Counseling. 2. Psychotherapy. WM 420 M931p]
RC480.M677   1990
616.89′1—dc20
DNLM/DLC
for Library of Congress   89–8852
                                                              CIP

For Claudette, Carol, Mari, and Norma
with gratitude and love

Editorial/production supervision: Lynn Alden Kendall
Interior design: Karen Buck
Cover design: Lundgren Graphics Ltd.
Manufacturing buyer: Ray Keating

© 1990, 1985 by Prentice-Hall, Inc.
A Division of Simon & Schuster
Englewood Cliffs, New Jersey 07632

Printed in the United States of America
10 9 8 7 6 5 4 3 2

ISBN 0-13-723131-8

Prentice-Hall International (UK) Limited, *London*
Prentice-Hall of Australia Pty. Limited, *Sydney*
Prentice-Hall Canada Inc., *Toronto*
Prentice-Hall Hispanoamericana, S.A., *Mexico*
Prentice-Hall of India Private Limited, *New Delhi*
Prentice-Hall of Japan, Inc., *Tokyo*
Simon & Schuster Asia Pte. Ltd., *Singapore*
Editora Prentice-Hall do Brasil, Ltda., *Rio de Janeiro*

CONTENTS

12 THE CARE AND FEEDING OF THERAPISTS 195

REFERENCES 216

INDEX 221

PREFACE

It seems rather odd, somehow, to be sitting down to write the very first part of a book after all the rest has been finished. But that's how prefaces are done—and for very good reason. Most authors, you see, begin to write a book with a pretty clear idea of what the book will be like. But books have a way of changing in midstream, of taking on a life of their own, of growing into something different from what was originally intended or expected. The preface, which serves to introduce the book to the reader, to explain what it's about and why someone should bother to read it, has to be written last, after the author discovers what that book has become.

When I began this book, I thought it would be a quite scholarly volume, heavy on theory, the sort of book I myself have used in teaching graduate courses in counseling and psychotherapy. But the book had other ideas. It wanted to be a practitioner's book, a book about being a clinician. It wanted to talk about the kinds of problems and solutions that people deal with day after day and week after week as they work with real live clients. And who am I, a mere author, to argue with a book-in-the-making? You have to give a book its head, I've learned, or you're likely to break its spirit....

So now I'm writing a preface, to introduce you to *The Process of Counseling and Therapy*, a book which grew out of my typewriter and tells, as honestly as I can, how to be a psychotherapist. It also tells a lot about me, about the kinds of things that are important to me as a therapist, and the kinds of things that are difficult for me, and the kinds of things that work for me. I hope some of them will work for you, too. And I also hope that some of them *won't* be right for you, because every therapist needs to build a unique style, taking and rejecting bits and pieces from all sorts of teachers and models. What you decide not to use from these pages will be as important for you as what you decide to keep, for in the very process of deciding you will be shaping your own personal way of doing therapy, your own way of being in the work.

There are a few things that may be helpful for you to understand before we actually get started. One has to do with pronouns—the bane of every modern American writer, forced to deal with a language that has no unisex words for her or him, he or she, hers or his. My solution has been to refer to the therapist consistently as "she" or "her" and to the client as "he" or "him" (except in cases where a client is obviously and necessarily female). I have two reasons for this choice: first, switching back and forth between masculine and feminine pronouns, in order to balance everything out, is something that I as a reader find confusing. Second, I have frequently been surprised at my own inertial sexist bias, my own unconscious tendency to assume that the "authority" in an ambiguous situation is probably male. If I, a professional woman, well aware of the issues of sexism in our society, still fall victim to this kind of thinking, then it seems likely that many others do too; referring to the therapist (who is usually regarded as a high-status person) as "she" helps to jolt both myself and you, the reader, into a different level of awareness.

Another shortcut I have taken the liberty of using is to omit the words "counselor" and "counseling" from most of the book, in favor of "therapist," "therapy," or "psychotherapy." Using both ("Counselors and psychotherapists..."; "...in the counseling or therapy session...") is cumbersome and unwieldy; switching back and forth seems, again, confusing. While a very good case can be made for differences between counseling and psychotherapy, the exact nature of the differences depends on who happens to be arguing about it. Moreover, it is increasingly true that many psychotherapists do a lot of counseling, and that many counselors do a lot of therapy, and that the dividing line between the two is pretty blurred. This is a book about what I would call "therapy"; it's also a book about what occupies much of the professional life of competent counselors.

The first half of this book is concerned with the general practice of therapy with the individual, "garden variety" client. Chapter 1 begins with a short review of the history of therapy, the variety of therapies being practiced today, and the values and assumptions underlying therapeutic work.

Chapter 2 discusses the foundation skills of therapy: the basic tools which all therapists, regardless of orientation, must master in order to work with clients.

Chapters 3 through 6 move us through the overall course of therapy, from the initial interview to the early stage of therapy, into middle stage work, and finally into the final or termination stage.

The first half of the book, then, is an overview, a general treatment plan, for working with a wide variety of clients. It also sets the stage for the special kinds of therapy situations which are discussed in the second half, when the book shifts from a how-do-we-move-through-therapy focus to a consideration of some of the special demands of various sorts of clients: career counseling, crisis work, groups, couples, families. And, last but not least, the therapist: what she (!) needs in order to continue to do good work with her clients.

Many people have contributed to this book, with or without their knowledge. First on the list is my dean, Dr. Wesley Becker, who helped me take the leave of absence from teaching that started the whole thing. My colleagues in the Division of Counseling and Educational Psychology at the University of Oregon have been both helpful and supportive. My family too: poor dears, they've grown resigned to bagels and cold meat for dinner when a chapter wasn't going smoothly....

My most heartfelt thanks, though, go to those who have patiently walked with me on my road to becoming a competent therapist. Norma Ragsdale, Claudette Hastie, Carol Ormiston, and Mari Panzer, to whom this book is dedicated, were among my first mentors. Roberta Roth encouraged and taught and believed in me, even when I didn't believe in myself. Richard Erskine and Rebecca Trautman taught me much about being a person as well as a therapist. All those with whom I have studied and laughed and wept: Helen, Joe, Karen, Marvin, Sally, George, Jerry, Mary, and many more. My partners, Sue and Lance. And, finally, all the clients who have so courageously worked through their own personal pain and problems, and allowed me to share in that working-through. I owe all of these people more than I can say.

I want to acknowledge the folks who have been so helpful in seeing the book through its final stages: Susan Finnemore, my editor at Prentice Hall; Lundgren Graphics Ltd., which executed the cover design; and Lynn Alden Kendall, production editor. Lastly, thanks are due to Prentice Hall's reviewers; to all of them, many thanks.

In readying this preface for the second edition, I was prepared to do a great deal of tinkering—maybe rewrite the whole thing. Somewhat to my surprise, it wasn't needed. What was true about the way the book wrote itself five years ago is still true today. The basic ideas have not changed. though details have been brought up-to-date. So, again, thanks to mentors, colleagues, clients, friends—and to you, the reader, who took the time to read this preface....

1 FIRST THINGS FIRST

Therapy Then and Now
The Therapy Supermarket
Evaluating Outcomes
Theory, Assumptions, Values

Psychotherapy, says Hilde Bruch, is "a situation where two people interact and try to come to an understanding of one another, with the specific goal of accomplishing something beneficial for the complaining person" (1981, p. 86). It is difficult to argue with a definition like that; but it is difficult to learn much from it, either. Already, in the first sentence of the first paragraph of Chapter 1, we are nose-to-nose with the problem that has plagued students and practitioners of psychotherapy down through the years: if a statement is general enough to apply across the board to what practitioners do, it gives us little practical, concrete information. As soon as our statements and descriptions get specific enough to tell us something useful about what we are doing, we discover that the statement or description no longer fits large segments of our practice. It is the old cliché of the blind men and the elephant all over again; depending on what part you are exploring, therapy is like a rope, or a wall, or a tree, or a bit of garden hose.

This is a book for people who are performing, or who intend to perform, psychotherapy. It is not a book just for psychoanalysts, or just for Gestaltists, or for behaviorists, or for transactional analysts, or Adlerians, or Rogerians, or any other *-ist* or *-ian* who intends to work exclusively within a single framework. It is a book about out there, in-the-trenches working with real clients in real situations. I am a therapist, and I work with real people who have real problems. To do so, I borrow ideas, insights, and techniques from anywhere I can find them. Of course, I have in my head a conceptual underpinning, a theory that helps me understand what I am doing and where I am going. To that extent, I too am an *-ist* or an *-ian,* but the specific variety does not matter. I have not yet shaken hands with a theory that is incompatible with most of the ideas in this book; if you know of one, I would very much appreciate an introduction.

1

Even though this is not going to be a historically or theoretically oriented book, and even though you (and I!) are eager to plunge into the real meat of being with clients, we do need to take a few pages here at the outset to clarify what will happen in the book and to calibrate ourselves to each other, so to speak, so that we will be able to communicate smoothly throughout our time together. That is a major purpose of this first chapter. We will talk a bit about psychotherapy in general, what it is about, and where it has come from. We will discuss the bewildering variety of forms and shapes it is packaged in today. We will look briefly at the evidence for its effectiveness. Is this enterprise that we are making our life's work worth doing, after all? Finally, we will lay out a few of the basic assumptions on which therapy depends. Then we will be ready to move on into the work itself.

To return to the perplexing question that we began this chapter with: is there any way to describe psychotherapy generally, to say what it really is? Can we make a rule that will divide therapy from other human endeavors so that an observer, applying the rule, might say "yes, this is therapy" or "no, this is not"? I do not think there is a single statement that can accomplish such a task. However, there are many which do part of the job, and by putting some of these together we can at least sketch in the outline of what *psychotherapy* means.

There are really two ways to go about defining psychotherapy. One way looks at what happens to the client or patient; it describes the intended product of the activity. The other looks at the therapist and describes what the therapist does; it focuses on the process. Among the former sorts of descriptions, one of the best comes from Jerome Frank: "All successful therapies implicitly or explicitly change the patient's image of himself from a person who is overwhelmed by his symptoms and problems to one who can master them" (1971, p. 357). Singer (1965), in a not-too-dissimilar vein, points to the narrowing of the gap between what the client would like to be and what he believes himself to be. Carl Rogers, one of the most widely quoted of modern therapeutic gurus, says simply that the goal of therapy is personal growth.

But do we really need a therapist in order to reach these ends? Surely people grow without professional help, learn to overcome problems, and learn to be more the sort of person they want to be on their own? Of course they do. Most of us do, most of the time. It is when that process breaks down, gets blocked, or is not moving along as quickly or as directly as we want it to that we call on a therapist. That is the first step in defining what a therapist does, then: she steps in to help when the natural growth process is not handling things well enough.

HOW does she step in? What does a therapist *do* that makes her different from a friend or a pastor or a mother or a bartender or hairdresser? Here is where variety rears its interesting head. Depending on what she believes to be growth-producing, the therapist will *do* different things. However, all therapists do what they do from a common perspective, and that is what makes us therapists: we put ourselves in a relationship with a client in a way that focuses on him and his needs. "The therapist," says Strupp, "may be said to develop, maintain, and manage a specialized human relationship, with therapeutic intent" (1986, p. 126). "Therapeutic intent" refers to exactly this focus, this concern with the client's welfare. The therapy relationship is unique in this regard: it is the only human relationship in which two people make genuine two-way contact at a deep level of knowing and caring, and yet have as their shared aim the personal growth and enrichment of only one of the partners.

I do not mean to imply that the therapist is not enriched through her relationship with clients. If she is doing her job well, she will and must grow in it. The point here is that her growth and learning are incidental side benefits. The reason for being in a therapy relationship is the enrichment of the client, and the client only. Some other professionals, such as lawyers, doctors, and teachers, have similar interactions with clients. But only in psychotherapy is the personal relationship with a professional person the primary vehicle for changes in emotional, cognitive, and behavioral areas. It is the use of a relationship to effect positive change and growth that makes our work unique.

THERAPY THEN AND NOW

The history of psychotherapy, as with so many other aspects of Western culture, really begins with the ancient Greeks. Classical Greek culture recognized disease, both physical and mental, as a natural rather than a supernatural process. The Greeks identified different kinds of mental dysfunction. Their distinctions may have been crude by modern standards, but the classifications are still recognizable today. While they did not recognize the healing potential of a relationship with a therapist, they began a tradition of treating mental illness through professional intervention.

This tradition spread through the developed nations of the Near East, and by the eighth century many large hospitals in cities such as Baghdad and Damascus had psychiatric sections for treatment of mental illness. The West lagged far behind, but in the thirteenth century hospitals in major European cities in France, England, Germany, and Switzerland were providing psychiatric care for the mentally ill. The mental health movement in the West was held back, though, by the fear and superstition of the Middle Ages. Witchcraft and demonology competed quite successfully with more enlightened views; the mentally ill person was thought to be possessed or cursed, and treatment generally consisted of punishing him so that the evil spirits would leave his body in search of a more congenial home.

By the middle of the seventeenth century, superstitious views of mental illness were on the wane, at least among the better educated. But what replaced them was a confused mishmash of treatment ideas: bloodletting, temperature extremes, isolation. There was at least as much concern in those days with protecting the sane from the insane as there was in curing mental illness. Mentally ill people were considered dangerous and unpredictable and were usually locked up when their behavior became too bizarre to be simply ignored.

Gradually, these views changed. In 1680, Thomas Sydenham wrote on hysteria as a specific illness which could be cured by drugs, a diet of milk, and much horseback riding. Interestingly, the 1600s also saw one of the first attempts to use blood transfusion as a medical treatment: a Parisian doctor, Jean Denis, put arterial lambs' blood into the veins of mental patients. (The practice was discontinued when it was noticed that most of the patients so treated died shortly thereafter).

By the eighteenth century, psychiatry had become a true science. The Age of Enlightenment was one that glorified logic and reason, and saw logical thought as the birthright of all humans. "As reason was their highest god, how they sympathized with those who had lost reason! Their optimism was boundless, as was their belief in attaining human perfection. Thus they overcame the fatalist belief in the incurability of insanity; they founded numerous institutions for the mentally sick, and improved the regime within those institutions until the day when, through the great symbolic gesture of taking off the chains of the 'mad men,' these were definitively reinstated as human beings" (Ackerman 1968, p. 34).

The movement continued: studies of hysteria, studies of neurosis, treatment through diet and drugs, and environmental manipulation. There is not the space here to trace the development of the great treatment centers in France and Germany, the use of hypnosis as a treatment method, the gradual realization that something could be done with and for patients by *talking* with them in one way or another. Of course, the great milepost along this developmental road was the work of Sigmund Freud, the young neurologist-turned-psychiatrist whose books shocked his own generation and have shaped the course of psychiatry and psychotherapy up to our own time. Freud's psychoanalysis, as it came to be called, spread throughout the Western world in the waning years of the nineteenth century and by the early 1900s had become the predominant, virtually the only, acceptable psychotherapeutic method. So it remained, right up to the cataclysmic years of World War II. Some of Freud's break-away students founded their own trends of psychotherapy, but these were (at the time) of minor influence and were, in any event, firmly grounded in traditional psychoanalytic principles. The only real rival to Freud's preeminence in the world of psychiatric treatment at the outset of the Big War was a young American upstart named Carl Rogers—who ever heard of him, anyhow?

The Rogerian, client-centered approach was a harbinger of things to come. Other approaches began to appear: Taft and Allen's relationship therapy, Frohman's "brief psychotherapy," Hertzberg's "active psychotherapy," and Thorne's "directive psychotherapy." By 1960, only about 40 percent of American psychiatrists surveyed still considered themselves to be doing psychoanalytic therapy (Garfield 1981). Even greater changes were occurring in two major areas. First, the community mental health movement was gaining momentum, bringing in its wake an emphasis on social and cultural factors in treatment, sanctioning the practice of nonanalytically trained therapists (many of them not even medical doctors!), and popularizing the notion of psychotherapy for the middle and lower classes. Second, the behavioral psychologists had begun to tire of rats and pigeons and were applying their theories of learning to human beings with great and well-publicized success. The dam had broken, and the full flood of mental health enthusiasm was about to inundate the country.

And what a flood it has been! The late 60s and the 70s saw the flowering of the human-potential movement, through which everyone was to experience consciousness raising. Commercial ventures such as Lifespring and est sprang up to introduce suburbanites to self-awareness and the power of "getting It." Marriage encounter groups became available for couples, primarily through churches; children and parents were invited to family weekends, treatment centers for every sort of psychiatric ailment and nonailment emerged almost overnight. The variety of approaches, theories, and fads has grown in an equally bewildering way.

THE THERAPY SUPERMARKET

In 1920 there was one psychotherapeutic approach; in 1930 there were, perhaps, half a dozen, all but one of only minor influence. Then explosion—the world turned upside down. Psychotherapy, like nearly everything else, changed dramatically in the 40s; it will never be the same again. In 1947 Frederick Thorne wrote: "Clinical psychology in America is still characterized by a primitive state of organization in which the leaders in the field operate more or less independently....Lacking any formally systematized viewpoint, the theoretical biases of clinical psychologists literally represent all the permutations and combinations of behaviorism, experimentalism, Gestalt psychology, Freudianism, Adlerian individual psychology, Jungian analytic psychology, and many other minor schools" (Ard 1975, p. 66). Much has happened since then, and the net result seems to be that Thorne's statement is even more true today than it was more than forty years ago.

Therapies pile upon therapies in the 1990s. Parloff reported more than 130 systems in 1976, and the number has continued to grow. It is even possible to buy a many-paged volume entitled *Consumer's Guide to Mental Health,* a kind of road map through the jungle of competing approaches and claims. It is this quality of competition that is perhaps the most disturbing aspect of the modern mental health scene. Each therapy stridently proclaims its superiority over all the others, and little or no progress has been made in determining any rationale for selecting a particular treatment for a specific problem. Indeed, the claims have become so exaggerated and the suggested forms of treatment occasionally so extreme, that one critic finally commented in utter disgust that in therapy development it often seems to be "a far, far better thing to have a firm anchor in nonsense than to put out on the troubled seas of thought" (Galbraith 1958; quoted in Chessick 1969).

Despite this complex tangle, however, it is possible to discover some order among the confusion. Just as virtually all of the therapies have their ultimate origins in psychoanalysis, so each can be traced back to those origins, and the tracing forms a sort of schematic design, a tree of therapies. Figure 1-1 shows one such tree in which therapies are seen as falling into two schools, behavioral and verbal; and within the verbal school into cognitive or dynamic or humanistic classes.

Building and understanding such schematics is a particularly useful task in that it forces us to notice the similarities as well as the contrasts among the various approaches. We are used to shouting about differences, to championing theory A because it takes into account the trauma of birth or theory B because it assumes that all humans are capable of logic or theory C because it focuses on the here-and-now. But we are less used to noticing similarities. As Frank says, "Features which are shared by all therapists have been relatively neglected, since little glory derives from showing the particular method one has mastered with so much effort may be indistinguishable from other methods in its effects" (quoted in Goldfried 1980, p. 991). Yet we all do more of what we hold in common, I am convinced, than of what is unique to one or a few systems. Were it not so, this book could not be written, for this is a book about psychotherapy, not about psychotherapies. All of us are involved in bringing about one form or another of what Freud called the talking cure. There are many tools available to us in that effort, and the great majority of them will be appropriate across the great majority of theoretical approaches. Thorne wrote in the late 40s: "With such a complex situation, it is inevitable that a wide armamentarium of therapeutic tools will be needed, each used as skillfully as possible based on a valid knowledge of what each tool can be expected to accom-

FIGURE 1–1   A Tree of Therapy Types. From *The Benefits of Psychotherapy* by M. L. Smith, G. V. Glass, and T. I. Miller. Baltimore, Md.: Johns Hopkins University Press, 1980. Reprinted by permission.

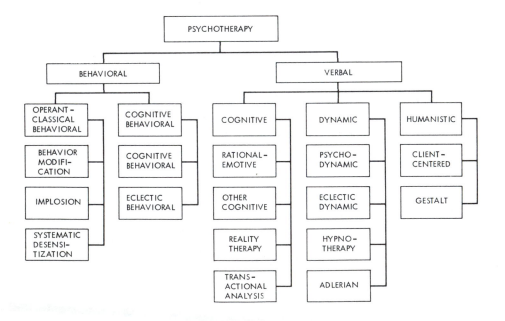

plish" (Ard 1975, p. 71). What was true then is true today: we do have many tools in the armamentarium, and we do need to know how to use them with clarity and skill. Perhaps a wiser generation of therapists will some day find a way to bring all of the different theories together, building on this common foundation. Until then, we can only remember that we are more alike than different, and that because of this each of us can teach and can learn from each of the others.

EVALUATING OUTCOMES

Just as the psychotherapeutic kettle was beginning to come to a boil, back in the early 1950s, an Englishman named Hans Eysenck did his best to clamp a lid down on the whole scene. Having spent much effort in an investigation of therapeutic effectiveness, he concluded that "roughly two-thirds of a group of neurotic patients will recover or improve to a marked extent within about two years of the onset of their illness, whether they are treated by means of psychotherapy or not" (Eysenck, 1952, p. 322). It is not difficult to imagine the reaction to that statement—the mental health community was up in arms! Almost forty years later, the dust still has not settled. Therapists of all stripes and colors were quick to claim that although such an outrageous statement might possibly have relevance for other approaches, it certainly was not true of *their* brand of treatment; they are still making the same sorts of claims.

Rebuttal of Eysenck's findings has been difficult for a number of reasons. For one thing, improvement in mental health is very hard to define in any specific, measurable way. The variables are elusive; the criteria are slippery. Does the client report that he feels better? That is probably because he wants to believe it; the same claims have been made for witchcraft, water cures, leeching, and nearly every other imaginable curative device. Give him some kind of tests, then, and see if his scores after therapy look different than they did when he started. But if they do look different, who is to say that the scores reflect real, meaningful changes? And if they do not look different, perhaps the test failed to measure what the real changes were. We could ask the therapist herself whether the treatment was effective, but she would obviously be biased in her reporting. What sorts of actual behavior could we look for that would indicate improvement? That depends on what was wrong in the first place, on the environmental constraints, on the number and kinds of options actually available for this or that client. Does it really make sense to look at psychotherapy as a single kind of treatment when there are so many different things that fall into that category? Maybe one kind of therapy is effective with some clients but not with others; maybe some kinds of mental health problems are amenable to some psychotherapeutic treatments but not to others. Truax and Carkhuff, working from this latter point of view, argue:

> Thus, to ask whether psychotherapy is indeed therapeutic, and to attempt to answer that question by comparing change in counseled and 'control' groups is very much like a

pharmacologist asking 'Is chemotherapy therapeutic?' and then conducting his research by randomly giving unknown kinds and quantities of drugs to one group of patients with various complaints and no drugs to a similar 'control' group. (1967, p. 18)

In the early 70s, a number of researchers went back to Eysenck's original data and concluded that there were significant errors in his research and statistical procedures. Two teams, in particular, were able to rebut the Eysenck report using Eysenck's own data; both concluded that psychotherapy does produce significant improvement in clients (Meltzoff & Kornreich 1970; Bergin 1978). Eysenck disagreed vigorously in print. So the argument raged on; the new studies did not succeed in dispelling the cloud of suspicion that Eysenck and others had raised. Is psychotherapy really just a big sham? Are these so-called therapists just taking people's money, making them believe they are getting something worthwhile? If some therapies are good (and some therapists) and some not so good, how can a prospective client know the difference?

The most comprehensive answer to this question comes from a study team led by Smith and Glass. These researchers searched the literature for all of the therapy outcome research published between 1900 and 1977 (a formidable task in and of itself!). They found 475 controlled outcome studies which they pooled and evaluated in a "meta-analysis." Their conclusions: "The results show unequivocally that psychotherapy is effective....In absolute terms, the magnitude of therapeutic effect is greater than most interventions of social science" (Smith, Glass, & Miller 1980, p. 124). On the average, Smith and Glass continue, the typical therapy client is better off after treatment than 80 percent of untreated individuals. Moreover, "despite volumes devoted to the theoretical differences among schools of psychotherapy, the results of research demonstrate negligible differences in the effects produced by different therapy types. Unconditional judgments of superiority of one type or another of psychotherapy, and all that these claims imply about treatment and training policy, are unjustified" (Smith & Glass 1977, p. 760).

Psychologists and other researchers have not been slow to join this new phase of the outcome battle. Obviously, since Smith relied upon old data, analyzed by old methods, the original flaws in those studies have not been eliminated. Moreover, some statisticians take serious exception to the meta-analysis technique that Smith employed.[1]

The therapists who are out in practice do not know if they have been vindicated or betrayed by Smith's work. The study did support the effectiveness of therapy, to be sure, but what is this about everybody's method working about as well as everybody else's? That's not right; I *know* that my brand of treatment is better than Brand X....

---

[1]The statistical argument even led to a very snide satire published in an otherwise sober and respectable journal. The article was entitled "Meta-meta-analysis: A New Method for Evaluating Therapy Outcome," and it concluded triumphantly: "Overall, psychotherapy was shown to be of definite tentative value for people in need of help excepting those who have psychological problems" (Kazren, Durac, & Agteros 1979, p. 399).

There is, in all of this furor, one important aspect of psychotherapy that the outcome research people seem to have overlooked, and it is a very important aspect indeed. Psychotherapy is intended not only to cure but also to help people to get through a troubled period in their lives with a minimum of pain and a maximum of growth and learning. Even if psychotherapy should not prove to cure mental illness (and the evidence is certainly unclear on this point), it may still reduce the duration of the illness as well as making that ill period more bearable. After all, aspirin has not been shown to "cure" anything; yet it is still one of the major items used by Americans in the treatment of physical illness. We take aspirin not to make us well but to help us endure being sick. Similarly, a cast on an arm or leg does not heal the broken bone; it merely provides support and structure while the bone heals itself.

I believe that psychotherapy may, in some cases, truly cure clients. It allows them to grow and change in ways that would be impossible without therapy. I believe that in many other instances psychotherapy substantially shortens the duration of an illness (and we could spend a great deal of time, indeed, trying to define what is meant by that word). I believe that, even when it neither cures nor significantly hastens the self-curative process, psychotherapy may significantly decrease the pain, anxiety, and other debilitating emotional symptoms that accompany illness. Finally, although research seems to have overlooked this possibility, psychotherapy has enormous potential as a preventive measure. Engaging in therapy at the point where things are just beginning to go wrong may allow a person to avoid a full-fledged illness later on. Further, therapy may prevent illness in the next generation: the client who deals with his own experience of abuse, incest, emotional deprivation, or alcoholism is far less likely to put his children through the same torment. In sparing them an abused childhood, he is also sparing them his own illness.

All of these statements are beliefs, matters of faith and hope, rather than facts. I have no data to support them, no research to prove their validity. Yet it is just such beliefs, borne out in session after session with client after client, that keep me working at being a psychotherapist. Research has a long way to go before it will be able to test hypotheses such as these. In fact, it may be time for practitioners to turn the tables on researchers and to ask seriously: "Does traditional research really work?" Can research, as it is now understood, ever hope to capture the subtleties of what goes on in that incredibly complex relationship that we call psychotherapy? That is another digression, although a fascinating one; it does not lead us where we need to go. Let us shift gears again, back to our major concern: the practice of psychotherapy.

THEORY, ASSUMPTIONS, VALUES

When I first began this book, I expected to include a number of chapters which would outline the major theories of psychotherapy. Theory is important, as Ard (1975) points out. It tells the therapist what she should and should not do and why. However, the idea of theory chapters soon got out of hand. There are so many to be assorted and categorized in such a variety of ways, and I soon realized that, if I was not careful, I would be writing a whole book on theory rather than a book on the practice of therapy. So (with some reluctance) I abandoned the theory chapters. The reader should be acquainted with theory. All practicing therapists should know at least two or three theories of therapy well, and have nodding acquaintance with several others. If you need to brush up in that area, there are many books available. Three of the best are Prochaska's *Systems of Psychotherapy* (1979), Corsini's *Current Psychotherapies* (1979), and Corey's *Theory and Practice of Counseling and Psychotherapy* (1986).

Although we will not discuss theory at length, we must still clarify the assumptions and values that will guide us throughout our work together. "The way we think about problems determines to a large degree what we will do about them," says Krumboltz (1966, p. 4). Psychotherapy is, in the last analysis, doing something about problems. What are the ways in which we think about problems of mental health, the assumptions we hold, that form a basis of our doing something as therapists?

There are two basic assumptions shared by all therapists, without which therapy cannot be performed. The first of these has to do with the worthiness of the therapeutic enterprise. "Simply by offering any form of therapy the therapist conveys his expectations that it will work, thus creating favorable expectations in the patient" (Frank et al. 1978, p. 30). If we do not believe it will work, we are no better than snake-oil salesmen, charlatans, and con artists. Frank goes even farther with this basic assumption: he sees faith in the efficacy of treatment as the major reason, perhaps the only reason, why it works. Therapy, for him, is a powerful and effective placebo. Although most therapists believe that they offer more than just a good placebo, the usefulness of the placebo effect is undeniable. Again, our own belief in what we are doing makes such an effect possible.

The second assumption shared by all therapists is that our client is capable of change and of making choices about his changes. This is a belief about the nature of man; it is untestable because it is a philosophy rather than a fact. It is "the image of man as capable of being (or at least becoming) free to know and able to make responsible choices on the basis of his knowledge. Only a system of values which places this freedom at the top of its hierarchy has any use for the idea of psychotherapy" (Singer 1965, p. 19). All therapists, from client-centered to analytic to behaviorist, must share this belief. It is one of the great paradoxes of orthodox behavioral therapy that, believing all behavior to be shaped by external stimuli, nevertheless the therapist first attempts to discover what behaviors the client wants to change.

Moving beyond these two fundamental and essential assumptions, we discover a host of questions about people and how they function. These are questions upon which therapists may legitimately differ, but which each of us needs to consider and answer in terms of our own beliefs. Brammer (1973) has provided us with an extensive list of such questions, including

> How is the human personality structured? What motivates him to behave as he does? How do thinking processes take place? What are the relationships among thinking, feeling, and valuing? How does man make choices?…How do we learn? Do we change

the environment first, or our personality characteristics first, and then expect behavior to change? Do we act first, then learn; or do we obtain understanding first, then act? What does it mean to be helpful to another person?...What is my view of the "good life"? What is my model of an effective, well-functioning, mature person for existing in our society at the present time? What do I want for this life? What is my responsibility to others? (p. 39)

Out of this barrage of questions, there emerge four major categories of enquiry, issues on which a therapist must take a stand. These are: (1) How/why do people get to be the way they are? (2) How/why do they maintain their thoughts and feelings and behaviors in a particular maladaptive or pain-producing pattern? (3) How can I facilitate their changing that pattern? and (4) What kinds and directions of change am I willing to support and assist? Your answers here may shift over time; you may not believe today what you will believe ten years from now. However, you must believe something, and you must know what that something is. The answers to these questions, and all the others that grow out of them, are the foundation upon which the whole structure of your therapeutic skill is built. Without a foundation, that skill collapses into an unrelated heap of tricks and nostrums, equally confusing to both you and your client.

With clear, consistent answers you are ready to become a therapist, with all that the word implies. Ponder, if you will, Strupp's description:

> Throughout therapy he sets an example and portrays an ideal. When the patient is anxious, the therapist is calm; when the patient feels guilty about his feelings or past actions, the therapist, through his attitude more than by any other means, disagrees with the patient's a priori assumptions and evaluations of his behavior. When the patient attempts to provoke the therapist, the latter does not participate in the maneuver. When the patient is horrified by the enormity of his demands and expectations of others, the therapist accepts his feelings as "scientific data," although he places them continually in the context of infantile wishes and questions their adaptive value. When the patient feels overpowered or helpless in the face of manipulations by significant others, the therapist displays a sense of mastery and competence and at times may suggest alternative courses of action. When the patient attempts to "act out" passivity, erotic longings, etc., with the therapist, the latter thwarts these wishes by nonparticipation. And so on. (Strupp 1973, p. 97)

Well, it is certainly something to aim for. I am not there yet, not all the way, not all the time. Maybe I never will be. Somehow, that's all right. As long as I continue to learn, to grow, to improve my skills, always building on a firm and consistent set of beliefs about myself and my fellow humans, I can be pleased with my work and my competence.

This brings us to the end of this introduction, the end of the beginning, and the beginning of the main course. How do we continue to grow and to improve our skills? What are the skills that contribute to good psychotherapy? It is a long journey that we are embarking on, one that will probably last a lifetime. The door is open, and the road lies before us. Shall we explore it together?

2 FOUNDATION SKILLS

Whatever the brand of therapy they use, all good therapists share some important skills. They know how to listen, to attend to what a client is saying, and to let the client know that they are attending. They know how to help the client deal with problems; clarifying what the problem is, considering various solutions, making decisions. They know how to encourage the expression of feelings, and they have some guidelines about what to do when a strong feeling is expressed.

It has often been asserted that good therapists, no matter how widely their theoretical frameworks may differ, seem to have about the same level of effectiveness. As was mentioned in Chapter 1, the Smith and Glass meta-analysis of therapy outcome research (1977, 1980) reached this same conclusion. According to Irvin Yalom (1980), one reason for this similarity may be the "throw-ins"—the things that each of us do so intuitively or automatically that they are not ever talked about or included in writings about the various theories.

One such "throw-in" is surely the set of behaviors I have called *foundation skills:* the abilities that contribute to getting a client to talk about his problems/needs/concerns, to focus on areas where useful change may occur, to explore new facets of himself and his situation. They are similar to the skills of a conversationalist, but they differ from conversational skills in that they focus on only one-half of the conversation dyad. Moreover, these foundation skills are goal-directed; they are not used to pass time pleasantly but to accomplish a specific purpose. They are used for the benefit of and in the service of the client. A conversationalist can monopolize the conversation with anecdotes about herself or can give up on an uninteresting partner and move on to someone else. The therapist, in contrast, must focus on the client who happens to be in her office. Here they are, the two of them. While the client, of course, shares in the responsibility for what happens, it is the therapist's job to ensure that the exchange is as therapeutic as the client will allow it to be.

The therapy session is not a "random encounter, a social conversation, an inquiry into pathology, an exercise in 'labeling,' or a veiled interrogation in which the client must establish his or her 'suitability' for service" (Wells 1982, p. 83). At the beginning of treatment, and often at the beginning of each session, the therapist must create an atmosphere for learning, exploring, problem solving, and growth. This atmosphere is determined more by the way in which therapist and client talk to each other than by what they talk about. You, the therapist, set the style. As Gilmore puts it, "Your client has the major responsibility for the content of the communication; you and your client together determine the purposes for communication; but you bear the major responsibility for the process of communicating with one another" (1973, p. 231).

That process of communicating is the stuff of which therapy is built. It determines the quality of the interaction, the openness of the relationship, and the degree of trust that the client comes to feel in you and in your ability to help. More than anything else, your task is to attend to the client. Everything else you do is built on skillful listening.

Good listening skills can be more than a foundation for psychotherapy; they can be a primary therapeutic intervention. A whole school of therapy has been built on the notion that, given the proper conditions of genuine attending, clients will respond by growing and changing in positive ways.[1] For these therapists, listening (and communicating that one is doing so) *is* therapy. For many others, the art of listening empathetically may not be the primary skill, but it is one upon which all other therapeutic activities depend. After all, whatever we do in therapy is accomplished by means of communication. That is what we do with clients. Communication is simply listening to and sending information, listening and responding.

We will begin this chapter with a consideration of some of the specifics of skillful attending behavior: how the good listener does a great deal more than simply listen quietly. Then we will discuss attending in the context of two major frameworks or focus areas of therapy, the cognitive (thinking) and the affective (feeling) focus.

---

[1]This is the belief of Carl Rogers, founder of client-centered therapy, one of the most influential of modern theories of therapy (Rogers 1951).

Readers who have had experience working as therapists or counselors may be telling themselves that this is going to be old stuff, a rehash of the done-to-death materials on listening skills and I-statements. To some degree they are right. We will, in this chapter, be reviewing some very basic therapy ideas. I have frequently been surprised, however, to discover how much I can benefit from a review of foundation skills. Almost inevitably I am reminded of some guideline or technique that I used more effectively in the past than I do now. Reviewing is like cleaning a cupboard. It brings to light all sorts of useful items that have been obscured by more recent acquisitions.

So as you read these pages, I invite you to try an experiment. Keep one or two of your clients in mind. If possible, review tapes or notes of their last session with you. As we discuss the foundation skills of therapy, pause now and again to ask yourself if you have utilized these skills fully in the sessions you reviewed, how you might have proceeded differently were you to have gone back to basics, and what the result might have been had you done so.

LISTENING

Listening is often thought of as a passive skill: the other person is the active communicator, while the listener simply takes in what is said. The therapist, whose stock in trade is listening, knows that good listeners are very active indeed. Her job is to make sure that she really hears and understands what the client is telling her. She makes sure that she receives and responds to the whole content of the communication. The therapist helps the person to talk about all of the parts of his concern, not just what is superficial or immediately apparent. The therapist is responsive in such a way that the client experiences being attended to and knows he has been heard. Therapeutic listening also helps the client to listen to himself, to slow down, attend to, and respect his own wisdom. By listening with skill, the therapist makes understandable what has been previously confusing to the client (Bruch 1981). In order to accomplish this, the therapist may use a variety of specific listening skills and techniques.

Paraphrasing

The most basic of the therapist's armamentarium of listening skills is the paraphrase. A paraphrase is simply a restatement of what the client has just said. The therapist repeats the message in her own words, perhaps using a concrete illustration, example, or metaphor to convey more vividly what she understands the client to be saying. Paraphrases involve more than just parroting what the client has said. Typically, they summarize whole units of the client's behavior—they mirror "the essence of the client's thoughts, feelings, and/or actions, usually providing a clearer picture for both client and helper" (Hutchins & Cole 1986, p. 55). Paraphrases allow the client to re-hear a statement and thus verify that the therapist did, in fact, listen to him. They also allow the client to correct any misperceptions on the part of the therapist, to deal with misunderstandings before they have a chance to derail the train of thought. In other words, these responses provide ongoing feedback for both therapist and client, a constant re-tuning of the communication channel, a way for each to ensure that they are on track with the other.

For many clients, the therapy session may be a first experience of talking to a sympathetic and attentive listener. Being heard without being judged, tuned out, argued against, or shouted down can be quite therapeutic in and of itself. The degree that you can use reflections and paraphrases to help the client experience this kind of acceptance and interest contributes to his growth and builds a foundation for future work.

Cornier and Hackney (1987) point out that paraphrases must do more than simply mirror back what the client has said. They must invite the client to explore further or to understand better whatever he is dealing with. While the primary focus of a paraphrase is on the cognitive aspects of a client's message, the paraphrase can also acknowledge feelings and behaviors. A client may be talking, for instance, of how close he and his father have been. He describes a heated argument with the father over the father's refusal to lend him money to buy a new car and as he talks of his rage, his eyes fill with tears. The therapist might paraphrase: "You're angry with your father for not giving you the loan, and at the same time you feel sad." This paraphrase takes into account both the content (my father would not lend me money), the verbalized feelings (I am angry at him), and the nonverbal behavior (tears suggest sadness).

It is important to invite the client to confirm or reject such responses, not only to give him the opportunity to correct any errors of perception you might make but also to help you to decide what to do next. The client described above might respond: "Yeah—I hate to see our relationship fall apart like this." Or he might say, "No, I'm not sad—I just get so mad and frustrated that I don't know what to do, and I feel like I'm going to explode." The former reaction is an invitation to pursue the sense of sadness and loss; the second corrects the therapist's perception and warns that (for now, at least) the client does not feel or does not care to discuss his sadness.

Paraphrases used appropriately are highly effective therapeutic responses. Used inappropriately, they can bog down the process and irritate the client. The therapist who uses only reflections may appear to be ducking the client's requests for help, information, or feedback or to be hiding her real self behind a facade of phoney professionalism. Pure reflection is seldom appropriate as a response to a direct question. The client who struggles to tell you of his problems with his son and then asks, "What do you think I should do?" is not likely to be helped much by a grave, "You'd really like me to tell you what to do." A more appropriate response might be to combine your paraphrase with some additional response. You could, for instance, summarize what the client has said, share your personal response to his situation, and add a question to help him move forward:

THERAPIST: I understand that you want my opinion about that, but I'd like to explore what you've already figured out about it and help you to find your own answers. Let me see if I understand where you are with this. You've told me of several possible choices open to you. You could try to discipline your son yourself, you could make an appointment to meet with his teachers, or you could let the school deal with the problem. You see some advantages and disadvantages in each of these possibilities and feel frustrated and confused. You've gotten advice from several different people, and you're still not ready to make a decision; none of the things you've heard feels like a perfect solution. I'm uncomfortable with giving you advice right now—even though I hear that you'd really like me to tell you what I think. Instead, let's make a list of the options you've already considered. What's one possible option?

One problem with using paraphrases is that you may fall into a set way of introducing them, using the same words over and over again. "I hear you saying that...." "So you're telling me that...." "Sounds like you're feeling...." All of these are good introductions, but overusing them can annoy your client and lead him to feel that you are using a formula rather than truly listening to him. Vary your way of leading into a response, and use a variety of examples and images to convey your understanding.

Finally, give yourself permission to paraphrase what you think the client is saying, even if you are not sure that you are right. Says Gilmore, "Within limits, it is better to risk giving an inaccurate paraphrase and stopping for clarification than to sit there with an all-knowing look, nodding your head as if you understand, just so the client will move on" (p. 242). Misunderstandings are a natural part of communicating and do no harm if they can be clarified and corrected. The client will not lose respect for you if you check out an inaccurate paraphrase or reflection. Your willingness to be fallible may help in establishing rapport.

Perception Checks

A perception check, like a paraphrase, is designed to clarify and underscore what the client has just said. It goes beyond the paraphrase in that it includes the therapist's inferences about what may be going on for the client and a request for feedback as to the accuracy of those inferences. "I get the impression, as you tell me about your husband's problems at work, that you're feeling angry. Is that true?" "You've given your friend lots and lots of advice, and she never seems to pay attention to it. Sounds like you may be wondering if she even listens to what you say to her. Is that what's happening?" Since perception checks do go beyond what the client has actually told you, it is especially important to check out your accuracy before proceeding. As the name suggests, the checking-out is an integral part of the perception check response. Beware of the too-facile or grudging agreement: "Sure—and so I went ahead and...." "Well, maybe that could be true...." The client may be so engrossed in telling his story that he has not really listened to your comment, or he may disagree but be unwilling to say so. In either case, the perception check statement was off target; it did not meet the client where he was or further the unfolding of his story. Your understanding may, indeed, have been correct, but your timing or your phrasing (or both) were off. Store the idea and the response the client gave for future reference, and come back to focus on what the client is doing and saying now.

Perception checks and paraphrases can be very effective if given in the form of a fantasy or a metaphor. "As you describe all the demands on your time and energy, I have an image of someone with ropes tied to all the parts of his body and people pulling those ropes in all directions at once. Is that how it feels to you?" "You'd like, just once, to have someone else do it and do it right—just like in the story of the elves and the shoemaker, when the shoemaker got up to find all of the shoes finished while he was asleep. Does that fit for you?" Using words from more than one sense modality will give your comments vividness: "You really didn't expect your wife to react that way—kind of like a little kid who's been having fun playing in a puddle of rich, squishy mud, and suddenly he hears someone scolding him. He feels surprised and scared standing there all covered with mud, 'cause he didn't even know he was doing anything wrong."

Combinations of paraphrases and perception checks can be used to comment on and ask about discrepancies or mismatches between different parts of a communication. "You say you get very scared when you are with a group of strangers, but I notice that you are smiling as you tell me that. What's the smile saying?" "Your voice sounds angry even when you tell me that you don't feel angry. Does it sound angry to you?" Remember, again, that the purpose of a perception check is not to persuade the client to accept your point of view or to catch him in some kind of error or omission, but rather to share your impression and invite him to correct you if you are mistaken. Sometimes a perception check will result in greater self-awareness on the part of the client and sometimes not. Either way, the therapist's job is to accept whatever correction the client may offer (perhaps with some mental reservations, some intent to return to the idea later) and to go on from there.

Summaries

A summary can serve a variety of purposes in therapy. You may use it to help to warm up the client in the early part of an interview or to close the discussion of a particular theme or issue. Summarizing what has been said can allow a check of your understanding of the progress of the interview, or it can encourage the client to explore an idea more completely and thus enhance his own understanding. It can reassure the client that the session is going well, or it can be used to focus thoughts and feelings when you feel stuck or confused.

Whatever the purpose, a summary has the same general form: it gathers together the main points which have been discussed and puts them out in a package that can be reviewed and confirmed or corrected. The response on page 16, in which the therapist summarizes the client's options in solving a problem, is a good example. The client may have taken twenty or thirty minutes to describe how he has agonized over studying and choosing among the three alternatives; the therapist's summary lists them objectively, separating out the content and yet acknowledging the underlying affect. The client now has a choice either to pursue the decision-making process or to focus on the feelings that he is experiencing.

Brammer provides a number of guidelines for summarizing in therapy. First, he advises, attend to the client's various themes and emotional overtones. Next, put together the key ideas and feelings into "broad statements of his basic meanings." Do not add new ideas to the summary, however good you think they might be; stay with the ideas the client has presented. In fact, it may be more useful to invite the client to do the summarizing rather than doing it for him. Finally, in choosing a way to implement a summary, be sure to take into account the purpose for which that summary is intended: opening, closing, expanding, focusing, etc. (Brammer 1973, p. 94).

I-Statements

Several of the examples given in this section have contained therapist I-statements. These are statements about the therapist's own feelings, thoughts, or behaviors, clearly labeled to differentiate them from what the therapist believes or understands about the client. Such differentiation and owning of your personal response is essential. "I feel uncomfortable about telling you what to do" is a straightforward owning of your feelings. "Your question makes me uncomfortable" or "that statement is confusing" gives the client responsibility for your feelings and muddles the therapeutic waters.

I-statements are often most effective when combined with a paraphrase or perception check. "You wanted to talk to her about it, but you were afraid of what she'd say. As I listen to your description of that, I find myself getting very tense and tight. Is that what happened to you?" By describing your own response, you can suggest that such a reaction is not unusual; at the same time you are not telling the client that he does or ought to feel the same way.

We began this section with a comparison of therapist foundation skills and the skills of a good conversationalist. One of the major differences between the two, it was pointed out, is that the focus in therapy is on only one of the participants. Paraphrases, perception checks, and summaries all maintain the focus on the client. I-statements, in contrast, shift the focus back to the therapist. In doing so, they relieve the pressure on the client. Just as blinking one's eyes helps one to see more clearly, so this brief shift in attention gives the client a chance to come back to his own reactions with a better focus. The contrast of the therapist's response with that of the client allows the client to hear his own comments more clearly. It also allows the therapist to step out of the role of neutral, detached, uninvolved observer and to be a real person. This creates the possibility of relationship. True contact is only possible between two people; the therapist who will not allow herself to be a person, owning her honest thoughts and feelings, cannot be a genuine participant in the therapeutic relationship.

The therapist must take care, of course, not to overuse I-statements. After all, the purpose of a therapeutic interview is to facilitate the client's growth, increase his self-understanding, and help him achieve his personal goals. I-statements, like every other response, must be used for that purpose. They always carry the implicit message, "with regard to you." Thus the therapist may respond, "I am feeling confused right now" (with regard to what you are saying) or "In that situation, I think I would be angry" (about the way your needs were ignored), or "I'm remembering what you said earlier about your brother" (and thinking about how that relates to what you are telling me now). Used with care, I-statements can form a bridge between client and therapist, moving the client into a deeper exploration of his own needs and goals while at the same time assuring him of the therapist's continuing interest and support.

PROBLEM SOLVING

The classic triad of client behaviors to be considered in therapy are *thinking, feeling,* and *doing.* "Doing" is the behavioral outcome of changes in thinking and feeling; it can also help create those changes by providing new experiences for the client to react to cognitively and emotionally. Since the advent of the behavioral approach to therapy, psychologists have been deeply divided as to the appropriate causal sequence for creating lasting change in a client. Do we help him to change how he thinks and feels, assuming that these changes will lead to new behavior (the traditional approach), or do we encourage and coach him in new behaviors, assuming that these will bring about changes in thinking and feeling (the behavioral approach)? In the remainder of this chapter, we will deal primarily with the traditional point of view, looking at ways to help clients to explore their issues from cognitive (problem solving) and from affective (feeling) perspectives. We will begin with problem solving.

Problems are the raw material of therapy. Clients come to therapy because of problems. "How can I deal with my spouse?" "How can I stop feeling scared when I'm alone?" "How can I learn to be more assertive?" "How can I develop a sense of purpose in my life?" If all goes well, they leave treatment with at least a partial solution. One way of looking at therapy, then, is as a problem-solving process.

There are many models of problem solving (Gibson & Mitchell 1986; Dixon & Glover 1984; Stewart et al. 1978; Egan 1975). Most involve a series of steps to be followed in order. Stewart et al. for example, suggests the following seven steps:

1. identify the problem
2. identify one's values and goals which relate to the problem
3. identify the available alternatives
4. examine the alternatives
5. make a tentative decision
6. take action on the decision
7. evaluate the results; cycle back through the steps if necessary.

Although this sounds straightforward and logical enough, most clients need help with many of the steps. Assisting in problem solving involves more than providing a model and watching the client work it through. In addition to the foundation skills we have already discussed, the therapist will often need to employ other skills more specifically designed to deal with the problem-solving process.

Goal Setting

It is a truism that clients often do not know at the outset what problem has really brought them to therapy. The client who begins by talking of troubles with his children may come to recognize a deeper problem in his marriage relationship; the client who initially complains of panic attacks may discover a need to become more assertive. Many clients are confused and bewildered by multiple problems: so many things are going wrong in their lives that they do not know where to begin.

A major therapeutic task is to help the client find such a beginning. It need not be the most important aspect of the problem, the basic, underlying root from which all of the other troubles develop; it must simply be something that therapist and client agree is causing trouble for the client. Just as the knitter trying to untangle a snarl of yarn must first find a loose end and work from there, so therapist and client work their way into the tangle of problems from this first, agreed-on starting point.

Agreement is a key issue here. If you have one goal, one problem-that-needs-to-be-solved in mind for your client while he is concerned about something else, you are likely to be working at cross purposes. A young college student, for example, may have sought treatment because he is failing in school. As he talks, you begin to see a pattern of procrastination, of overuse of alcohol, of too many parties and not enough studying. You are convinced that he needs to develop better work habits, an ability to delay gratification, a less egocentric view of the world. He, on the other hand, wants to figure out why his professors are being so unfair to him. Treatment is likely to go nowhere until you can establish some goal that both of you can agree is desirable and possible, toward which you can work together.

The confused and overwhelmed client presents a different kind of goal-setting challenge. For him, everything is going wrong. Things are falling apart at work, at home, socially, physically. No matter what he starts to talk about, he soon switches to something else; troubles with his boss remind him of the fight he had with his wife; he could not ask his friend's advice because his friend recently moved to California and now he has nobody to talk to; he got so upset about that that he wrecked his car, and he does not know what to do because he let his insurance lapse and cannot afford the repair bill; he cannot fix it himself because he gets these terrible back pains; sometimes the pain is so bad he cannot sleep, and then he lies awake and feels anxious and wonders if he is going crazy....This kind of client needs to be helped to focus on one part of the problem, one single thing that he can, in fact, do something about. You may ask him to go back and list the major points he has covered (writing these points on a chalkboard as he talks can further aid the focusing process), or you may summarize for him. When the summary is complete, invite him to choose one item that he wants to concentrate on now. "We can't deal with all of this at one time. Which of the things you've mentioned is most important to work on today?"

Having chosen a focus, further work may be necessary to frame it as a solvable problem. "I want my wife to stop nagging me" cannot be dealt with directly in therapy. "I want to learn to respond differently to my wife's nagging" can. A solvable problem is one in which the desired change can be made by the client. A successful solution does not depend on someone else's behavior. The wise therapist will never accept as a therapeutic goal some change on the part of family, friends, co-workers, etc., no matter how desirable such a change might be. Therapy can help the client change only those things he is in charge of: his own thoughts, feelings, and behaviors. Others may change as a result of his changes and often those changes in others are quite desirable, but they are not the major goal of therapy.

It is often extraordinarily difficult for a client to accept this kind of problem framing. "The only thing I want is to get my husband back; I'll never be happy without him." "If only I had a better job, everything would be fine." The therapist must call upon reserves of patience and empathy, understanding the feelings of frustration and despair that the client experiences while continuing to search for some goal, however small, that the client can experience as both desirable and reachable. Such a goal is often introduced as a first step in resolving the total problem; neither client nor therapist need know at the beginning exactly where it will lead. For example, both may agree to sort out the sequence of events that leads up to a spouse's nagging. Understanding what happens is an achievable goal and, once achieved, can be a jumping-off place for further problem identification and solution.

"The therapeutic response," says Hale, "is one which looks forward as well as backward. It is the task of the psychotherapist to respond in a manner which will elicit the most fitting response from the client, not merely to respond with a socially appropriate answer" (1976, p. 299). Finding a common, mutually acceptable goal is this sort of a look-both-ways achievement; it requires not only sensitive responding to what the client has been telling you, but also framing your comments so as to invite him to move ahead in a productive way.

As the client explores his situation, as you work together to find a point at which further steps in problem solving can begin, he will often wander off the track. He may become confused, change the subject, forget the point he was trying to make. Gilmore suggests that a delayed paraphrase is useful here to recapture the focus. "Whether a client loses track of what he started to say because he got on a side issue suggested by the original topic or perhaps because you stopped to ask for clarification or to check your perception, it is important that you are able to assist him back on track. One of the best ways to accomplish this is to quote exactly what he was saying just before he got off track" (p. 248). Either a direct quote or a close paraphrase will usually take him back to that point and reestablish him on his original course.

Helping the client to focus on identifying a solvable problem requires that you, the therapist, maintain your own sense of direction. You cannot afford to get lost in the client's confusion or to become overwhelmed by the difficulty of his situation. Two guidelines will help you here. First, remember that *there is always something that can be done*. No matter how desperate the client's plight or how helpless his circumstance, he is not condemned to stay depressed, miserable, guilty, or crazy. Ultimately, each of us is in charge of how we respond to our lives; there are always alternatives among which we can choose. The client may indeed feel trapped and helpless; the therapist must remain grounded in the knowledge that the client can, in fact, change. Second, *you are not responsible for solving the problem.* Your task is to make yourself and your skills available to the client, not to do the work for him. You can help. That is what you are paid to do. Ultimately, however, it is the client who must set the goals, make the decisions, and implement the changes.

Using Questions

You, the therapist, need to understand what your client is saying, why he is saying it, why right now, why in this context, why he is not telling you about something else, what other things are going on for him, etc. To the extent that you both can discover answers to these questions through other kinds of dialogue, questions should be avoided. Sometimes they cannot. Then you will need to ask.

Many experienced therapists avoid asking direct questions because of the way in which questioning can interrupt or distort the flow of an interview. There are dangers in using questions. Knowing what these dangers are will help you to frame your questions productively and help you to ask them in ways that will enhance rather than detract from the therapeutic process. Questions, used with care and discretion, are not necessarily bad and may in fact help to move things along. Let us look, then, at some of the pitfalls into which question-asking can lead; knowing these dangers will help you to avoid them.

The most common result of therapist questioning is that the therapist inadvertently takes control of the session. She decides what will and what will not be discussed. After a series of question–answer transactions, the client may settle back and wait for the therapist to indicate what topic shall be covered next rather than volunteering information on his own. The therapist is in charge, and the client follows directions. Once this pattern has been established, it will be difficult to change; the client will have learned that the therapist is supposed to figure out what to talk about. Not only does this kind of expectation practically guarantee that you will miss hearing about things which are, in fact, important to the client, but it also gets in the way of the client's learning to take responsibility for his own behavior. It leads to an attitude in which the client passively waits for the therapist to produce a magical idea or suggestion that will solve the problem, make the bad feelings go away, or change the world for him.

Another danger in using questions with clients is that of coercion: asking questions in such a way that the client is maneuvered or pushed into saying or accepting something he does not want to say or accept. "Don't you really think...?" "Isn't it true that...?" "Do you agree that...?" are lead-ins to such coercive questions. More subtle coercion includes techniques such as coming back to the same question again and again (until the client finally gives up and tells you what he thinks you want to hear) or setting a verbal trap and then triumphantly snapping it shut ("You told me that you..., and later you admitted that...; how can both those things possibly be true?"). Questions are appropriately used to help the client tell his story, to clarify that story when it is not clear to one or both of you, and to fill in gaps where pieces of information are missing. It is not appropriate to use them to bludgeon a client into accepting your point of view or revealing more about himself than he is ready to trust you with.

Beware of the question that is really an interpretation in disguise. The need to interpret, says Brammer, "is one of the strong temptations to which helpers must not submit in the early stages of the relationship" (1973, p. 85). "Do you still resent your mother for treating you that way?" or "Do you want the same things from your husband that you wanted from your father when you were a little girl?" are examples of this kind of interpretive question. Interpretations may be very useful, especially when therapy has progressed beyond the early stages, but they should be clearly labeled as such, owned as the therapist's hypotheses. "It seems to me that you still resent your mother for treating you that way" is a clear interpretation. It can often be followed by an equally clear request for feedback: "Does that fit for you?" "How do you react to that idea?" "What do you feel when you hear me say that?"

The goal of the problem-solving process in therapy is not primarily to solve the client's immediate problem. It is, rather, to teach the client skills and confidence in solving this and future problems. The good therapist makes herself obsolete; she helps the client to move to a point where he no longer needs her. Her questions are designed with this in mind; they continually encourage the client to develop his own ability to analyze, create alternatives, and make choices.

From all of the foregoing, we can extract some specific guidelines for using questions in problem solving. (1) Do not ask questions unless you need to. The client will feel more responsible and in control when he is not following your structure but is rather building his own. (2) Ask for clarification when you do not understand what the client is saying. Make it clear that the question arises out of your own confusion rather than something the client has done wrong. (3) Avoid yes-no questions or questions that can be answered in a single word. Questions like "Do you work days or nights?" or "What time did you get home the night you had the fight with your wife?" shift responsibility for solving the problem from the client to the therapist. (4) If there are major gaps in the client's story, ask for information to fill them; do so with open-ended questions. Say "What did you do next?" rather than "Did you talk to her about it?" (5) If the client avoids answering, do not insist on an answer at that time; you can always get the information later if you need to. (6) Ask questions which direct the client toward constructing new alternatives and finding his own solutions. Do not ask "Did you ever think of…?" Instead, ask "What are some of the things you've thought of doing?"

Feedback

At some point in the problem-solving process, most clients will find themselves stuck. If they were not stuck, they would not need help in solving their problems. Sometimes a paraphrase or a carefully constructed question will help them find their own way out of the stuck place. At other times, though, they may need additional input. Feedback from the therapist—a statement about her own reaction to what is happening in the therapeutic interchange or about her own perception of some dimension of the problem—is another technique which can help a client get unstuck.

Just as with questions, therapist feedback can be misused. It is all too easy to impose one's own perception or solution on a client, to move in too quickly to do the work for him rather than to help him do it for himself. We therapists, like anyone else, want to be seen as wise, perceptive, clever folk; it is hard to refrain from giving answers or sharing some (to us) crucial insight with a client who seems to be floundering. The most important rule in using feedback is: wait! Use feedback sparingly, and use it only when the client is ready to listen to what you have to say. In many cases the client will ask you directly or will give you some nonverbal indication that he wants your input. If not, ask him if he would like to hear your reactions to what he has been saying, and pay attention to his nonverbal as well as his verbal responses. The best feedback in the world will be useless if the client is not ready for it.

Feedback, says Brammer, "should be given in small amounts so that the helpee can experience the full impact of the helper's reaction. Too many items may overload him and create confusion and possible resentment" (1973, p. 99). You will probably notice many things in the client's behavior with you, as well as in the behavior he relates as he describes his problem, that he does not seem to be aware of. Pick one of these things to share with him and let him react to and work with that piece before moving on to the next. You may not even have to give him the rest of it; the part that you have shared may be just enough to change his focus and let him begin, on his own, to consider other new-to-him aspects of his situation.

If your feedback has to do with your own reactions to the client's behavior, describe the behavior before giving your reaction to it. "I notice that your voice is getting softer and softer, so that I have to strain to understand you. And what's happening for me is, I find my thoughts drifting, so I'm not listening to big chunks of what you say." "You say that when she finally did get home, you sat with your paper up in front of your face and wouldn't talk to her. If you did that to me, I might feel angry and sulky toward you." Describing the behavior first and then giving your response helps to keep clear boundaries between what you are doing and what the client is doing. The client is not pushed to take responsibility for your response but is merely asked to be aware of it. He can choose to explore that line of thinking further or to move on to something else.

Usually, the client will share his reaction to your feedback without being asked. "I never thought of it that way." "You mean when I talk softly people kinda stop paying attention?" If he ignores your feedback and goes on to another topic, it may mean that your timing was off, that he was not ready to deal with what you had to say. If he does this several times in succession, you may want to give him feedback about this process: "I've noticed something interesting that happens when I share an observation with you. I'd like to tell you about what I see." Another common response to therapist feedback is silence. The client may be thinking through what you have said or may be feeling confused or may be annoyed by your comment. It is important for you to find out what is happening behind the silence, and it is entirely appropriate to ask about it.

In general, feedback should be used sparingly and only when the client is ready to hear it. It should contain only one idea at a time and should be phrased simply and in the client's own language so that he can easily understand it. It should clearly differentiate between what the client is doing or saying, and what the therapist is thinking or feeling. And, finally, the therapist should invite the client to share his reactions to the feedback including whether or not he found it helpful and whether it tended to enhance or diminish his trust in the relationship.

Advice

Giving advice is a great temptation to therapists. So often we think we know just what a client should do. "But, as you know, advice and instruction can be overused. Advice must be used carefully, and mainly at the request of the client; otherwise the client will say 'Yes, but....' Any time the client responds with 'yes, but...' it is generally time to change your style" (Ivey et al., 1987). Even if the client does not "yes, but" your advice, advice-giving can still short-circuit one of the major goals of therapy: it can prevent the client from experiencing the power of solving his own problems.

Advice-giving may be appropriate in crisis situations where some action must be taken and the client is unable to think clearly enough to make responsible choices. It is inappropriate for decision-making in which there is time for the client to work things out for himself. "I think you should take action right now to have your husband hospitalized" may be a caring and responsible therapist intervention. "I think you should go to graduate school" is neither responsible nor respectful of the client's own decision-making ability.

Be careful, though, not to confuse advice with information. When the client makes a clear request for information, and you have the information he wants, it makes sense to share it with him. "Do you think I could handle the academic demands of graduate school?" is a different kind of question than "Should I go to graduate school?" In answer to the former question the therapist might appropriately respond: "Based on your test scores and on your college records, I think you would have to work pretty hard in graduate school, but I think you could handle it." An appropriate response to the latter question might involve commenting on the difficulty of making a decision, on the client's apparent desire that someone tell him what to do, or on the therapist's own conflict around wanting to give advice and yet knowing how important it is for the client to make his own choices.

Even when the request clearly has to do with information rather than advice, it is still important to note whether the underlying affect is one of dependency and helplessness. Asking for information can be an indirect way of asking to be taken care of or a means of putting off making a decision. If you suspect that this is happening, try reflecting the feeling of helplessness or neediness first and deal with the content of the request later.

All of these techniques—focusing on a problem, questioning, feedback, and information-giving—may be used at any stage of the problem-solving process. They can help the client identify options, explore consequences, choose a plan of action, or evaluate his success. They can also be used to deal with the affect associated with any stage of the problem-solving process. Working with affect, though, requires some additional considerations. We will talk about them next.

DEALING WITH FEELINGS

Few clients come to treatment without an emotional component to the problems they need to solve. The cognitive work may be most apparent to them—they need to make a decision about this, figure out how to manage that—but more often than not, their cognitive functioning is undercut by some kind of emotional disturbance. Clarifying the feelings that surround the problem area is a major, perhaps *the* major, part of middle-phase therapy. The therapist must be sensitive to both aspects of therapeutic need. She must not focus on thinking, on cognitive problem-solving, to the exclusion of emotional work. Nor must she deal exclusively with feelings and ignore the client's need to think constructively about the changes he needs to make in his life. In actual practice, cognitive and emotional work are intertwined: clients need to feel, to process information, to experience the emotions that accompany their decision-making dilemmas, and to think clearly about their feelings. For the purpose of this discussion, though, we have separated the two. We now turn to the area of feeling work: what are some of the foundation skills needed to help clients to deal with emotional issues?

The first step in helping a client work through his emotional problems is to recognize what the problem is. Many people spend years repressing painful feelings, learning to push them out of awareness, to think about something else. Others are confused about the feelings they experience: they cover sadness with anger, fear with guilt, or hurt with resentment. They feel very intensely, but they do not identify those feelings. Both kinds of clients, those who repress feelings and those who mis-identify them, need to bring the feelings out in the therapy hour, experience them, know them for what they are.

A first step in this process often involves teaching the client to describe his emotions. Many clients have a small vocabulary of feeling words. Even if they recognize a familiar or recurring emotional response, they don't know how to talk about it, to compare it to other sorts of feelings, to find out if other people ever feel that way too. Hutchins and Cole (1986) have put together a useful chart of feeling words (Table 2-1); clients who have difficulty talking about feelings can be encouraged to find the word or words on the list that best describe what they have experienced or are experiencing now. Therapists, too, may use the Hutchins and Cole chart to expand their emotional vocabulary, so that their paraphrases and summaries can be richer and more accurate. Reflecting the feeling component of a client's statement, including feelings in your summary statements, and asking questions about emotions, all serve to legitimize the expression of feeling, to let the client know that emotional expression is an appropriate therapeutic behavior.

We must be careful, though, not to move too quickly into feeling expression. Emotions can be scary: the client worries about looking foolish or losing control or being overwhelmed by a painful emotional response out of which he cannot move. He may experience intense guilt about his feelings. In our culture many girls learn that they are not supposed to be angry; boys are often brought up to believe that fear and sadness are inappropriate reactions for men. The expression of forbidden or fear-producing feelings may need to be a gradual process, one for which the therapist has prepared the client by providing permissions ("It's okay to feel what you feel;" "Your emotions are neither wrong nor crazy") and protection ("You don't need to go into that feeling any more deeply than you want to;" "It's important that you know how to take care of yourself as you let yourself experience your fear/rage/sadness").

Pushing too hard or too fast for feelings may move the client back into a more strongly defended place. Experiencing strong emotions for which he is not ready can lead to denial or distortion, and one facet of the denial or distortion is usually some loss of trust in the therapist. Moving too quickly detracts from the therapist's ability to give the client the kind of potent protection and permissions that he needs in order to do his emotional work.

Brammer (1973) suggests that therapists be particularly careful in encouraging emotional expression if: (1) the client is known to have a severe emotional disorder; (2) he is under so much internal or external pressure that he is liable to respond with more intensity than he can handle; (3) he has a history of badly handled emotional crises; (4) he is strongly and explicitly resistant to exploring feelings; or (5) the therapist has doubts about her own adequacy in helping people deal with feelings. In these situations, the best guidelines come from the client himself. If you

TABLE 2–1   Feelings Chart

RELATIVE INTENSITY OF WORDS	FEELING CATEGORY				
	Anger	Conflict	Fear	Happiness	Sadness
Mild Feeling	Annoyed	Blocked	Apprehensive	Amused	Apathetic
	Bothered	Bound	Concerned	Anticipating	Bored
	Bugged	Caught	Tense	Comfortable	Confused
	Irked	Caught in	Tight	Confident	Disappointed
	Irritated	a bind	Uneasy	Contented	Discontented
	Peeved	Pulled		Glad	Mixed up
	Ticked			Pleased	Resigned
				Relieved	Unsure
Moderate Feeling	Disgusted	Locked	Afraid	Delighted	Abandoned
	Hacked	Pressured	Alarmed	Eager	Burdened
	Harassed	Torn	Anxious	Happy	Discouraged
	Mad		Fearful	Hopeful	Distressed
	Provoked		Frightened	Joyful	Down
	Put upon		Shook	Surprised	Drained
	Resentful		Threatened	Up	Empty
	Set up		Worried		Hurt
	Spiteful				Lonely
	Used				Lost
					Sad
					Unhappy
					Weighted
Intense Feeling	Angry	Ripped	Desperate	Bursting	Anguished
	Boiled	Wrenched	Overwhelmed	Ecstatic	Crushed
	Burned		Panicky	Elated	Deadened
	Contemptful		Petrified	Enthusiastic	Depressed
	Enraged		Scared	Enthralled	Despairing
	Fuming		Terrified	Excited	Helpless
	Furious		Terror-	Free	Hopeless
	Hateful		stricken	Fulfilled	Humiliated
	Hot		Tortured	Moved	Miserable
	Infuriated			Proud	Overwhelmed
	Pissed			Terrific	Smothered
	Smoldering			Thrilled	Tortured
	Steamed			Turned on	

are sensitive to everything he tells you, and to your own feelings about what is happening, you will know when it is time to take that next step inside to move to the next layer of genuine experiencing.

Timing

The key idea here is, of course, the issue of timing. Our responses—paraphrases, interpretations, confrontations, questions—need to be accurate, and they also need to be precisely timed. Too soon, and the client either does not understand or feels pushed or trapped. Too late, and the affect has changed, the moment has passed, the client has moved on to something else. Make use of the natural pauses in the client's speech to insert your responses; do not interrupt the flow of his thought. Where possible, respond to the most recent part of what he has told you. If you have to go back to some earlier comment, acknowledge what you are doing. "You said a minute ago that…, and I noticed that your face tightened up. What were you feeling just then?" "I'm very interested in what you just said, but I'd like to go back first to what you were telling me about….Would you say more about what that means for you?"

It is usually more productive to deal with feelings experienced by the client during the therapy session than with those that are simply talked about. You may comment about inconsistencies between what the client says he felt and what he appears to be feeling now. (Again, such a response must be timed to catch the feeling as it is experienced.) You may encourage him to allow himself to reexperience the situation he describes. Sometimes just asking the client about his present feelings opens the door to such reexperiencing: "Are you feeling some of the same feelings now that you experienced back then?" At other times, a more direct invitation is useful: "Let yourself feel right now the way you felt when that happened."

Remember that the more directive your intervention the more certain you should be of both accuracy and timing. When in doubt, don't. It is better to miss an opportunity to explore something that looks promising than to push the client where he is not ready to go. Tuck your observation away for future reference. (After all, if it really was that important the client will surely circle around eventually and give you another chance.) Then refocus on what is happening between the two of you now.

Therapist Feelings

Therapy is an interaction between therapist and client, and the client's emotional responses occur in the context of that interaction. But the client is not the only one who experiences an emotional response; the therapist has feelings too. One of the differences between more and less effective therapists is that the former use their own feelings to further the therapeutic exploration while the latter tend to ignore or discount the value of such feelings.

The inner experience of the therapist can be a finely tuned guide to what is important in the client's communication. Sometimes we are immediately aware of our emotional response: We feel annoyed, anxious, or disappointed as a consequence of what is happening in our interaction with a client. At other times, we are less tuned-in to our emotions but may be very much aware of our physical sensations. Physical sensations can be a bridge to the underlying feelings if we let them. Tenseness in neck and shoulders, persistent needs to yawn or clear the throat, sweating palms, twinges of headache, frequent shifts in position—each can point to one's own anxiety, sadness, or anger. Often our body will recognize the significance of a remark or a nonverbal communication before our brain has had time to process it through.

But how can you focus on your own sensations and feelings and, at the same time, be aware of all that is going on for the client? For many therapists the answer lies in a kind of shuttling, a back-and-forth movement of attention from self to other and back again. I hear the client's words, see his facial expression and posture and gestures, notice his voice tone; I shift to an awareness of my own response, both internal and external. I notice my reaction to him and his reaction to what I do. His state, his communication, blend with my own state and my own reaction and that reaction leads me back to him again. I follow the flow, now with myself and now with my client and now with myself again. Gradually, as my comfort with this sort of shifting movement increases, I am aware not so much of conscious shifting from one to the other as of a kind of blending, a process that occurs between the two of us. "The helper's ability to communicate at high levels of empathic understanding," say Carkhuff and Berenson, "appears to involve the helper's ability to allow himself to experience or merge with the experience of the helpee, reflect upon this experience while suspending his own judgment, tolerating his own anxiety and communicating this understanding to the helpee" (1977, p. 8). But as I tolerate my anxiety, I do not push it out of my awareness. Rather, my anxiety, or my confusion, or annoyance, or whatever is going on in me becomes an integral part of my understanding of that other person's communication. My own emotional response both is called forth by his behavior and helps to trigger that behavior. We are two people interacting, with all the richness of meaning and response that true two-person contact implies. I am able to respond to my client's feelings and experiences more deeply and accurately as I am able to respect and respond to my own feelings and experiences. I am, in a very real sense, a sounding board: what he communicates is expanded and elaborated upon in my reactions to him.

There are a number of specific signals or red flags to which the therapist should pay particular attention as she works to enhance her skill in this self-to-other shuttling process. Often we get so caught up in what the client is telling us that we forget to attend to our own responses; we need some kind of signal to bring us back. One such signal is discrepancy. The longer I stay just with the client, not noticing my own internal process, the more likely I am to become split: some part of me outside my awareness will be taking care of my own reactions even as I continue to focus consciously on my client's behavior. This splitting will eventually result in a mismatch between different parts of my communicative behavior. My voice tone will not fit the words I am saying, or my gestures or body posture will be at odds with my facial expression. Whether or not the client responds to this mismatch, I need to notice it; it can be the signal that I have been neglecting something important in me. Focusing on the nature of the discrepancy, asking myself just what it is that I have been saying with the out-of-awareness part of my response, will put me back in tune with my own process.

Another signal that the therapist can use is her own postural shifts. Ask yourself at intervals: "What is my body saying?" Are you leaning forward or sitting back in your chair? Did you just cross your legs or your arms? Do you find yourself cupping your chin in your hand, scratching your head, or rubbing the back of your neck? Large body movements call attention to themselves and can put you on notice that something may be happening, something you need to attend to.

Speaking of attention, notice when you stop attending to the client! We all have those moments when we realize that we have been thinking about something else while the client was talking and have not really been a part of the therapeutic process. Such lapses are not accidental, random occurrences. They are warnings that something is going on for us that we need to take care of. More often than not, the something in us was set off by some part of the client's communication. Go back to what the client was saying or doing just before you tuned out and use that as a bridge to your own internal state at that time. If you discover something relevant to the interaction, plug it into the ongoing process; if not, if you were dealing with some external-to-therapy issue of your own, you will be better able to put it aside after recognizing and acknowledging it to yourself as a concern.

Sharing Your Feelings

It is easy to begin to feel overwhelmed by all of the things one is supposed to attend to as a therapist. How can I notice everything about my client, everything about myself, and at the same time choose appropriately among the dozens of responses I might make at any given moment? Unspoken in this question is often an underlying assumption that the therapist must keep hidden from the client all that is going on inside herself. While it is true that the focus of the interview must be on the client's needs, wants, problems, etc., this does not mean that the therapist may never share her own personal reactions or should not pause to take stock of the whole of the communicative process. At times it may be very appropriate to ask the client to wait a moment while you sort out what has been happening or to share with him some of your own internal response to what he is presenting. Gottman and Leiblum point out that this kind of sharing can be a very useful therapeutic intervention: "Rather than hide his own reactions from the client, the therapist's reactions should be used as relevant data. If the therapist tells the client about reactions to him, the client is better able to understand others' reactions to his communications and may better monitor his behavior. Acceptance of all of a client's behavior without comment is neither realistic in terms of generalization to the extra-therapy world nor respectful of the client" (1974, p. 126).

In doing this kind of sharing, the first rule to remember is to own your own feelings. Describe them as your response rather than as something that he is doing to you. "I need to stop a minute and think about what we've been saying." "I'm aware that I'm beginning to feel very tight and tense as I listen to you talk about your relationship with your girlfriend." "Wait—something happened to me just now and I stopped listening to what you were saying. Would you tell me again what happened when you went in to talk to your supervisor?" Obviously, responses like this can get in the client's way if they occur too often; but used judiciously and honestly, they serve a number of therapeutic purposes.

First, the statement which openly takes responsibility for your own feelings serves as a model of communication. You are showing the client how to sort through and report on internal processes. After all, this is one of the things he must learn to do if he is to profit from therapy. Teachers have long known that demonstrating a technique or skill is one of the most effective ways to help someone else acquire that technique or skill. In therapy, modeling personal openness not only gives information, but also provides permission. It tells the client that sharing here-and-now feelings and reactions is acceptable in the therapy setting and invites the client to do the same.

As Gottman and Leiblum suggest, the therapist's response to the client provides him with important information about how others may react to him. If the therapist becomes annoyed or tense or tunes out when the client talks in a certain way, then maybe other people do the same thing. Awareness of the therapist's response may be the first step for the client in figuring out how he sets up unwanted responses in other people. This, in turn, may help him choose alternative behaviors that will lead to different and more enjoyable kinds of interactions.

Perhaps even more importantly, as you share your own honest responses with your client, you are conveying to him a sense of respect and trust. You respect him enough to be honest about what you are feeling; you trust him to be able to handle your reactions. This kind of openness is rare in today's social climate; much more common is the polite, socially acceptable response which protects both speaker and listener from the risks of being genuine and open with each other. The absence of this kind of open and intimate sharing may be a major reason why so many people seek psychotherapy! By trusting and respecting your client enough to share your feelings honestly with him, you invite him into the kind of relationship which is healing in and of itself. You invite him to experience contact with another human being, contact that goes beyond social convention and polite avoidance, contact that affirms the tender and vulnerable parts that most of us work so hard to protect. And it is in the affirmation of this core of self, this essential inner me, that the therapeutic process takes root.

CONCLUSIONS

Throughout this chapter, we have focused on specific techniques which the successful therapist uses to achieve her therapeutic goals. We have talked about paraphrasing, questioning and summarizing. We have discussed approaches to problem-solving. We have looked at how to help clients express their feelings and at what the therapist herself may choose to express.

Although you have now read about these techniques, reading alone will not make you a master of them. Using the techniques smoothly and appropriately, choosing fitting and timely interventions, knowing when to follow up in the same vein and when to switch to another focus all require practice. Beginners and experienced therapists alike can profit from an occasional return to the basics, from examining their work in terms of how they employ these fundamental therapeutic tools.

All of the techniques we have discussed in these pages have as their goal the improvement of communication. Many of them may have other benefits as well: they may provide the client with useful information, teach him a social skill, or help him to think more clearly. But they are primarily communication skills. As such, we must use them with one final caution: they are not ends in themselves. Clear, open, and effective communication is a tool to be used by client and therapist to achieve the client's overall goal. Gilmore puts it well: "Because communicating is generally rewarding to humans and particularly prized by persons attracted to counseling as a profession, you have to guard against allowing communicating to become the goal of counseling, instead of the means for achieving counseling goals" (1973, p. 229).

Clear communication skills are an essential ingredient of good therapy just as a tasty crust is an essential ingredient of a good pie. But a pie crust all by itself is not much fun to eat. Communication by itself is not enough in therapy. In the next chapters, we will look at the various stages of the therapeutic process and the goals and focus areas of each. At every stage in every phase, the basic communication skills are the vehicle through which therapeutic change is achieved. These skills are not the goal of therapy; they are, though, the raw materials of which therapy is made.

3 THE INITIAL INTERVIEW

Therapists are likely to feel a certain amount of anxiety before the first interview with a client. This may, especially for beginners, be an understatement. I was flat-out scared the first time I saw a client: scared that I would do something wrong, that the client would not like me, that I might look foolish. I conjured up a hundred things that might go wrong. Some of that anxiety is inevitable, and it can work to your advantage. You can use it to keep yourself up, alert to what is going on in the client and in yourself. But some of it is not helpful at all, as well as being downright uncomfortable. Knowing what you are about and what you want to accomplish will help you to reduce your anxiety to a manageable level and to ensure that both you and your client get what you need during the first contact.

PREPARATION

The business of the first interview really begins, in most settings, some time before the therapist actually sits down with her client. She or someone else will have scheduled the interview. She will have the client's name and some information about him. In an agency setting, a counseling center for instance, the client may have been seen by an intake worker (or a secretary) and asked to provide some data about why he has decided to seek help, what he expects out of therapy, etc. If the therapist has made the first contact, often by telephone, she herself may have asked some of these kinds of questions. Getting a general idea of what is going on for the person and what he wants, prior to that first interview, is a good idea; it gives both therapist and client some sense of structure with which to begin. It is also important, during that first contact, to get the client's address and telephone number as well as the referral source. Then, if for any reason the client does not show up at the time of the appointment, the therapist has the option of following up to find out what happened. Mistakes do occur in scheduling, misunderstandings about time and date, so one need not assume that the client has changed his mind about coming in. Therapists disagree about checking back with a new client who fails to make a first appointment. Some maintain that calling after a missed initial session sets up an "I am responsible for you" kind of framework which is antitherapeutic. Others are willing to make an extra effort at the beginning to ensure that at least one session actually takes place. I tend toward this latter view. After all, new clients are usually scared too, and I am willing to give them the benefit of the doubt in order to get us both into the same room looking at each other and talking to each other.

If some prior information is available about a client, such as a completed agency questionnaire, a letter from a referral source, or a report from an intake worker, a decision must be made about what to do with it. Some therapists choose not to read information about the client ahead of time, preferring to start clean with what the client chooses to present to them rather than forming a preconceived notion of what the client is going to be like. The problem with this approach is that the client knows that the information has been given. He may know that the therapist has talked with the referral source. He may have put considerable energy into filling out a questionnaire or spent a significant amount of time talking with an intake worker. He may resent having been asked to give information which is now going to be ignored; he may wonder if the therapist is being honest with him, if she really has drawn some conclusions about him but is not willing to share them. Maybe she thinks he is really crazy! Obviously, these kinds of fears, suspicions, and resentments do not help to advance the purposes of the early sessions.

On balance, I think it is best that the therapist does familiarize herself with all available information about a new client. She should treat all that information as hypothesis rather than fact. The therapist will be able to decide as she goes along whether the information is useful to her or not. She can speculate about what it may mean in terms of working with this client. Is he likely to be talkative? Apprehensive? Will he be eager to get to work or is he likely to resent having been referred for therapy? Has he had therapy before? If so, what kind? What expectations does he have about this process and how it will work for him, and do those expectations fit her own therapy style? The answers to these questions can help in planning how to handle the first interview, selecting strategies to use in establishing rapport, exchanging necessary information, and launching into the process of treatment.

GETTING STARTED

Imagine yourself as a client, about to sit down with a therapist for the first time. You are hurting about some part or parts of your life. Things are going badly for you, and you have not been able to figure out what to do about it. At some level you are feeling inadequate, incompetent, somehow less valuable or worthwhile than other people you know. You are simply not as good a person as others or you would be able to handle this thing on your own. The very fact of seeking help is, in most people's minds, an admission of personal failure. Pascal describes the situation well:

> In most instances the patient is having his first interview with a professional. It took a strong need and a real feeling of humility to come to that interview. The patient is confronted with a stranger. This stranger asks that the patient psychologically undress. To most people, this is a threat. It is much easier to physically undress oneself for a physician. Besides, a physician is a known quantity. To the average patient, the mental health worker is an omniscient person who can strip the patient of defenses and leave him a quivering, unintegrated blob. (1983, p. 30)

No wonder the client is anxious!

The first task of the therapist in the initial interview is to create a climate in which the client can begin to relax and to focus on what he wants and needs. As Wells points out, "The therapist has about fifty minutes—sometimes less—to establish a relationship that can make helping possible" (1982, p. 83). Establishing this relationship takes precedence over any other goal; if it is not accomplished successfully, whatever else you do may not matter a great deal. Within this context, your second task is to get enough information from the client to make some tentative decisions about what to do, whether to offer him therapy, on what terms, and toward what sorts of therapeutic goals. There are three rules of the road which will help you to accomplish these tasks: (1) Keep yourself centered; (2) follow the client's lead; and (3) be yourself.

Centering

Therapists, like clients, can find themselves off-balance. In order to help a client find his own balance again, you yourself need to be centered: you need to have put aside your personal concerns and preoccupations so that you can be fully available to work with your client. You need to be aware of your purpose, confident of your own ability, and ready to devote your attention to the task at hand. By staying centered in this way you can offer him a model for his own functioning; in addition, you will give him a sense of protection and of permission to deal with his own issues freely and openly. This is as important in the initial interview, when you are primarily concerned with groundwork-laying and information-gathering, as it will be later on when you formally embark on the actual treatment phases of therapy. Rioch et al. see it as primarily a matter of making contact, of letting the client begin to experience the therapist as clear, focused, ready to be involved in the therapeutic process. "I do not mean," says Rioch, "that you waste the clients' time by giving them your life history or any other irrelevant information. I mean making it clear by your attitude that you are there for a job that is in their interest, and you are there *only* for that during the time you have set aside" (1979, p. 15).

A good check on your own centeredness involves breathing. If you are feeling awkward, anxious, or uncertain, your breathing is likely to be shallow or jerky. Before your client comes into the room, take the time to steady your breathing pattern: take several deep breaths, letting the air out slowly. Let yourself experience the tension draining out of your body as you exhale. Give yourself permission to focus on yourself for a few moments, on attending to your own body and your own feelings. Let yourself know that there is plenty of time and that it is okay to be here in the present without hanging on to what happened earlier in the day or worrying about what may happen next. Your agenda can come later; for now it is quite enough to be here, fully responding to and being with another human being. If you are not able to do this, to put your own personal issues aside in the interest of availability to your client, then you should probably seek out a colleague, supervisor, or trainer to work through whatever unfinished business is intruding on your attention and awareness.

Follow the Client's Lead

Once you have slowed down, focused, and centered yourself, you are ready to respond. Now it is time to be aware of the client's needs, actions, and desires. If he is waiting for permission to plunge in, give that permission. If he is already beginning to talk, just listen. If he seems confused and needs some structure, go ahead and ask a question that will help him to focus on what he wants to tell you.

In order to get to know a client, the therapist must find a way to allow him to tell his story. There may be some parts of that story that are especially important, some set of facts that will need clarification. But do not worry about them right now; there is time enough for that later. At the beginning, the client should be encouraged to follow his own agenda, to talk about whatever is in the foreground for him. Especially for beginning therapists, there is a temptation to ease into an initial session by making some sort of social comment. "Did you find my office with no trouble?" "Pretty warm out there, huh?" "My desk/office/waiting room is kind of messy today...." This kind of beginning, while it may feel like a good ice-breaker, is generally counterproductive for several reasons: it doesn't set the proper tone for a counseling session, it can mislead the client as to what kind of relationship you and he will have, and it can increase his anxiety and confusion as he tries to figure out what is expected of him in this new situation (Seligman 1986).

There are any number of opening questions or statements that will invite the client to begin to talk without conveying that there is a right way to go about it. "I'd like to know something about you and how you decided to come for therapy at this time." "Where would you like to begin?" "Later on I may have some specific questions, but right now I'd like you to talk about whatever you most want to tell me." "How can I be of help to you?" At the beginning of the initial interview, it does not really matter where the client starts; what matters is that he simply begins and in so doing starts to experience the quality of the relationship that will be built during the course of treatment.

As the dialogue progresses, the therapist listens at many levels. The easiest and most obvious level is that of content. The client is talking about what is important to him; he is sharing facts. He wants someone to attend to this information; he has a right to expect that the therapist will remember it and understand his later remarks in the context of what he has already said. Another level is that of nonverbal communication: posture, voice tone, facial expression. The nonverbal communications of the client provide a constant commentary on the actual words; they often explain what the words really mean. Words and nonverbals are a kind of duet, in which each part is important and yet the whole conveys the real message.

Yet a third level of listening is that of style, of pattern; the rhythm of the dialogue, its coherence and logic, the client's active or passive stance, the general rapport that is developing. The therapy hour is a microcosm of the client's whole pattern of interacting with his world and much can be learned about his social relationships, his sense of self, his strengths, and his weaknesses by attending to the overall ebb and flow of the early therapy interaction.

Be Yourself

Finally, the therapist must be aware of the dangers of pseudo-professionalism. In our anxiety and uncertainty about how to present ourselves, in our fear that the client may see us as fumbling amateurs who do not really know what we are doing, we may bend over backwards to appear competent. This can lead to brusque or stilted behavior, can erode the warmth and genuineness that is so essential in establishing rapport. Wolberg, in his classic and exhaustive volume, *The Technique of Psychotherapy,* makes the point: "No better rule can be followed in the therapist's first contact with the patient than to heed the injunction to 'be himself' " (1954, p. 201). Your own self—spontaneous, human, real—is your most important therapeutic tool. Of course, if you are just beginning as a therapist, you will not be able to use that tool as effectively as you will later on, when experience has sharpened and shaped it a bit; still, the sharpening and shaping come from getting out there, out from behind facade and pretense.

Be yourself is a simple rule, but it is not always easy to follow. You will find yourself slipping into insincerity at times, pretending to be what you are not or to know what you do not. You may be tempted to pretend to agree with the client, joining her in blaming friends or relatives for her plight or promising her more than you can deliver, even though you (in a more relaxed moment) know better. Do not despair: real people make mistakes and being genuine always carries with it the possibility—in fact, the inevitability—that you will sometimes stumble. That is all right; the relationship you are building as you risk genuine contact with your client can tolerate your errors. Admitting them to yourself and then moving back into a genuine stance of concern, respect, and honesty is what getting started is all about.

Gather Information

Much of what I have said about rapport has to do with letting the client know the therapist as a genuine and trustworthy person. Part of that sense of trust develops as clients see their therapist coming to know them, accepting their concerns and their pain. Another part comes from experiencing the therapist as knowing what to do in the session, as being in control, as getting the information that will be needed in order to begin the process of therapeutic change. Colby (1951) points out that these two themes, getting the client acclimated to the therapy process (and to the therapist) and gathering information about the client, determine the whole course of the initial session. Therapists differ as to what kind of information to get, in what order, and in what detail; yet most agree that there is an optimum balance between an attitude of "give me the following facts" on the one hand, and of "I have no idea what may be important" on the other. "Inexperienced students may either become too task-oriented or too person-oriented. That is, they become overly concerned with gathering information and neglect the client's concerns; or they are overly concerned with the client's feelings and, as a result, end up with little or no information" (Zaro et al. 1977, p. 41). It is useful to decide ahead of time what basic facts you want to know about your client and to make sure that you do find out those things. Once you have made that decision, you can relax and be open to all of the additional information that will emerge as you go along.

Depending on her therapeutic orientation, the therapist may choose to use the first interview to get a clear and detailed picture of the kind of person she will be working with: demographic details such as occupation, marital status, number and ages of children, specifics about the onset and duration of the symptoms which led him to seek therapy, medical history, and so on. Wolberg provides a convenient checklist for this sort of informational interview:

1. Statistical data—name, address, telephone number, age, sex, marital status, education, occupation, employment status, income
2. Complaint—history and development of symptoms, other complaints, previous illnesses, effects of present condition on functioning
3. Causal factors—family history, environmental stresses
4. Personal resources—maturation level, interests and hobbies, interpersonal relationships, coping mechanisms (1954, pp. 208–209)
5. (I would add to this list: medication and drugs—what medicines are currently being taken, and for what; how much alcohol, caffeine, tobacco, and other drugs are used).

While not a formal outline to be pursued point by point in the interview, this list may be referred to occasionally as a reminder of what has been covered already and what may have been overlooked in the developing interaction. Some of the points will be self-evident, some may deal with information already collected, and some are conclusions and generalizations which will be made as the therapist watches and listens to the client. Direct questions may be inserted as a way of eliciting information that does not emerge naturally. It is also true that a judicious amount of structure, in the form of specific questions, can provide reassurance to an anxious or confused new client.

A major drawback of systematic questioning is that it tends to set up an expectation on the part of the client that the therapist will take charge, will tell him what to do and when to do it. Such an expectation can be a real hindrance for later therapeutic work. It is important not to suggest to the client "that he has relatively little to do with his own growth and development, that in effect he can remain passive and yet be 'cured,' an obvious contradiction in terms" (Singer 1965, p. 131). For this reason, if you choose to use most of your initial sessions to gather information, you should let the client know that this first session is conducted in a different way (and serves a different purpose) than future sessions. Cornier and Hackney give an example of how to open such a session: "Before counseling gets started, it is helpful if I have some preliminary background about you. So this time, I'd like to spend the hour getting to know you and asking questions about your school, work and family background, and so on. Then at the next session, you will be able to start discussing and working on the specific concerns that brought you" (1987, p. 66). This lead-in clearly distinguishes between what will be going on this hour and what will happen when the "real" therapy begins.

As I suggested earlier, the amount and kind of information gathered in the initial interview will depend in part upon the therapist's theoretical orientation, the kind of therapy she intends to provide. A behavioral therapist will need to know the specific behaviors that are to be changed and the specific circumstances under which they occur. A more psychodynamically oriented therapist will want to know more about the client's developmental history, his early relationships with parents and siblings. A client-centered therapist may deliberately choose to have no agenda at all but to encourage the client to talk about whatever is in his awareness at the moment.

Whatever the strategy you choose, remember that the client can only tell you of his own experience. This experience comes, not just from the events of the present, but from the interaction of the present situation with his whole history of being in the world. "The stimulus situation is not only clothed with its physical attributes but with the past experiences of the responding organism to a similar stimulus situation" (Pascal 1983). Part of the client's inability to solve his present problems has to do with his inability to step out of his frame of reference, to see new possibilities, different ways of reacting and responding to all-too-familiar stresses. The information you collect should help you to begin to identify the perceptual ruts—the old, limiting habits of thought and feeling and behavior—that the client, because of his personal history, literally is unable to see. Keeping this in mind will help you to be efficient and purposeful in your information gathering, rather than simply asking a set of general questions.

One last word about information gathering: the client should not be pushed or bullied to give information that he does not want to give. The first interview is not, with most clients, the time for confrontation and coercion. Demanding that a client reveal things that are sensitive, embarrassing, or painful casts the therapist in the role of inquisitor. It not only suggests to the client that the therapist's agenda is more important than his own and that the therapist (rather than the client) will be doing the work of therapy, but it can also begin a power struggle that may set the tone of the sessions for weeks or months to come if the client even comes back for another visit. It is much better to let the client set the pace for self-revelation and to provide the protection he needs in order to feel safe, even at the expense of waiting a few sessions to fill in the map of what his life has been like. First trust, then data, is a good rule of thumb for the initial interview.

DIAGNOSIS AND ASSESSMENT

If I go to a medical doctor because my head aches or I have a persistent cough or my wrist is swollen and painful, I want that doctor to examine me and tell me what is wrong. I expect a diagnosis of my ailment. Many clients, seeking therapy for the first time, have that same expectation, and beginning therapists often expect themselves to be able to provide a quick diagnosis. The pressure to diagnose is increased by requests from agencies or from insurance companies who want a form filled out, complete with diagnostic category. Unfortunately, the medical model, in which diagnosis logically precedes treatment, is not always appropriate for psychotherapy. Accurate psychological diagnosis may require a whole series of sessions, and thus becomes inextricably interwoven with the therapy process. Diagnosis emerges from what occurs in therapy, just as therapy can occur in the process of gathering diagnostic information.

Not only is it often impossible to make an accurate assessment on the basis of one session with an anxious, defensive, or ambivalent client, but also the kind of assessment that you make will depend on the kind of treatment model you are using. The base-line data of the behaviorist, the script analysis of the transactional analyst, the lifestyle description of the Adlerian therapist—none of these fit the neat categories of the DSM III-R (the *Diagnostic and Statistical Manual of Mental Disorders,* 3d ed. rev., published in 1987 by the American Psychiatric Association) standardly used for reporting diagnoses in the United States. The therapist's first priority must be to gather data and formulate hypotheses that will generate a treatment plan, a sense of what can be done therapeutically for this particular client. "Without some skill in clinical assessment," comment Howard et al., "the therapist is like the lost traveler who has no map to tell him where he is and where he is going. To assess a client appropriately is to pinpoint where we are. To identify what needs to happen in treatment tells us where we need to go" (1987, p. 121). It is important to have such a map in mind as you work with a client. It is equally important to remember that the map is tentative, subject to change as your understanding of this particular client continues to develop week after week.

If you must submit a formal diagnosis because of the circumstances of your employment as a therapist, you will do well to keep two facts firmly in mind: first, the diagnostic system you are using (whether it is DSM III-R or any other) is an abstraction, a set of categories that may or may not provide a good fit for what your client is telling and showing you. You may be required to make a diagnosis of this sort; you are not required, once having made it, to believe in it absolutely. It is at best an approximation of what is true for any individual. Second, your diagnosis is subject to change as you learn more about the client. New information may turn up that will drastically alter your initial impression. There is a great temptation, after having made a diagnosis, to use it to filter all subsequent information. This creates a self-fulfilling prophecy: no matter what the client does or says, the therapist can distort that behavior to support her belief that the client is paranoid or has a major depression or an anxiety disorder. Initial diagnoses can take on a life of their own; like weeds in the garden, they tend to persist beyond the time when we think we have chopped them down and replaced them with something more useful.

For all of these reasons, it is not a good idea to share a formal diagnosis with a client. Telling someone that he has this or that "disorder" can be as frightening to him as it is misleading. The diagnosis sounds so formidable, so real. The client will not understand it as tentative, as a hypothesis, as a shorthand way of summing up a host of partially formulated impressions. Instead, it becomes Truth; it becomes His Illness; it leaves him helpless and ignorant, waiting passively for treatment by someone who knows him better than he knows himself.

ANSWERS

Clients, of course, do want some answers from you. They want to know what is wrong with them and whether you can help make them better, and they have a right to your best answers to such questions. The most useful way I have found to give this feedback is in two steps. First, summarize what you have heard the client say. "It sounds like you're under a lot of stress in your life right now. You feel that your wife and your children are making a lot of demands on you, and you don't know how to deal with them. So you tie yourself in knots, get angry, and then feel guilty about it." This kind of summary statement *is* a diagnosis and is probably at least as accurate (and certainly more understandable to the client) than a phrase filled with psychiatric jargon.

Having dealt with how things are now, the second step is to consider what will happen next. Does it make sense for this client to be in therapy? If so, are you the best person for the client to work with? If you do work together, what will that work be like? These are all questions to be dealt with before the first session comes to an end.

Will You Continue?

While you might like to offer your services to every new client who approaches you, there are a number of possible reasons for deciding not to do so. For instance, some prospective clients will simply not be appropriate for the way in which you prefer to work. As an example, I generally do not work with clients who come to me in order to meet the demands of someone else—the alcoholic (perhaps) who comes because the court insists that he get some sort of treatment, or the spouse who comes in order to please his or her partner. Other therapists with other styles and skills may choose to accept these clients. It is up to you, the therapist, to decide; your decision will be easier to the degree that you have thought out such policies ahead of time and set up guidelines for yourself. Moreover, clarifying your thinking here can prevent you (and your client) from being caught off-guard and having to make an unexpected decision in the middle of an initial interview.

Another reason for refusing to accept a particular client may be that he can get better help from someone else. You may not feel that you have the skills to deal with some kinds of problems. Treatment of substance abuse or sexual dysfunction, for example, calls for specialized training. Part of the purpose of an initial interview is screening and referral, making sure that the client gets the treatment most likely to help him. If you do not feel competent to help with the problem the client is presenting, say so and make a referral to someone who does work in that problem area. To do so is not only required by our ethical code, but also simply makes good, practical sense.

Another part of the process of deciding whether or not to work with someone is discovering whether therapist and client share the same goals. One way to further this discovery is for the therapist to summarize her perception of what the client wants to get out of therapy. Alternatively, she may state her tentative goals for the client and ask if this fits with what the client wants. It is important to make such statements open-ended, to give the client ample opportunity to add, amplify, or correct. It also is helpful for the therapist to expect that her first formulation will need some sort of editing by the client. "This is what I see us working toward. How would you change that to make it fit better with your expectations?" is a good invitation to this sort of editing. Johnson and Matross say,

> When a client enters therapy, both the client and the therapist have a set of goals for the relationship. A client may wish to improve his feeling state and have a more meaningful career and the therapist may wish to improve the client's general interpersonal functioning. Given that the goals of the client and therapist may or may not have a large overlap, the two must negotiate a set of goals which they can mutually commit themselves to achieve. (1977, p. 408)

It is not necessary that client and therapist agree on every particular of these goals, but rather that they find some area of intersection that both believe important and worthwhile and that neither be working toward some goal that the other finds objectionable. Goals can shift and change, and they often need to be renegotiated as treatment progresses. The initial menu is a starting place, a firm basis for beginning to work together rather than a final, carved-in-stone plan that must be followed throughout the course of therapy. Some initial agreement is necessary, though, in order to begin to learn how both client and therapist will use this particular therapeutic relationship. If a common ground cannot be reached, it is the therapist's responsibility to acknowledge the disagreement without blaming either herself or the client and to send the client elsewhere.

The "not blaming" part is critical here. If you decide to send a client somewhere else for treatment, do so matter-of-factly: you believe that he can get better help in some other place, that someone else would work better with him than you would. Nobody is bad or wrong, incompetent or incurable; you simply want this person to get the kind of help that you think would work best for him. Give the client this information as soon as you're sure of it yourself—don't string him along or let him commit himself to working with you only to feel rejected at the end of the session.

If you do want to work with him, let him know that, too. That's part of the information he needs in order to make his own decision about continuing. Only one part, though; there are other things he needs to know as well. Hare-Mustin et al. (1979) point out that the therapist has an ethical responsibility to let a prospective client know something about the procedures that the therapist will use and the possible side-effects (if any) of those procedures. He also must be informed about the qualifications and the policies of the therapist (the fee scale, for instance, and whether he will be charged for missed sessions). Finally, he must know what other alternatives exist—can he get help for his problems anywhere else? Before asking the client for a therapy commitment, the therapist must find a way to give him this information.

After giving him these facts and letting him know that you are interested in working with him, find out what *he* wants. Ask directly; don't just assume that he will want to schedule another session. "Do you want to work with me on these problems?" Or tell him what makes sense to you: "I'd like to meet with you once a week, at least for a while. How does that sound to you?" You may want to encourage him to take some time to consider his decision carefully: "Sometimes people like to take a day or two to think about how things have gone in a first session before deciding whether or not to continue. Would it be helpful for you to have some time, and then let me know what you have decided?"

How Will You Work Together?

The client's decision about continuing in treatment may have been made before you get around to asking him about it, or it may emerge out of a discussion of what therapy is going to be like for him. By the end of the first session, each of you has begun to form some ideas about what the other is like and how therapy will be structured. The client, though, is at a serious disadvantage here. He has experienced you only in the initial interview, and the structure of that initial session may be very different from later ones. Or his idea of therapy may have been shaped by experiences with other therapists or by movies or books or TV in which treatment procedures are quite different from your personal style. Failing to spell out some of the basics may lead to awkwardness and confusion, with each of you wondering why the other is not doing the right thing. Not only is it an ethical requirement to tell the client in a straightforward way what you expect will happen during future sessions, it also makes good therapeutic sense. "Our hours together will be your time to use to talk about whatever you want," is a good frame for a nondirective approach. Other therapists may want the client to use a contracting method. "At the beginning of each of our sessions, I'll be asking you what specific behavior or problem you want to work on during that session." Still others will be most interested in emotional exploration: "Much of what you've been telling me has to do with painful feelings, feelings that are interfering with your ability to enjoy life. In our work together, we will explore those feelings and find out what can be done to get them under control."

Before sharing your own expectations, though, find out what the client expects or hopes will happen in therapy. "Do you have any expectations about how we might work together?" Or, "Assuming we do decide to work together, what's your fantasy of what that will be like?" Questions such as these help the client to clarify for himself what he wants; his answers also give you some guidelines for how much and what kinds of structuring you will need to provide.

Remember that, even though your own behavior makes perfect sense to you, it may seem strange or incomprehensible to the client. Tell him what you are doing and why. If you plan to take notes, explain how they will be used and whether you will continue to do so after the first few sessions. (In my opinion, taking notes during an interview, except possibly the initial one, is a poor strategy. Taking notes while the client is talking can derail his train of thought as well as distract your attention from what he's saying now. It is much better to allow yourself a few minutes after each interview to jot down your notes while the session is still fresh in your mind.)

Many therapists record their sessions, and some agencies regularly use videotape for training and supervision. Again, explain to your client why you are taping the sessions and what use will be made of the tapes, and make sure that the client understands and agrees with your plans. It is particularly important to reassure clients as to the confidentiality of the recordings, who will be allowed to hear or see them, and what provisions are made for protecting the client's identity. Are the tapes saved week after week, or are they reused so that no permanent record is kept of the sessions? How can the client be sure that some friend or acquaintance (another student in the training program, a friend who works at the clinic, an acquaintance of his wife who works for another agency in town) will not hear one of the tapes? A simple explanation of how the tapes will be used and what will happen to them when the therapist is done using them usually is sufficient to allay client anxieties on this score.

How Often, How Long, How Much?

Obviously, before telling the client how often sessions will be scheduled and how long they will be, the therapist needs to decide for herself what sort of pattern would be most helpful. In a structured situation in which all clients are seen weekly for the traditional fifty-minute hour, the decision has already been made. If not, a particular client may be seen more frequently or less frequently. For most clients and for most therapeutic styles, the once-a-week format works reasonably well; it has the added advantage of simplifying the task of keeping track of appointments. At the beginning of treatment, most clients need to be seen at least this often in order to build up therapeutic momentum; with longer intervals rapport development is much slower, and the work tends to be choppy and disconnected rather than cumulative. Some clients may need to be seen more than once a week.

> Patients who do a lot of acting out, evoking recurrent crises in their lives with friends, at home, and at work, may...require more frequent contacts. Otherwise we could spend one hour administering first aid each week, our work would be limited to exploring that week's crises without ever moving beyond them into what there is within the patient which necessitates all this furor (Kopp 1977, p. 45)

The fifty-minute hour, like the weekly session, facilitates schedule keeping. It is almost certainly the therapist's convenience, rather than any theoretical consideration, which has made it so common. Yet, it does seem to be a workable length of time—long enough to explore in detail and with some leisure, yet not so long as to fatigue either therapist or client unduly. In my practice I deviate from the fifty-minute hour only when I have some specific therapeutic reason for doing so. A child or a severely disturbed adult may be unable to maintain concentration for a full-length session, and for him a twice-weekly, half-hour session may work better. For couples or families a single hour may not be enough to deal with all that is going on in the session.

How much is all of this going to cost? You can be sure that every client thinks of this question, whether they ask it aloud or not. Clients should be informed of the fee per session at the time scheduling is discussed; if some sort of sliding fee scale is available, this is the time to settle the whole question of payment. Dealing with money issues is difficult for many therapists. (We will discuss this issue further in Chapter 13.) They should be met head-on and matter-of-factly, for no amount of hedging will make them go away. The client is paying for his time with you, and he needs to know what that payment will be and how the payment is to be made.

Ideally, clients have the right to know how long their treatment can be expected to last. Practically, it is often difficult or impossible to make such a prediction, especially on the basis of a single interview. An estimation of the overall length of treatment needed may be received by the client as a promise that you will cure him in that length of time. (Notice who is active and who is passive here.) It is usually better to suggest that you and the client work together for some specific number of sessions after which you can evaluate together what has happened and determine whether the client will continue.

ENDING THE SESSION

The first contact with a client establishes a whole set of precedents that will flavor future sessions for weeks to come. From relatively minor matters, like who sits down first and where, to more important patterns of talking and silence, choosing a focus for discussion, and how limits will be respected or not respected, the client is developing beliefs about what therapy will be like for him. It is particularly important, at the close of the first session, to set a pattern for ending the interview that will be comfortable for both of you. Many beginning therapists are tempted to stretch out the first hour, to allow more time if the client seems to want it. There is an awkwardness about ending, a social sense that we should not cut people off or leave a conversation before the other person is ready. After all, we have been taught all our lives to be polite. Yet the end of the first session is often the first test of the therapist's limits, the first opportunity for both client and therapist to discover whether and how the therapist really will say "no."

Although it is important to keep to an established time framework, it is obviously unwise and unhelpful to cut the client off too abruptly. To say, "I'm sorry, our time is up" when the client is in the middle of a long explanation, especially if he is dealing with emotionally charged material, seems very cold and unfeeling. Yet not interrupting can allow the session to stretch well beyond its allotted time. The best way I know to avoid this dilemma is to begin to wind up the interview at least ten minutes before it must really end. "We have only a few minutes left of our time together today, so some of what you are talking about may have to wait until we meet again. Let's see if I've got the main points, though...." or "Our time is almost up, and there are a few things I need to clarify with you before you leave today..." are good examples. Having given notice in this way, it becomes easier for both therapist and client to accept the reality of the clock when the hour does end: "There's no more time left. I really want to hear more about what you've been telling me, so let's plan to pick up next time where we left off today."

Notice that all of the examples I have in that last paragraph involved taking charge of the conversation, shifting from the client's to the therapist's agenda. This can be the lead-in to the whole discussion of continuation of treatment, and must be done early enough in the hour to allow you to finish that discussion. If there's time left over, you may choose to go back to whatever the client was talking about before you shifted gears. Or you may end the session—there's no magic rule that the first session must last a certain length of time, and if everything feels comfortably closed, there may be no need to open it up again.

The hour ends. A smile, perhaps a handshake, and your client is gone. If you and he have chosen to continue, you have set the stage for one of the most exciting and challenging relationships possible between two human beings. In fact, though you may not realize it, the relationship, with its challenge and excitement, has already begun.

4 THE EARLY PHASE

The first phase of therapy is a period of building trust, of testing limits, of discovering what the therapeutic process is and what kinds of learning and changing it can bring about. Everything is new and strange; neither client nor therapist knows quite what to expect of the other. The client wants relief from the pain that brought him to therapy in the first place, and he wants it soon. The therapist, particularly if she is a beginner, may want to prove to the client (and to herself) that she can help, that therapy can make a difference. The danger is obvious: hurry up and fix it, hurry up and make something change. In our eagerness to get results, it is all too easy to overlook the importance of creating a situation in which the client can begin to discover his own strength, his own rhythm of change and growth, his own self. And yet it is that internal process, not some set of quick tricks from the therapist, which will allow him to change in the most lasting and meaningful ways. "The relationships are the effective ingredients (of psychotherapy), not the techniques," says Hynan (1981, p. 13). The best advice I know for this first phase of treatment is: slow down. There are a number of rather technical tasks which need to be taken care of during the early stages of therapy; if you attend to them and do them well, the client's changing and growing and initial symptom relief will usually take care of itself.

BUILDING RAPPORT

We talked in Chapter 3 about the sense of defeat and one-down-ness that is typical of the new client, the conviction that he has failed in managing his life (otherwise, why is he here?). Depending on the kinds of defenses he has developed over the years, he may react to the therapy situation by appearing super-strong ("I've really got it mostly together; I just want to talk things over and get a little help on one or two minor points"), by freezing up and not knowing what he really wants, or by spilling into tears or rage or sullen hopelessness at the first possible opportunity. However he reacts, there is one basic thing he needs from his therapist: acceptance. He needs that therapist to accept him as he is, to listen to and care about what he has to say. And at the same time, he is likely to resist that acceptance, to distrust it. Paradoxically, the better the relationship feels to him, the more accepted and comfortable and invested he becomes, the more fearful he may be. He does not trust those feelings because many of his past experiences with relationships have ended in pain and disappointment, and he has learned that it is not very safe to expect things to be any different (Stiles 1979).

So there in the other chair sits your new client: scared, belligerent, discouraged, strong, whatever. Underneath the mask that he chooses to present is usually a frightened, angry, or hopeless human being. Your first job as therapist is to accept all of this person—the mask as well as the underlying feelings. It is too soon to start digging past the front he presents, and it is too late to pretend that the front is all there is. You are there for all of this person, for what he chooses to show you and for what he chooses to conceal. You value whatever he presents, and you respect his right and his need to reveal himself at his own pace. Later you may decide to push, to confront, to employ any of the techniques that you know how to use, but not now. Now your job is to accept, to listen, to be there with the client as fully and completely as you possibly can be.

Rapport, that almost tangible sense of contact and trust between client and therapist, is created out of acceptance. And acceptance is conveyed by listening patiently, without judgment or prompting, to all of what the client has to say. The therapist's genuine interest will show not only in the words she uses, but also in her facial expression, her body position, her inflections, her gestures. "My posture and attitude," says Kopp, "are meant to communicate my interest in getting to know the patient, and my willingness to let the patient get to know me" (1977, p. 40). Interest without demand, the unforced willingness to know and to be known, is rare indeed in the currency of human relationships. The client may not know quite what to do in such a situation; he will be wary of trusting it at first; yet, out of his first hesitant tests (of the therapist and of himself), trust can begin to grow.

Listening, respecting, and being in contact with a client are relatively easy when the client is willing and able to talk freely about his problems. Often, though, clients do not know where or how to start. Everything is confused, complicated. They do not really know what the central problem is or how to describe it. Things just feel generally bad. Many clients come to therapy with an expectation that they should be able to lay the whole problem out, step by logical step and, since their life does not seem to follow that kind of logical pattern, they do not know how to begin talking about it. Others come expecting the therapist to take over, to provide some kind of magical structure that will begin the healing process, and so they wait for direction, for questions, for someone to tell them what to do. With such clients, one can be supportive in providing some structure while at the same time giving them assurance that whatever they choose to begin with is all right. "Tell me something about how you are feeling right now," or "What have things been like for you over the past few days?" are good lead-ins, as is Kopp's marvelously reassuring; "Of course it's hard to begin, but you can start anywhere. It's all attached" (1977, p. 40).

It *is* all attached and by reminding ourselves of that fact we can do much to calm our own anxious impatience to make something happen. All the verbal reassurance in the world will not make much difference if we are communicating nonverbally that we do not, in fact, want the client to be saying whatever he is saying. We define ourselves to the client by everything we do in these early sessions and by everything we do not do as well. We define ourselves more clearly and fully than we know. Clients are amazingly sensitive to the tiny signals that we put out. Unfortunately, they are likely to distort the meaning of those signals, reading into our behavior disapproval of themselves rather than our own sense of uncertainty or anxiety. The most therapeutic thing I can do for a new client is to take care of myself, to give myself permission simply to wait and listen, to not be responsible for the client's behavior. The paradox is obvious: by not making something happen, I do make the most important something of all happen. I begin to build rapport with my client.

Waiting and listening, however, do not require that the therapist take a passive role. On the contrary, she is actively representing herself as concerned, involved, open, willing to accept seriously whatever the client wants to present. A good therapist will not be discounted, will not take on the role of critic or unable-to-help or frightened bystander (and any of these roles may be offered her by a new client). Good therapists value themselves and their skills just as they value their clients; one's respect for clients is conveyed, in part, by one's respect for oneself and what one is doing.

Johnson and Matross have outlined a three-step model which very neatly describes the process through which therapeutic trust is built and maintained. The first step occurs as the client "takes a risk by disclosing his problems, feelings, behavior, and ideas." Even as the client is speaking, the therapist is initiating step two: she "responds with warmth, accurate understanding, and cooperative intentions." The final step has to do with the actual content of the therapist's response: she discloses her perceptions of the client, her reaction to what is happening within the therapy session, and where appropriate, she shares relevant information about herself (1977, p. 412). Notice that this process recurs over and over again; it is a basic figure in the therapeutic dance. It begins with the risk that the client takes every time he enters the therapist's office, and it continues with every comment, every response, every tentative step of growth that he makes.

Whatever techniques you learn to employ, and however well you employ them, the rapport between you and your client will always be your most valuable tool. Ivey et al. (1987) assert that a client cannot be "creative" unless the therapist provides a warm and supportive environment. The sense of rapport that grows out of honest warmth and interest and support is the foundation, the catalyst that allows all the other things to work. If you communicate genuine interest in and acceptance of your client, along with a sense of your own confidence and competence, that rapport will grow. Fostering it is, without doubt, the single most important task of the early phase of therapy.

THE THERAPIST AS TEACHER

Establishing rapport does not occur in a vacuum. It is built in the context of the activities of the therapy interview, and your competence and confidence will manifest themselves in the way in which you carry out those activities. One of the therapist's roles which is especially important in the early phase of therapy is that of teacher. Therapists do teach. They teach the client how to use therapy, and they may teach other skills as well. As a rule clients rely upon the therapist-as-teacher more heavily early in treatment rather than late in treatment (Howard et al. 1987). Let us look explicitly at some of the kinds of teaching that a therapist may engage in early in the therapy process.

How to Talk

Bernard Steinzor, in his book *The Healing Partnership,* quotes a new client's description of a previous therapy experience: "Most of the time I was hearing something like 'tell me about your parents,' which I found very abstract. It meant almost nothing at all to me. I think maybe you will have to help me somehow...to know how to talk about it" (1967, p. 68). Steinzor was fortunate in having a client who was articulate about his not knowing, able to communicate his difficulties in understanding how to use talking as a tool for growth. More often, clients feel embarrassed about not understanding what is expected of them, and do not or cannot make such explicit requests of the therapist. They try this or that approach, they flounder, or they retreat into silence. Many do not realize that there are ways to use talk as a vehicle of change; they are locked into old patterns of accusing, complaining, or self-blame. They talk about others or describe incidents mechanically as if they themselves were somehow not there. The therapist struggles to find the person behind the words, to make contact with the feelings and the needs that go with the content. It is easy to get frustrated and angry with such clients, to label them defensive, resistant, or not really interested in changing. Rather than framing their behavior in this way, though, it is well to find out if they simply need to be taught some other ways of responding.

One way to teach is to give direct instructions or ask direct questions. "What were you feeling right then?" Be aware, though, that some clients may not know how to respond even to such a direct question. *Why is my therapist asking this?* they wonder. *What kind of feeling does she mean? Does she want to know what I'm thinking about, or what sensations I have in my body, or whether I like what's going on?* It's best, with a new or inexperienced client, to prepare the ground for feeling-oriented questions. "You have a brand-new look on your face, a look I've never seen before. I wonder what you're feeling." With such a lead-in, the client can begin to attend to just what is going on inside (Polster 1987).

A less directive method of teaching is that of selective attention. The therapist can attend to the personal response component of what a client is saying or to the feeling tone which appears to underlie a client's words. This conveys permission for and approval of further exploration of such issues. From a behaviorist point of view, she reinforces the client for certain kinds of talking and withholds reinforcement for other (hopefully, less productive) kinds. Since people learn to continue doing those things for which they are reinforced, selective attention can be a very useful teaching device. Beware, though: the principle operates whether you want it to or not. If you inadvertently get caught up in a long and fruitless digression, or if you over-respond to nonproductive client behavior out of some needs or fears of your own, you will inevitably be teaching that client to continue in the same vein.

Modeling appropriate client behavior, if it is not over-used, can also be a good teaching strategy. "If I had been in that situation, I think I would have felt..." "As I listen to you tell me about that, I feel sad." The danger is that such statements shift the focus from client to therapist and may also convey to the client that the therapist's reaction is the right one. It may be tempting, if you are a naturally verbal person, to begin to fill silences with examples of your own processing rather than allowing ample time for the client to work things through. The self-example, used sparingly, can be powerful as permission-giving, as teaching device, and as rapport-building; but used too often it can slow or halt the whole therapeutic process.

A Common Vocabulary

Every therapist builds up her own set of jargon, words and phrases which she has found particularly useful to describe concepts she employs in therapy. Some of these come from her theoretical background. Behavior modifiers use words like stimulus and response and base line; neurolinguistic programmers may mention minimal cues or fuzzy functions; transactional analysts talk of ego states and scripts. Too much jargon, of course, hinders therapy. It forces the client to move into your territory instead of you coming into his. Some teaching of terminology, on the other hand, can enhance the process. The words not only provide a quick and easy reference to important concepts, but also the very teaching process can focus the client's attention on parts of himself or of his behavior that he may not otherwise have noticed.

There may even be a special vocabulary that develops between therapist and client, unique to that relationship. Such vocabularies provide shortcuts in communication as well as reaffirm the uniqueness of the relationship. I had a client, for example, who created a fantasy of a nurturing grandma figure on whom she could call during times when she felt depressed and alone. She referred to this figure as "my Lady." Months later, in a quite different context, she talked about "my Lady." For both of us, the words evoked a rich recall of the fantasy work and a sense of the continuity and directedness of the whole therapeutic relationship.

At the beginning of treatment, you will need to check back many times with clients to find out if the words you and they are using mean the same things to both of you. If it feels comfortable, learn to use your client's vocabulary; but do not use speech patterns and words that are alien and will sound awkward and phoney coming from you. Similarly, give the client a chance to learn and use those concepts of yours which are comfortable for him. You will both be the richer for learning from each other, and the common vocabulary serves as one more strand in the bond of rapport that is growing between you.

Skill Building

Skills to be learned in therapy come in at least two varieties. One is the set of skills to be used in the therapy hour itself; the other consists of new behaviors which will be used in the client's life, replacing old pain-producing ones. In reality, most skills turn out to be useful in both arenas. The outside-of-therapy changes may be practiced and used during the therapy session, and many of the activities of the therapy hour can turn out to be quite useful in everyday life.

One of the most fundamental skills that most clients need to learn is that of monitoring their own behavior. Surprisingly often, people simply do not notice what they are doing or thinking or feeling. Some will be very alert and sensitive in one area and quite cut off in another. Others will confuse what is going on, will mistake thoughts for feelings, for instance, or will project their own internal behavior onto others or assume that other people's reactions are their own. "Of course I feel sad when my wife is upset!" "Whenever I get discouraged, I make everyone else blue." "What am I feeling? I'm feeling that I should have done it a different way." All of these comments were made by clients who needed to learn how to be aware of their own behavior and how to differentiate between the thinking, feeling, and acting aspects of that behavior.

Learning how to monitor oneself is a significant, if not necessary, precursor to change: it is very hard to do things differently if you do not notice when and how you are doing them now. Even if changes do occur in such behaviors—fortuitously or as a spin-off of other more conscious changes—they are less likely to last if the client does not notice them. Clients need to learn to be sensitive to their internal and external responses, to separate their own reactions from those of others, and to differentiate among the different aspects of their own behavior in order to make and to keep the kinds of changes that they want.

Closely related to self-monitoring is the ability to relax. Many clients cannot relax because they have not learned to recognize when and how they are tense. For such clients, self-monitoring leads to awareness of the need for relaxation skills. Others know that they are tense but do not know what to do about it. Here the concern about tension may preclude other kinds of self-monitoring so that relaxation training would logically precede training in behavioral awareness. Teaching clients to slow down, attend to their breathing, focus awareness on body processes, and practice progressive muscle relaxation can facilitate other therapeutic work, and it can also provide a useful tool in coping with the bustle of everyday life. Teaching relaxation techniques is commonplace in behavior therapy; it is increasingly done in other therapeutic settings as well. It is appropriate to do such teaching during the early phase of therapy so that the client can use the skills he has learned as he moves into later phases of his work.

Another important set of skills has to do with communication. Many clients come to therapy sadly deficient in this area. They do not know how to express themselves clearly, nor do they know how to listen. Learning to say what one means has obvious benefits for therapy; learning to listen well has equally obvious usefulness for out-of-therapy relationships. Lack of skill in communication is so common that a whole network of classes, workshops, seminars, and the like have sprung up to meet the need for such training. This gives the therapist a new set of options: rather than teach the client yourself, you may choose to refer him elsewhere for this kind of skill-building. Your decision will be based on considerations of how else you would rather use your time (practice in communication may be a very helpful structure to use during an early rapport-building period) and what the client's level of readiness is (clients who are very disturbed or discouraged may simply not be open to a group training approach). However it is accomplished, communication training is a highly appropriate adjunct to the early phase of therapy.

How to Be a Client

As therapists, we come to recognize rather quickly that some kinds of client behaviors are likely to be therapeutically useful, while others generally lead to frustration and wheel-spinning. Talking about what other people ought to do differently is the classic example of a nonprofitable therapeutic occupation. There are other behaviors which may be useful for some clients and not for others: the client who habitually hides his feelings behind a smokescreen of words may benefit from some silent, internal processing, for instance, while a shy and withdrawn client may need to learn to talk more freely.

You, the therapist, are likely to have a sense of what the client needs to do long before the client does. Part of your teaching job is to teach him how to use therapy or how to be a client. You do this in two ways: by attending and responding to the most therapeutically useful portion of every communication and by directing his attention to those topics and behaviors that he may be avoiding or overlooking. Says Zaro: "A topic must be dealt with in some way if a client repeatedly brings it up as a matter of concern, even if you do not judge it particularly relevant to the treatment. You must be responsive to the client's needs to talk about certain issues, yet you must also try to educate him or her about the most profitable way to approach discussion of the problem" (1977, p. 104).

Learning what to talk about and how is, in essence, learning to focus on change. After all, the purpose of therapy is change, growth, making things different than they have been. As you help a client to acquire this kind of focus, you are engaging in a kind of contracting process. Together, you and the client are building a contract to work toward new behaviors, new ways of being in the world. While contract-building does involve teaching on the part of the therapist, it is important enough to deserve a section of this chapter all to itself.

CONTRACTING FOR CHANGE

Making a therapeutic contract is an integral part of some therapeutic approaches. For others it is an optional attachment. There are few theoretical orientations in which contracting for change would be inappropriate. In these next paragraphs I will be describing an approach to contracting which I have found useful in my own practice. As you read it, be aware that this is only one way to deal with the topic; you will undoubtedly develop variations of your own which will fit your personal style just as mine fits for me.

Steps in Negotiating a Contract

A change contract is simply a statement of what the client intends to accomplish by means of therapy; negotiating such a contract is in part "an educative process in which the patient learns the behavioral expectations that the mental professional holds—and vice versa" (Group for the Advancement of Psychiatry 1987). As we discuss the making of a therapeutic contract, we will focus primarily on the behavior of the client. We do well to remind ourselves occasionally that the therapist, too, learns and bends and changes in the contracting process.

There are many kinds of contracts, some more useful than others. The most useful ones often involve a series of steps. The first of these steps is to agree on the problem. In order to make a contract to change something, the client must know what part of his life situation needs changing. The focus of the contract may shift as treatment proceeds, or the initial contract may become one of a whole set of interrelated contracts, but he must start somewhere, and the starting will be easier if there is a focus, a clear identification of the problem area, shared by client and therapist.

Next, the client must make a commitment to solve the problem. He may not yet know what the solution will be, but he must decide that he is, in fact, willing to make a change in his thoughts, feelings, or behaviors in order to make things different for himself. Having made that commitment, he is ready to move to step three: choosing a plan of action related to his goal. Here, as with the first two steps, much therapeutic work may be done. Different possibilities can be explored, together with the client's reactions to them. Often the first two steps will be reexamined, defining a new goal as a result of insights derived during the plan-of-action phase.

The final step, once problem and decision to change and plan are synchronized, is to decide upon a way to evaluate whether or not the contract has been met. A good contract includes an objective criterion for success, so that both therapist and client will know when the work of that particular contract is complete.

Claude Steiner (1974) points out that a therapy contract, like a legal contract, must have four characteristics. First, it is arrived at through mutual consent. Both therapist and client must agree to the terms of the contract. If I, the therapist, am working to change the client in ways that he does not want, we are not working on the same contract; similarly, if the client is using me to accomplish changes of which I do not approve, he will not get very good therapy for his purposes. Second, both legal and therapeutic contracts involve valid consideration. Both parties must get some benefit from carrying out the contract. Looking at it another way, each party to the contract must contribute something. The therapist gives her time and skill, and the client must give something too. Says Steiner: "When consideration does not exist, then the situation becomes a Rescue" (p. 297). Neither rescuing nor being rescued is, in the long run, therapeutic.

The third characteristic of a legal contract is that both parties be competent to enter into the agreement. Translated into therapy terms, this means that the therapist be qualified to do the kind of work the client needs, and that the client be competent (not psychotic, drunk, or severely retarded) to decide what kinds of changes he wants to make. Finally, legal contracts must have a lawful object. Neither the contract itself (the kinds of changes being contracted for) nor the consideration may be contrary to the law or to the ethical and moral standards of the participants. Steiner comments that this is seldom an issue but must be carefully considered when working with clients involved in such activities as drug use, violence, or other criminal behaviors.

Contracts can be built for different time lengths and different situations, and many therapists invite clients to become involved in contracting in a variety of ways. The overall therapy contract or treatment contract is a statement about the long-term or final goal of therapy. "How will you know when you are done with your treatment?" or "How do you want to be feeling and acting when you finish therapy?" are good ways to introduce contracting at this level. Within the overall contract, it is often useful to build session contracts. "What do you want to accomplish during our time together today?" can help the client move from a passive, you-tell-me-what-to-talk-about position to being an active and responsible choice-maker. A third kind of contract is the homework contract, in which the client agrees to try out some different kind of behavior, to experiment with acting or thinking or fantasizing in a new way, during the time until his next session.

Each of these kinds of contracts is related to the others. The session contracts define sub-goals of the overall treatment contract. Homework contracts often grow out of the work around a session contract; conversely, session contracts are often suggested by the client's experience as he carries out his homework.

Building a Contract

It is very well to describe the different kinds of contracts and talk about how useful they are, but how do we help a client to build one? Muriel James has developed a series of questions which form a very handy outline or framework for the contract-building process (1977, pp. 106–107). First, she asks the client, "Is there anything you want that would enhance your life?" Few of us can resist the open-endedness of this sort of question; it invites us to look at what we really want to have and to change. It also points in a positive direction, focusing on what we do want, how we would like things to be, rather than on how awful things are now.

Having described his ideal situation, the client is next asked, "What would you need to change in order to get what you want?" If the client says that someone else must change—wife must do thus and such, children or boss or friends must behave differently—the question is restated: "Well, unless they come in for treatment, we are not likely to change them. Are there any changes *you* could make in yourself that would enhance your life?" The client may then begin to look at things he could do for himself or at things he could do to get others to change. If he does the latter, it is important to focus the contract on his own changes. Do not make success contingent on someone else's behavior. "I could start asking my wife directly rather than hinting around for what I want" is a good beginning for a contract, provided that the contract is defined as successful whether or not the wife meets the requests.

The next question is often an eye-opener, even though it seems on the surface to be very similar to the preceding one: "What would you be *willing to do* to effect the change?" Many clients are surprised by their own reluctance to make the first move or by their desire to be given a magical solution at this point. Others are excited by the idea that they can begin right now to bring about the changes they want. Still others begin to realize how they defeat themselves by deciding ahead of time that whatever they try will not work, how they set themselves up to stay stuck in their old, pain-producing patterns.

Once the client has decided what he is willing to do first, he is asked, "How will other people know when the change has been made?" This question helps him to choose a means of evaluating his success objectively. Objective evaluation allows clients (and therapists) to pause and congratulate themselves when they make progress; it can also provide ways to get reinforcements for new behaviors from other important people in the client's life. "My wife will see that I'm not raiding the refrigerator every night" can be a springboard to a decision to ask the wife to reinforce the change by telling the client that she has noticed or by giving him a hug.

The last (and perhaps the most important) question is, "How might you sabotage yourself?" As the client describes the banana peels that he might throw in the way of carrying out his contract, he inoculates himself against such self-defeating behavior. He may recognize that the sabotage is a pattern, repeated many times in the past, and move to a contracting focus that will deal explicitly with a change in that pattern. He may also discover the emotional underlay, the fear or anger or grief that has helped to maintain his unproductive behaviors over the years.

Each of James's questions can precipitate useful therapeutic work, work that may well extend beyond a single session. Often getting a contract, or a series of contracts, constitutes the major part of the therapeutic treatment. At other times, dealing with the whys and hows of contracts that fail turns out to be the focal point of therapy. Either way, using James's model of contract building can be an excellent way of maintaining direction, of continuing to move the client toward getting what he came for and making the changes he wants.

Closing the Contract

Once the contract has been decided upon, there are still a few loose ends to clear up. You, the therapist, know the characteristics of a good contract, so share these with your client and ask him to check out his contract to make sure it is the way he wants it. Is it clear and understandable? A good way to get a clear contract is to phrase it in language that an eight-year-old child could understand. Is it objective, does it include some observable change, some unmistakable signal by which both the client and those around him can know that the contract has been completed? Is it achievable? It is important that the client be sure he has not built a contract for failure, a contract which is too long-term, or involves too many changes all at once, or depends on someone else's behavior. Is it something he believes he should do? Does it fit with his value system? Finally, will he enjoy doing it? A contract which has no fun in it, which generates no sense of excitement or anticipation, is also a contract for failure. Like most New Year's resolutions, it may be followed grimly for a while, but there is little chance for it in the long run.

As you work with the client in finalizing his contract, watch out for words like "I'll try" or "maybe" or "I'd like to." These are hedge words, words that leave the door open for not following through. They often are an indication that the client has not yet clearly committed himself to the contract, or that he is contracting to do something that he really does not believe he can do. You can invite him to experiment with stating the contract in a more positive way—"I will" instead of "I'll try to," for instance—and to let himself know which feels more comfortable. If he still opts for the perhaps version, ask him to try the opposite—"I won't..."— and discover how that feels.

Be alert, too, for the open-ended contract, the one that involves doing more or better or less often. These contracts cannot be completed, because no matter how much or how little one changes, one can always do more. Ask the client how much more is enough, or how he will know when he is done. Similarly, watch for no-observable-change contracts, contracts to "think about" or "get in touch with." A client who wants to contract for some internal, nonobservable behavior can be encouraged to build in a reporting clause, a commitment to tell someone (telling is observable behavior) at regular intervals how he is progressing.

The last step in formally closing the contract is to invite the client to actually write it down and then read it out loud. Seeing the words and hearing his own voice saying them carries a strong impact. Having done this, and agreeing that it is the way he wants it, the client signs the contract, using the signature he uses for legal transactions. Some therapists invite clients to post their contracts in a place where they will see them every day, to serve both as a reminder and an affirmation of their decision to change.

Writing and signing the contract and posting it in an obvious place are useful and powerful elements, but they are not absolutely essential. If the client is uncomfortable with these last steps, do not be rigid about them. The essential point is that the contract is clearly stated and clearly accepted. "If the client is not able (or not willing) to make even an ambivalent acceptance, then therapy, in its usual form, cannot proceed" (Wells 1982, p. 99). When it is accepted, moving on into the actual process of therapy is a natural next step.

LIMITS

As you and your client begin the work of therapy and begin to use the therapy relationship as a vehicle for change, there will inevitably be setbacks. Therapeutic change is not a smooth unfolding from beginning to end. It has its ups and downs, its leaps forward and its slidings back. For your own welfare, as well as for that of your client, you will need to recognize this unevenness as a natural part of the therapeutic process. Anticipating the rough spots can help you to know that they too can signal progress.

Of all the things that appear to disturb the smooth flow of therapy and can certainly disturb the peace of mind of the therapist, the most common is limit-testing. It is a rare client who does not check out his therapist's limits in one way or another, consciously or unconsciously. Because limit-testing is so common (I am tempted to say inevitable), an important task for the early phase of treatment is spelling out just what the limits are. It is hard to confront a client about limit-testing—or deal with it in any other way, for that matter—if you haven't clarified the ground rules in the first place.

The therapist needs to know for herself exactly what her limits are, what she can expect of herself, and where she will draw the lines of involvement with and service to her clients. Beginning therapists find it especially easy to get sucked into giving more and more to a needy or demanding client; knowing ahead of time what you will and will not do helps you to be clear about your degree of involvement without feeling guilty for not doing more, or feeling resentful over having been conned into providing more than you had intended. Clients need to be told early in treatment what they can expect from the therapist, so that they have clear permission to use that therapist to the fullest and at the same time know what they will not be allowed to do or demand.

Among the most frequently tested limits are those of time. I make it clear to my clients that they are expected to be on time for their appointments, and to let me know well in advance if they must cancel a session. Sessions end at the scheduled time, even if the client was late. I am not willing to punish myself for a client's tardiness. Appointments missed without advance notice are to be paid for. I impose the same limits on myself: I am on time for my appointments, and I give ample notice if I must reschedule a session.

Having set limits around time, it is important to respect them. Tacking an extra ten minutes on the end of an hour, to make up for the client being late by that much, tells the client that the therapist is willing for him to be late and will, in fact, inconvenience herself to help him continue that pattern. Similarly, providing extra time, extra sessions, or frequent phone check-ins (unless these have been clearly contracted for) is not helpful to a client who needs to deal with his own issues around living with limits. Therapists who find themselves frequently on overtime with clients would do well to question their own motivation, their own need to please or rescue or prove themselves.

As for behavior during the therapy hour, I have found it useful to begin by setting just two absolute limits: (1) the client may not hurt either himself or me; and (2) anything that he breaks, he will be expected to pay for. Beyond this, we may need to negotiate if either of us engages in behaviors that get in the way of the work, and we will deal with these if and when they become a problem. Stating the rules in this way startles a lot of clients; it had never occurred to them that they might want to hurt someone or break something. The surprise effect can be beneficial in itself; it underscores the notion that this therapy stuff really is different from other kinds of relationships. If those are the only two things I cannot do in here, what in the world *will* I do?

Depending on your own personal style and your theoretical orientation, you may impose additional constraints on your or the client's behavior. Some therapists, for instance, will not physically touch a client or allow a client to touch them. Some have a particular chair they want to sit in, or a particular chair (or couch) for the client. Whatever your limits and ground rules are, the first and most important thing is to clarify them for yourself. The second is to share them with your client. And the third is to hold to them, unless you have a clear therapeutic reason for making a change.

Spelling out limits like this may feel awkward at first, but it is important that they be stated, and stated explicitly, from the start. You can soften the statements by prefacing them with: "There are a few things I require of all my clients" or "There are only two requirements for how you use your time here at the clinic." But spell them out one way or another. You may never need to bring them up again—but if you do need to, you will be very glad that you laid the groundwork earlier.

Of course, different clients may need different sorts of limits. What is hurtful to one may be helpful to another. The rule of not hurting oneself in therapy may be extended and elaborated upon in many different ways. "It's not helpful for you to come in and be angry week after week with no sense of how you want to change that behavior, and I'm not willing to support you in continuing to do that," says the therapist to a rebellious teenager. To another client, she might confront different but equally self-destructive behavior: "When you refuse to share your feelings with me, or even to let yourself know what those feelings are, you are following the same pattern that gets you into trouble with your wife and your friends. If you aren't willing to work toward changing that behavior, then I can't help you." In other words, the rule that the client may not hurt himself or the therapist goes beyond physical injury; it includes all sorts of behaviors which get in the way of positive change. Neither the client nor the therapist may know what these specific behaviors are when the initial rules are laid out; it is the therapist's responsibility to clarify, explain, and insist that protective limits be respected as the problem behaviors emerge.

As the therapist sets and maintains limits with her client, she demonstrates her respect for both his welfare and her own. She will not allow him to discount his own needs or values; nor will she herself be discounted. To do otherwise invites him, in the long run, to feel guilty, one-up, or cheated of the protection he needs—any of which will ultimately interfere with his treatment.

CONCLUSIONS

There is much more that could be said about the early phase of therapy. We could list typical presenting problems or describe the many ways that clients approach the idea of therapy. We could talk about how people get stuck and stay stuck, how they are frightened or hurt or angry and, because of their pain, fail to discover more comfortable ways of behaving. We could describe the frustrating moments and the joyful ones, the times when the therapist feels she could cure the world and the times when she wonders why she did not go into some other line of work (like painting doorknobs, for instance).

These are the things that you will discover for yourself. You will learn what to expect in your early sessions with clients, and you will learn that you can never predict everything, that there are always surprises. Most important, you will learn that you can cope with the job, that you can handle the demands that therapy makes, and that you can even survive your own errors.

About the time you are beginning to believe all of this, you will discover that one of your clients has moved out of that now-familiar early stage and has entered (snuck in, really) a different phase of treatment. Middle phase work is different from early phase work, and so you will feel new and strange again for a while. When that happens, one way to take care of yourself is to review all that you do know about providing therapy; by now, that is quite a lot. And another thing you can do is learn more about middle phase work. That is what the next chapter of this book is about.

5 THE MIDDLE PHASE

I want to stipulate right from the beginning that just about everything that I will be saying in this chapter can sometimes be shown to be untrue. For every generalization about the middle phase of treatment, there will be clients who do not fit, who do not follow the rules. Or, from another perspective, every client you see can be expected to vary from standard middle phase behavior in at least one respect. Middle phase work is as varied as the clients themselves; it requires of the therapist sensitivity, flexibility, and an enormous tolerance for ambiguity. It requires that we follow the client's lead and trust in his innate capacity to learn and to grow and to know what work he needs to do.

Paradoxically, middle phase work also demands that the therapist keep the work focused and on track. The paradox is resolved when we realize that our clients operate at many levels and can move in many directions at once. One of the signals of middle phase work may be a sense of confusion, of muddledness, of not really knowing what is going on. The therapist, if she is to be most helpful, must be able to step back from the muddle enough to sense the overall direction in which the work is proceeding and to invite the client to explore material which will further that overall direction.

Contributing to the confusion of middle phase work is the frequent discovery that the problems which first brought the client to therapy are well on their way to solution. "The first indication of completion of Phase 1 may come in the form of the patient's finding that there no longer seems to be much to talk about. This is often expressed in terms of having solved the problems that first led to seeking treatment" (Kopp 1977, p. 139). Many clients will terminate therapy at this point: they got what they came for; they are satisfied; they are done. Often with a sense of regret for possibilities not realized, the therapist bids them farewell. Others, however, want more. Even though the immediate problems do not loom as large, these clients sense that there is more to be learned, more growing to be done. The focus shifts from external problem-solving to internal growing and changing. Emotional issues take precedence over cognitive ones, and the therapeutic relationship itself is often the arena in which these issues are worked through.

Indeed, within some therapeutic orientations the relationship between therapist and client is considered the major legitimate vehicle for therapeutic change. These orientations focus on the development of the transference, the process through which the client uses the therapist as stand-in for the important persons throughout his life. As the transference develops, the therapist sees to it that the old, maladaptive patterns with these important people are not recreated. This allows the client to reexperience old relationships in new ways. The therapist helps the client to understand the old patterns, both intellectually and emotionally, and to find new and better working replacements for them. In such a framework, the relationship *is* middle phase therapy. "The middle phases of therapy therefore concern everything to do with the tending of the therapeutic relationship and the exercise of technique so that the process can unfold. The therapist learns more all the time, as does the patient while he experiences the situations and conflicts" (Balsam & Balsam 1974, p. 90).

The transition from early to middle phase work, then, is marked by a shift from focusing on external problems to focusing on internal experiences, from primarily cognitive-level work to primarily emotional-level work, from looking at relationships outside of therapy to experiencing relationships within the therapy session itself. Theoretically, it sounds good; it makes good sense; but often it is not nearly as clear-cut as I have made it seem. We cannot always tell just which phase a client is in. Even when he seems to have entered, worked through, and left a particular phase, he may do the same sorts of things again when he moves on to deal with a new issue. "Often the work proceeds in fits and starts (and often does not seem to be proceeding at all, but rather unraveling or working backward). The 'typical' case is in fact quite atypical" (Wachtel 1982, p. xiii).

When you stop to think about it, there is no particular reason why anyone should progress evenly from phase to phase. Your client has a number of external problems which might typically be dealt with in Phase 1. He has some internal issues which involve typical Phase 2 work. As he works on some of the Phase 1 material, his sense of trust in the therapeutic relationship grows. He experiences a new kind of being-with-another, and he uses that experience and that trust to begin to work with some internal (Phase 2) issues. Later, he may go back to rework some of the earlier material from a different perspective, or he may return to a Phase 1-type stance with regard to a new set of problems. He may run into a particularly scary or painful spot in his Phase 2 work and regress in the relationship as a way of staying safe or keeping control. Or he may choose to deal with less threatening material or to slow down and not open up new areas for a while. All of these are normal and appropriate shifts over the course of therapy.

We should not expect or demand that a client, once involved in middle phase work, continue to work at that level. The permission to shift, to change, to draw back as well as to move forward, is an important facet of the therapeutic relationship, as we shall see in a later section of this chapter. If we give such permission genuinely, honestly supporting his need to move more slowly or to pull away from some kinds of work, we can be sure that, when he is ready, the client will move forward again.

EMOTIONAL WORK

Problem solving or figuring out is useful. Together with relationship building, problem solving is one of the major activities of the early phase of therapy. As we move into Phase 2, however, we move into the period of personality change. Not only is the client figuring out how to deal with his world, he is learning and experiencing new ways to react, to feel, literally new ways to *be*. It is not enough that you understand his old patterns or even that he understand them. "Knowing the initiation of a pattern is not sufficient to produce therapeutic change—just as knowing what pushed a stone over a cliff is not sufficient to stop its fall" (Bugental 1987, p. 158). In order for change to occur at this level, he must experience new patterns. Most often, such experiencing takes place in the context of feelings. The client allows himself, because he trusts the relationship, to let go of his old defenses. He opens himself to emotions and sensations and memories which he had previously walled off or distorted. Like a forest stream when the warmth of spring begins to melt its ice and invite new life, the client very slowly begins to change, to come alive.

Hans Strupp points out that "psychotherapeutic change does not depend on the education of historical antecedents but on the reliving and modification of historically meaningful patterns that come alive in the patient-therapist relationship *in vivo*" (1977, p. 17). Talking about how things were with my mother can be a useful way for me to find my way into middle phase work; but if I do not ever go beyond simply talking about it, I'll not make many lasting changes in myself. I must somehow reexperience that relationship emotionally and learn at an emotional level that it is possible to respond differently. Only then will I be ready to take that learned possibility out into the world of my present-day relationships. Indeed, once such an emotional reexperiencing has occurred, I may not even have to make an effort to experience my everyday world differently: it will literally feel different to me. I may have to work hard to change my habitual response patterns, my behavior, but I will surely notice that behavior in ways that I never would have been aware of before.

The therapist's first responsibility in the middle phase of therapy is to facilitate this kind of awareness. She must use the relationship she has established with the client to provide protection and permission for the client to relate to her and to others in new ways. Bugental (1987) suggests that we occasionally pause and ask ourselves such questions as:

> If our talk continues pretty much as it is now will the client become more deeply immersed or less so? Will he, of his own accord, move to a level at which we can deal more effectively with his issues, or must I intervene in the flow in some way to encourage that movement? In the way he's responding now is there a hint of his being threatened? Do I need to change the way I'm taking part to reduce the possibility that he may withdraw from our involvement? (p. 62)

It is a delicate dance, with movements forward and back, changes in tempo, pauses to rest, and surges of enormous growth and high adventure. Through it all the therapist must never lose sight of the client's overall goals. We are not hired by our clients to entertain them, to dazzle them with our intuition or our deductive skills, or even to make them feel better. Our purpose is to help them change and grow. Strupp says that the therapist "cannot—nor should he—escape the realization that his assigned task is to effect or participate in the process of producing personality or behavior change in another person. That is his job; that is his *metier*. To deny this essential core of his function is to rob it of its basic meaning" (1977, p. 4).

Emotion and Discomfort

To change, especially if the change is from something familiar to something quite unknown, usually requires some amount of discomfort. It seems safe to say that nobody is likely to make significant behavior changes unless the behavior patterns they are giving up are not working any more. If I am happy with how things are, why should I change? "It is only when the familiar, the ordinary, repetitive, the predictable is made impossible by the therapist—only when the *gestalten* are destroyed—that the client is forced, kicking and screaming in terror—to give birth to something new" (Kovaks 1976, pp. 324–325). The kicking and screaming in terror part may be something of an exaggeration, but the idea is sound: without discomfort, nothing really new is likely to emerge. Discomfort, then, is not a bad thing (though the client may certainly experience it as such). It is very much an ally of the therapeutic process.

In order to better understand the function of discomfort in therapy, let us look again at how maladaptive responses get learned in the first place. As children (and throughout our lives, for that matter) we learn how to cope with life. We make thousands of choices, learn thousands of expectations. Because some of these learnings occur during times of stress, or when we are not well-informed about all the variables that are operating, they may not represent the best possible choices or decisions or beliefs. They may lead to behavior patterns that will cause us pain later on. At the time, they are the best we can manage; given our resources, we make the choices and decisions that we believe will work. The point here is that these decisions and choices were often made so as to minimize pain. We learn how to avoid being terrified, how to escape punishment, how to not hope for that which we will not get. We hang on to those patterns because, at some level, we are still protecting ourselves from the same pain. To give up an old protective behavior, or to try a new behavior that we learned in the past might hurt us—why in the world should we do that? There are only two possible reasons: either the pain of not changing is so great that it makes the risk worthwhile, or we imagine that the possible benefits of change may outweigh the possible losses. Most, though not all, of our clients come to treatment wanting to escape pain. Those who come to us motivated simply by the desire to feel good ("Nothing is really wrong in my life; I just want to learn to make things even better") will probably discover some painful spots in the process of growth. Sooner or later they, too, will need to deal with discomfort and anxiety.

As we work to assist the client to change, we must be careful not to provide him with the same kinds of responses he is used to getting from others. These responses have been a familiar framework within which his old patterns have become stable, tried-and-true, there's-no-other-way-to-be kinds of habits. Instead, we ourselves must begin the process of doing something different. By reacting to the client in a new way, one which does not fit the old pattern, we shake the framework. We move, as in a game, so as to block the client off from the familiar, forcing him to try the unfamiliar.

A major part of the therapist's task is to help the client to hold anxiety and discomfort at an optimum level, enough to energize and motivate change, but not so much as to scare him irretrievably back into his old patterns or out of therapy altogether. Zaro et al. describe the therapist as "aiming for a state where the client is not overwhelmed or paralyzed by excessive anxiety but sufficiently uncomfortable to demonstrate his or her coping skills and emotionality" (1977, p. 36). To this I would add that he also demonstrate (to himself) his ability to experience new feelings and responses and that this ability provides a vehicle for working through and making changes at a feeling level.

The "Basic Six"

Emotional work with clients can be based on the whole range of feeling responses. Just as behavior patterns may have their origins in experiences of sadness, fright, or anger, so the therapeutic work may center around any of these. It has been suggested that there are just six basic feeling states: sad, glad, mad, scared, sexy, and curious/excited. It may be that emotional work always involves one of these six or a variant of one of them. It has been my experience that clients, in looking back at a particular piece of work, have little or no difficulty in assigning the feeling tone of that work to one or two of the six categories. Many have found it helpful, as they struggle to define in a precise way what it is they are feeling, to go back to a less intellectual base: "So maybe you could describe it as annoyed, or upset, or irritated—at any rate, some part of you was *mad*."

It can also be helpful to encourage clients to be aware of feeling more than one emotional response at the same time: "Sounds like you are really scared of what might happen, and also you are very sad that he would treat you that way." Often a client will feel immobilized as he experiences two intense feelings at once, and can be invited to deal with them one at a time. "It's hard to feel all of that scare and all of that sadness at the same time. Would you be willing to choose one or the other, sadness or scare, and just focus on that part for now?" Permission *not* to feel one facet of an emotional response, but rather to focus on only the part which is most prominent at the moment, gives the client a new kind of freedom to work through and explore. He may finish the work by moving to deal with the aspect he originally set aside; or he may discover that he no longer needs to, that working through one set of feelings has effectively taken care of the other as well.

Permission to Feel

The notion of permission has come up several times in these pages. As clients begin to let go of old defenses and allow themselves to experience their feelings in a more immediate and genuine way, they often find themselves dealing with emotions at a level of intensity that is very new and strange for them. Many times they experience these responses as forbidden: they are doing and feeling things that they should not be doing and feeling. The therapist's job is to provide the support and encouragement they need in order to move past the defensive prohibitions and to discover that it is all right, that they can survive breaking the old taboos and experiencing themselves and their world in a new way.

The therapist's acceptance of intense feeling responses is a potent source of permission for clients. Wolberg advises "calmly and sympathetically verbalizing for the patient how he must feel—if the interviewer perceives, from verbal and nonverbal cues, the nature of the patient's distress. Putting the patient's feelings into words does much to help him accept the fact of the interviewer's understanding, and non-punitive role" (1954, p. 202). At times it may be useful to go beyond simple acceptance and to provide direct permission and reassurance. "It's okay to let yourself feel angry about that." "Of course you were scared, and it's natural for you to experience that same kind of scare right now." Some therapists go even farther, acting as a sort of modified cheering section: "Stay with whatever you're feeling...you're doing fine!"

It is not uncommon, as clients try out new ways of responding emotionally, that they later experience guilt or shame about what has happened. Clients may castigate themselves for having revealed themselves so completely to the therapist ("What will you think of me, now that I've shown you all those horrible parts of myself?") or for even having had those unacceptable feelings at all ("I hate to think of myself as being so selfish/cowardly/vicious/etc."). If a client shows signs that he may blame or punish himself in this way, it may be useful to contract with him not to do so. "Are you willing to decide not to beat on yourself for doing the piece of work you have just finished?" cr "I will help you find a way to express your anger/grief/fear, but first I want you to be very sure that, whatever feelings emerge, you won't use them as an excuse to put yourself down." Having decided at a conscious level to accept his feelings, the client is better prepared to deal with his unconscious resistances and prohibitions in a caring and self-nurturing way.

Another situation that often requires explicit permission is the return of previously worked materials. The client may discover anew some pain or discomfort which he thought had been dealt with earlier and experience a great deal of shame or discouragement or guilt that the issue has reemerged. Here the needed permission is to recycle, to deal with old feelings again from a new place. He needs to know that the work will not be the same as before, that he did deal with that issue appropriately for his needs at that time, and that it is natural and growthful to come back to it now.

Perhaps most threatening to the beginning therapist are those situations in which the client's expression of feeling turns upon the therapeutic relationship itself. The therapist may find herself the target of a client's anger, discover that the client is afraid of her, or that he is sad and disappointed about something she has done. The client may become very demanding, determined that you provide him with the (magical) answers that he is sure you have (Stiles 1979). Or the intense feeling may be a positive one; clients frequently feel dependent on a therapist, as a child depends on its mother, or experience strong sexual feelings toward the therapist. When a client expresses such strong feelings toward you, either positive or negative, it is important that you recognize that you are probably a stand-in for some other person in the client's life, that your relationship with the client is a convenient (and appropriate) vehicle for him to use in exploring old and new responses. Knowing that it is not you personally who has done something to arouse all of this intense feeling helps you to remain calm and accepting and eventually to guide the client to an awareness of how his feelings toward you fit into his whole pattern of behavior.

To Touch or Not to Touch

One final issue needs to be mentioned in the context of emotional work, and that is the question of physical closeness between therapist and client. Let me say first that there is never any justification whatsoever for sexual intimacy between people who are in a therapist/client role. No competent or ethical therapist uses clients to meet her own sexual needs. It is easy for clients to mistake the emotional closeness and vulnerability that they feel toward a therapist for love, and the therapist who is looking for sexual involvement with clients will find ample opportunity for it. Indeed, it is often difficult to find the most therapeutic way to avoid such involvement. It can also be easy for therapists to make the same mistake, to become emotionally confused about the close and caring feelings that they experience toward clients. Because of this danger of confusion of feelings, and because we therapists (like most other people) have a great capacity for self-deception in the area of sexuality, I believe it to be a useful guideline not to touch or hold a client if I find myself sexually attracted to him or if I am feeling overly mothering or protective of him. The key is to be quite clear who the touching is for—myself or my client. Whose needs are being served? If it is my own, then I had best take those needs elsewhere; the therapy hour is not the place to gratify them.

Many therapists, of course, do touch, hug, and hold clients. And most clients, at some point during the middle phase of therapy, want to be physically close to their therapist. Says Steinzor:

> The desire to be physically close to me I expect will be awakened in every patient. Whether or not from the very beginning there is an immediate physical attraction, the longer the patient and I talk together, the more reason there is to expect an urge to touch. I do not see how it can be otherwise. Feelings and intimacies shared between any two people cannot be so contained that their expression can occur without at least an impulse to hold hands and to embrace affectionately. (1967, p. 62)

Hugging a client can be a spontaneous way of expressing caring and joy over a shared breakthrough. It can be a potent nonverbal expression of support during a time of emotional turmoil and pain. Clients who have not experienced good parenting in their own lives may benefit from being held or rocked; reparenting is an integral aspect of some therapeutic orientations, and part of the reparenting process often involves physical closeness.

What is important here is not whether you touch a client, but when and why you do so. Touching as a way of meeting your own needs, or as a mechanical or awkward or distasteful technique, is not therapeutic. Hugging or holding can interrupt a client's process as well as advance it. In order to promote growth, touching must be neither phoney nor exploitative. "Touching has powerful immediacy as an experience, and a profound primitive quality that bypasses verbal defenses. Therefore, I never enter into this on a purely technical basis without genuine feelings of wishing to participate in this intimacy with a patient" (Kopp 1977, p. 90). Be sure, too, that your timing is appropriate. It really does not matter how clear *you* are about the therapeutic usefulness of physical closeness, if the client is not ready for it. In fact, the safest rule for beginning therapists (and maybe for all therapists) is: when in doubt, do not. Clients can continue to grow and change in the absence of touching, but there are many circumstances under which physical closeness can seriously damage, if not actually destroy, the therapeutic relationship.

PLUNGING INTO THE PROCESS

There will be many occasions when you will not know what the client is working on, or when you will think you know only to discover later that you were quite mistaken. Ambiguity comes with the territory. Part of the permission of the therapeutic setting is the permission to not know, to explore without a clear sense of where it is all heading. There is an apparent contradiction here. In the first part of this chapter, I commented on the need for the therapist to keep track of the "strands" of the work, so that pattern and direction will eventually emerge. Yet we must, at the same time, be alert to the possibility that the direction may change, that a new focus may become more useful than the old. If you try to make yourself responsible for planning the process, mapping it all out ahead of time, and keeping your client on task (as defined by your map) at all times, you may miss working on the area in which your client most needs help.

We walk a tightrope, then. We strike a balance between being too task-oriented on the one hand or giving too little direction on the other. To complicate matters still further, whatever we do is likely to be magnified in the eyes of the client. Because we are important to him, because we have been invested with power and authority by the role relationship of therapy, and often because we are to some degree mysterious and unknown, anything we do may take on great significance. Unfortunately, this is true of our errors as well as of our strokes of genius. We must be ready to backtrack, to clarify, to apologize, and to be intensely interested in what our clients perceive us to be doing and how they react to those perceptions.

The beginning therapist is likely to discount the impact of many of the unimportant things she does. She knows what is foreground for her, what she is focusing on, and what she is interested in, and she tends to assume that the client is similarly focused. Later, after clients have come back and repeated what she told them the previous week or how she reacted to something they said, she will become more convinced that she does, indeed, affect clients in unintended and often unexpected ways. As Singer puts it:

> Any relevant comment or question expressed by the therapist defines him to the patient; abstaining from comments and questions has a similar effect. There exists a mass of experimental evidence indicating that the most innocuous noises produced by the therapist are picked up by patients as signs and signals concerning the therapist's attitudes and that they will be responded to consciously or unconsciously. (1965, p. 137)

These responses, in turn, help us to know whether to become more active, to provide more structure, or to ease up and encourage the client to find his own way. Both by what he asks us to do and by how he reacts to our behavior (or what he believes to be our behavior), he will tell us what he needs.

The Client's-Eye View

It will never be possible, of course, to know exactly how your client is responding to you during the therapy hour. You cannot keep track of all that the client sees in you, for that would require you to monitor all of your behavior—every breath, every twitch—and to filter all of it through the same perceptual frame that your client is using. What you can do is accept the client's perceptions of your behavior as valid for him. It is not necessary to defend yourself, to prove that you in fact did not say that or feel or react that way. "How did you feel when you heard me say that?" "What does my reaction mean for you right now?" Questions like this allow you to avoid an argument about what was really done or intended, while using the client's perceptions as part of the therapeutic process.

If you find yourself arguing with a client, trying to correct his misperceptions, or justifying your own behavior, it usually means that you are uncertain, deep down, about your effectiveness. "Did I really do the right thing?" "How could he possibly think I said that? What *did* I say?" We tend to expect (illogically and often unconsciously) that clients will always make the best possible use of our interventions; if they do not, we worry about our therapeutic skills. One way to minimize unnecessary self-doubts is to frame your success in any given session in terms of what *you* do rather than what the client does. Not only will this lead in the long run to greater client progress, but it will also allow you to assess your own behavior more realistically. And it will keep you out of the hurry-up-and-help trap that catches so many unwary beginning therapists. "Unattached to the *outcome* of the process for the patient," says Kopp, "the therapist is free *not* to meddle. I mind my business by concentrating on doing the work I am paid to do" (1977, p. 116). A significant part of that work is to be the object of misperceptions, to tolerate the state of not having all the answers, to maintain your faith in the client's ability to find and correct his own course.

Clients, like customers, are always right. That is, at any given moment, the client may be presumed to be dealing with reality as he understands it, in the best way he knows how. You must work with him within the frame of his reality, rather than trying to argue or cajole him into yours. This is not to suggest, of course, that the client cannot change his ideas, or that you must never confront or interpret his self-destructive or pain-causing misperceptions. It does mean that your confrontation or interpretation must not be insisted upon. When the client is not ready to hear what you have to say, do not keep after him with it. Let it be; if the intervention was accurate, there will be another time for you (or the client) to rediscover it. "Should the patient disagree with an interpretation or some other type of intervention, the therapist must *never* attempt to persuade, to argue, or to justify the intervention. Instead the therapist must accept the negative response, silently reconsider the formulation, and listen!" (Kopp 1977, p. 119).

Similarly, learn to distrust an interpretation that is received with too much enthusiasm. Out of each client's awareness there lurks a scared but very clever child, ready to use any available ploy to keep the therapist away from the real pain. This child will seize on a useless interpretation with delight. If I can decoy the therapist here, she may not discover what I do not want to deal with! "Marked glibness...in response to an offered interpretation is indicative of its being doomed to therapeutic ineffectiveness for the time being," says Fromm-Reichmann. "It is ill-timed and working on it should be postponed" (1950, p. 151).

Silence

Silence, simply waiting and saying nothing, may be the most useful single intervention available to a therapist, especially during the middle phase. When you are silent, you are not talking. You are listening. Your silence is a very powerful statement: it tells the client that you are there, waiting for him, open to his communication. It tells him that you will not jump in and solve problems for him, criticize him, or restructure what he has been saying. It gives him permission to take his time, think things through, go where he wants to go at the pace that feels right to him. Fromm-Reichmann points out that many clients need quiet spaces to think over what has just been said by either the therapist or themselves, and the therapist most certainly should not interfere in this process.

Another possibility is that the client may interpret his therapist's silence to mean that the therapist is angry or critical or withholding or uncaring. So much the better: since the therapeutic session is a microcosm of the client's whole life space, such a reaction is invariably part of a general pattern of relating to people. As such, it is excellent therapeutic fuel, excellent material to be worked over in the session.

More potentially damaging than client misunderstanding is the possibility that the therapist herself may misinterpret her silence. Beginning therapists are apt to be highly self-critical and to believe that, when they are silent, they are doing nothing. They castigate themselves for not knowing what to say—as if every space in the dialogue somehow should be filled with words. Fear of silence can lead us to do foolish things during the therapy session, as Hutchins and Cole point out. In order to avoid the discomfort of silence, we may:

Not listen fully to the client
Ignore important relationships between client thoughts, feelings, and actions
Interrupt before the client is finished talking or thinking things through
Randomly sputter out any old thought to fill the silence
Cut off productive client thinking about what has just happened in the session (1986, p. 64)

The reality of therapy is that much of the time, you will *not* know what to say and, more often than not, this not knowing is a very dependable indicator that you should say nothing at all. What you must do, though, is recognize the difference between saying nothing and doing nothing. To say nothing is to do something: silence is a therapeutic behavior, and the competent therapist uses her silences with the same skill as she uses any other intervention.

One more word about silence. We can talk ourselves out of being quiet with a client if we believe that we have to share everything we discover about him. As the client tells his story, we discover a pattern, a theme. Suddenly we are bursting to make this interpretation to the client. We want to check it out, to see if he will validate it. We want to impress him with our perceptiveness. We want to follow up on this delightful insight, to use it to march the client off down the road to health and growth. So we talk, interrupting the client's own work, derailing his train of thought. Stating, by implication, that what we are thinking is of course more important than what he is thinking. "The most likely timing error," says Kopp, "occurs in the premature intervention. I am *not* there to tell everything I know, but to offer that which is most likely to be useful to the patient at any given point. Premature interpretations confuse the patient, arouse undue anxiety, and evoke characteristic defenses against such distress" (1977, p. 146).

THE IMPASSE

Early phase therapy can be a time of extreme pain and despair on the part of the client. Often he has come to therapy in crisis, as a last resort after everything else he could think of has failed. It can also be a very exciting and hopeful time, as he learns new skills and experiences changes in his life. Seldom, though, in the early phase will your client experience being stuck in the therapy itself. In fact, that feeling of stuckness may be one of the defining features of middle phase work, one of the clear indicators that you have moved into a new kind of process.

It is hard to be explicit in describing a therapeutic impasse. Therapists and clients can get stuck around any issue, any problem, any symptom, any relationship. The content does not matter; what makes it an impasse is that feeling of nowhere to go, nothing will work, no answers. It is a frustrating, itchy kind of feeling. And it is very easy for therapists to respond to all of this by being either self-critical ("What's wrong with me that I'm not helping my client?") or critical of the client ("He obviously is resisting my efforts"). Neither of these therapist responses is particularly useful; they tend to pull the therapist right down into the stuck place with the client rather than providing a clear perspective about what is going on.

One part of that example, though, is true: the stuck client is resisting. At some level, he is refusing to do what he needs to do in order to change. But the word "resistance" has such a punitive, critical flavor that it is often misunderstood. Resistance is a part—a natural, necessary part—of the client's overall problem. Were there not resistance, he would not need treatment; he could solve the problem by himself or at worst would need some help with the kind of skill-building or information that is provided during the first phase of therapy.

> Resistance is the impulse to protect one's familiar identity and known world against perceived threat. In depth psychotherapy, resistance is those ways in which the client avoids being truly subjectively present—accessible and expressive—in the therapeutic world. The conscious or unconscious threat is that immersion will bring challenges to the client's being in her world. (Bugental 1987, p. 175)

Such a challenge is terribly threatening—How could I survive as somebody who isn't me?—and will be strongly defended against. The stuck client does not want to resist change. It is just that the pain of changing, or the fear of what such change may involve, is so great that self-protection becomes his first priority.

Unfortunately, from the outside, that process of protecting himself may look as though nothing is happening. We cannot actually see the fear, the sense of being overwhelmed, the terror of losing the only self one has ever known. What we do see is the defensive bluster, the whining, the ineffective trying of one tactic after another, the critical or passive or hopeless waiting to be transformed by some powerful bit of therapeutic magic. Or the opposite: we may see frequent cheerful hours or great enthusiasm that lasts over several sessions; they do not quite fit and signal that some opposite sorts of feelings are being warded off. Something is happening here, something very important. The experience of being at an impasse, of trying all that stuff that does not work, may well be the critical factor in bringing about lasting change. Confronted with the client's stuckness, the therapist neither abandons nor rescues nor attacks. She continues to support the client's exploration, helping him to discover the permission (to change, to try new responses, to be different) and the protection (from all the catastrophic possibilities with which he threatens himself) that he needs.

Resisting the Therapist

It should be pointed out here that there are two major kinds of therapeutic impasses, two ways in which clients get stuck. One of these is internal to the client: it is his old conflict pattern, his own push and pull around knowing and doing what he needs to know and do. That is the kind of impasse that I have been talking about up to now. The other is an impasse between therapist and client, a stuck spot in the therapeutic relationship itself. Therapist-client impasses are less often an avenue for change and more often a symptom of therapist error. Speaking of this kind of being stuck, Kopp says that "a therapeutic impasse is simply a time when the therapist is trying to make a patient do something that the patient is not ready to do" (1977, p. 13). If you are too intent on your own agenda, too concerned with hurrying up the process or with proving that you know what is wrong and what should be done about it, you are very likely to create such an impasse. Clients do not come to therapy in order to change in ways that will please their therapists. Many do not really want to change at all, and those who do want the change to come about with little effort and no discomfort on their part. Pushing them to move faster, to work harder, or to risk more will only help them to become further entrenched in their old system.

The therapist's greatest enemy in working with a stuck client is her own impatience. Impatient therapists can forget to use the skills they have, forget to be silent, and push both self and client harder and harder. Like struggling in quicksand, such pushing will only serve to further mire the process. Even more damaging is the angry therapist who uses her intervention to punish the client for his resistance. Punishment does not usually enhance growth; it stifles it. You cannot bludgeon a client into changing or moving on.

Getting Unstuck

What can you do, then, when you feel stuck with a client? How can you help him to move through his impasse? The basic technique involves joining him, being sensitive to the pain and the fear from which he is trying to protect himself. Seeing resistance as a signal that the client is dealing with very important issues, using it as a clue to the kinds of responses that he has learned to use in the past and that are no longer working for him, will help you to overcome your own frustration. You may want to share that perspective with your client, helping him to understand his own stuck feelings as an important phase in his ongoing process. Or you may choose to wait, being content with what is happening, knowing that the words and movements of the treatment hour are only the tip of the iceberg, that the client is working at many levels invisible to both you and himself. Whatever intervention you choose, the most important thing is to continue doing your job: supporting and guiding your client toward increasing awareness of his own process and of alternative ways to think about and respond to his life situation.

Your very frustration, by the way, your sense that the client is pushing you away and working against your efforts to be therapeutic, may be your first and best indicator that an impasse has been reached. If you feel excluded, discounted, treated as the enemy, use these feelings as a signal to step back and regroup. Notice what's happening to you, and what client processes you may be responding to. Take your time; be gentle with yourself and with him. The stuck client is very likely to experience your observations as criticism, since he is already criticizing himself for being stuck. Compassion and genuine respect for his efforts will allow you to accept him as a partner, rather than an antagonist, in the process of growth. After all, he has managed to survive in spite of all the pain and confusion in his life. By recognizing this, you will help him to take pride in his own strength and perseverance; his pride can, in turn, give him the necessary impetus to break through the impasse.

TIMING

Although timing is an important aspect of therapy throughout the entire length of treatment, it is perhaps most critical during the middle phase. It is here that the therapist may use the widest variety of therapeutic techniques and must choose among possible approaches from session to session and from moment to moment within a session. It is here that the complex and shifting interactions between the client's internal process, the therapist's own responses, and the relationship itself give clues as to when to move ahead, when to wait, when to speak or be silent, when to support, and when to confront. Strupp sees these decisions as the very essence of psychotherapeutic skill: "The art of psychotherapy may largely consist of judicious and sensitive applications of a given technique, delicate decisions of when to press a point or when to be patient, when to be warm and understanding or when to be more remote" (1977, p. 11). There is no way (or, at least, I know of none) to spell out the specific rules governing the timing of these interventions. Their effectiveness will depend upon your sensitivity to the client's readiness, your knowledge of what he is doing at any given moment. If he is quietly working on an issue, pondering a new insight, searching through his awareness in order to push out the boundaries of what he has discovered about himself—let him be. If he is fearful or hesitant, he may need support and encouragement. If he is truly confused, honestly not knowing how to proceed, it may be useful to provide him with a suggestion, some structuring, or a question to guide him further in his process. The main point here is not to get in his way, not to let your agenda be more important than his.

The therapeutic relationship is continually growing and unfolding. Like any other growing thing, it will not thrive if it is pushed to grow too quickly. We are often tempted to try to hurry things, to expect the client to trust us and take risks before he is ready. It is easy to misjudge the strength of the relationship. After all, we know him so well by now! We know (or think we know) what he needs to do, and we know we can help him to do it. Force-feeding a relationship can damage it badly, just as too much fertilizer can damage a young plant. "Some therapists, most likely beginning ones, are so eager to form a relationship that they do so on terms that forever destroy any therapeutic potential. Other therapists are so eager to force a client toward maturity that they bring pressures to bear on him that are beyond his ability to withstand; unwittingly they drive the client out of the relationship" (Tate 1967, p. 60).

There is an ebb and flow, a kind of organic rhythm, in good therapy. New insights and new awarenesses on the part of the client strengthen his sense of trust in both himself and his therapist; thus the relationship grows stronger. This new level of relationship, in turn, provides a base for further exploration. The rhythm can be sensed, too, in a kind of alternation of movement and rest. Hard work is often followed by lightness and laughter. A highly emotional session may be succeeded by a very cognitive one in which the emotional awareness is integrated into the client's overall understanding of what is happening. The therapist who does not understand this may wonder why the client does not work hard during every session, or may become frustrated that the surge of movement during one hour seems to dwindle away or stagnate during the next. In other words, the therapist's pacing and the client's pacing may not mesh.

When they do not—when you are all ready for another grand breakthrough and the client seems to set his heels and refuse to go anywhere—adjust your rhythm to his. "We therapists," observes Goldman, "do not have the ability to speed up the process beyond the patient's schedule" (1976, p. 46). Depending on your own style and orientation, you may choose to go along with some period of idle conversation, to remain silent, or to comment on what you think may be happening: "You did some pretty heavy work last session, and it sounds as if you'd like a breathing spell before you plunge back in again." Or, "I'm aware that you aren't talking about any of the things you worked on last week. Is there some particular reason for that?" The client may agree that he does want a breather, or he may take your comment as an invitation into a more meaningful content area, or he may choose to explore with you his feelings about wanting to avoid further digging. Whatever he does, you have evidenced your willingness to respect his process and to support him in growing at his own speed.

Closing a Session

There is one exception to the general rule that the client be allowed to decide when he is ready to plunge ahead into the next piece of work. This has to do with managing the end of the session. It is not therapeutic, usually, for a client to involve himself in some highly emotional issue only to be told that his time is up and the session is over. The therapist needs to be aware of the time, and invite the client to save the issue for the next session if it looks like there will not be time to deal with it. "I think that's a very important thing for you to talk about, and I notice we only have five minutes left. I don't want you to get into it and then feel cut off. Would you be willing to bring it up at the beginning of our next hour, so that we'll have plenty of time to discuss it?" This kind of an intervention is evidence of the therapist's interest in the topic and her respect for the client's judgment that the topic is important; it is also an explicit statement of her commitment to manage the therapy sessions in a way that is protective and growth-enhancing.

In spite of your best efforts, though, there will be occasions when a client gets into an issue and does not have time to work it through. Indeed, bringing up a critically important bit of information at the last minute is a typical game for some clients, a way of hanging on to the therapist or of maneuvering for extra time or attention. "By the way," says the client, with his hand on the doorknob, "I've decided to quit my job." It takes a lot of self-control to avoid the hook in this kind of comment, to not get sucked back into another five or ten or thirty minutes of discussion. Insisting that time limits be observed in the face of such maneuvers will probably guarantee that the client goes away in some sort of negative frame of mind.

We would like our clients to leave their sessions happy, excited, serene, or at least in a neutral emotional state. We do not like to send them away miserable or angry, any more than we like to end the hour feeling uncomfortable ourselves. "However," comment Zaro et al., "as therapy progresses it may periodically be necessary to end an hour with some obviously bad feelings on the part of your client or yourself. This does not necessarily mean that the session has gone badly. The greatest amount of change may occur after such a session" (1977, p. 123). Dealing with some issues will invariably be uncomfortable if not downright painful for your client. Sometimes growing hurts, and some growing pains cannot be avoided. Moreover, some of the issues and the pain will occasionally have a carryover from one session to another. Sessions do not always end comfortably. Finally, sometimes therapists make errors. Some sessions will end with bad feelings because you made an inappropriate intervention, pursued an issue better left until later, or failed to provide something that the client needed. If the therapeutic relationship has been carefully nurtured, it will survive a few of these bad endings and may even emerge stronger for having survived them. If the therapist's timing is consistently off, so that the bad outweighs the good, the client may well decide that the benefit he is receiving is not worth the pain.

Using the Client's Guidance

As a therapist, you will soon learn to sense when your timing is right and when it is wrong. You will know when things are going badly and have a chance to do something about it. Usually the best thing to do is pull back, listen harder, and let the client tell you what he needs and wants. Sometimes the client, who is at least as much aware of being stuck as you are, will ask for direction: "What should I work on today?" "I don't know what to talk about." "Do you want me to tell you about what happened at work yesterday?" It is seldom helpful to tell the client what to do at such times; doing so only tends to reinforce his sense of helplessness or incompetence. Instead, help him to develop his own ability to know what he needs, to know what is foreground for him at this moment. Bugental, for example, says:

> Typically, my answer to such questions is along these lines: "You have the only valid compass, so look into yourself and see what (or which) really matters to you right now." Sometimes I link that up with a reflection, "You seem to feel that I know what's important to you better than you do. That's a startling idea. Do you really believe that?" (1987, p. 216)

Every client knows at some level what he wants and needs. He knows where his treatment needs to go in order for him to grow and change. Sometimes the knowledge is part of his conscious awareness, so that he can answer a direct question like the one in the previous paragraph. At other times the knowledge is at a deeper level; one part of him may be busily resisting what another part is urging him into, and he is conscious only of a sense of confusion and discomfort. The knowledge is always there, somewhere. The art of therapeutic timing is largely that of listening to all of the levels your client presents and of responding to what he tells you from all of those levels.

CONCLUSIONS

As I read what I have written in this chapter, I am painfully aware of how nonspecific much of it sounds. Some clients will do this, sometimes thus-and-such is useful, sometimes not....The beginning student would be quite justified in throwing up her hands and demanding a set of clear and understandable rules.

I wish that I could provide them. However, as I said at the outset, middle phase work really defies being outlined or categorized. It usually does involve emotional work, but not always. Much of the time you will not know exactly where the work is going, and many times you will. Often it is true that silence is the best intervention, and occasionally silence can be harmful. Most clients will find themselves stuck at least once during the middle phase, but a few will not. Your timing will depend on the unique characteristics of each therapist-plus-client relationship as it unfolds over time.

The ambiguity and unpredictability of middle phase work can be painful and frustrating, but it can also be a source of endless fascination. It is difficult and stressful to work in a situation where you often do not know what will happen next. It can also be exciting! If you demand of yourself that you always do well, always make good interventions at the right time, you will almost surely begin to dread the middle phase and be relatively ineffective with it. If, on the other hand, you allow yourself occasional confusion, allow yourself to not know, you will begin to learn how to really listen to your client. At that point you will have begun to be a therapist.

6 THE FINAL PHASE

The final phase of therapy is at once easy and difficult to describe. It is easy because its central issue is clear: termination. The ending of therapy, the ending of the therapist-client relationship, is the major theme. There are other themes, other issues, as well, and these are as variable as clients and therapists themselves. The end of therapy is not just the end, not simply the process of saying goodbye (although one would be quite foolish even to call that a simple process). It is a microcosm of the entire course of treatment.

Musical productions in the theater often end with something called the reprise, in which the major musical themes are repeated in a shortened and connected fashion. Perhaps the reprise is the best metaphor for therapeutic endings as well. The major themes, conflicts, and fantasies of the entire therapeutic process are reworked in the context of termination, of ending. Part of this reworking has to do with uncovering new issues that may bubble up as the client contemplates moving out into life without the now-familiar support of ongoing therapy; another part involves practicing, reporting on, and taking in reinforcement for the new behaviors and responses that he has acquired. Yet a third aspect is that of the relationship itself: the reality, for both client and therapist, of ending an interaction which has been a meaningful and important part of their lives.

In this chapter we shall discuss a number of issues relating to Phase 3, the final phase of treatment. We will talk about planning for termination, about recognizing the point at which clients begin to deal with termination-related issues. We will talk about the kinds of work that clients often need to do during the final phase and the predictable emotional components of that work. We will discuss some of the issues that the therapist may need to face in her own response to termination. Finally, we will introduce some special cases, some situations which differ in important ways from the traditional ending phase of long-term treatment. Even as we do this, however, it is important to recognize that we will not cover everything, will not deal with all the issues that may emerge for you and your clients. Termination is too varied, too individualized, to hope for that. What you can expect is an outline, a series of guideposts, that will help you to recognize and to plan for each of the varied termination processes which you will experience as a professional therapist.

GETTING INTO THE FINAL PHASE

It is a hallmark of our culture that we are reluctant to talk openly about ending relationships or cutting off contact. We say "see you later" instead of "goodbye," and disguise the finality of long-term partings (graduation, moving away) with promises to keep in touch. Even death, that most final of endings, is referred to as passing on, and Western religion is replete with reassurances that important relationships need not end—that, in the words of the old hymn, "we shall meet in the sweet bye-and-bye." Ending a meaningful relationship is unpleasant if not downright painful; none of us likes to give up something we care about. It is easier to pretend that it will not happen, that it is not happening, that it did not happen, and then deal with the reality later, when we have found new friends and new interests and the pain of parting has had time to subside. It is a great temptation to therapists and clients (being, after all, people like everyone else) to treat their endings in the same way: to ignore the fact that termination is coming, to disguise its reality with pseudo-plans to meet again in one way or another, or to slide through the last sessions without knowing that they will, in fact, be the last.

That is a mistake for at least two reasons. First, it encourages the client to continue to exercise the very defensive maneuvers he has probably been struggling with throughout treatment. Whatever is maladaptive in his system is most likely to reemerge under stress, and termination of therapy is clearly stressful. By allowing him to go ahead and reactivate his old behaviors—or, worse, to actively collaborate with him—may undermine much of the progress he has made. Second, dealing explicitly with feelings around the termination issue may provide opportunity to explore new and important areas which have not been discussed before. These issues may relate directly to endings, partings, leaving and being left; or they may involve other parts of the client's system which he has been reluctant to talk about. Now, knowing that therapy will soon be over, he may be ready to deal with them.

When to Terminate

As in any relationship, therapy can be terminated by either of the parties involved. Should the client decide to end treatment, the therapist cannot force him to stay. Similarly, once the therapist chooses to stop working with a client, the client cannot force her to continue. Ideally, of course, neither of these situations will arise, and termination will be a joint decision on the part of both client and therapist.

As you find yourself moving through the middle phase of therapy with a client, you will need to consider the whole question of termination. How will you know when it is time to quit? How will you know when it is time to begin talking about quitting? The beginning of the end may be more difficult to recognize than the end of the end. Part of the problem here lies in the fact that therapists are trained to recognize lots of reasons why treatment should not be terminated—defensive maneuvers, unfinished issues, transference, acting out, etc.—but we are not so well trained to recognize the signs that termination is appropriate. After all, who could not benefit from more therapy? Who has all their issues solved, their life perfectly in order? The most common criterion for termination is well enunciated by Zaro: "It is generally appropriate to bring up the question of termination when you believe either that the client has reached his or her therapeutic goals or that further progress is not possible at this time" (1977, p. 143). But to many of us (particularly if we are relatively new and unsure of ourselves), suggesting that a client has reached his goals seems arrogant and even dangerous. What if we have overlooked something important? Saying then that he can go no further is an admission of failure. So we plod ahead, keep trying, until the client tires of the whole thing and decides on his own to quit, leaving us feeling even more inadequate than we would have felt if we had met the issue head-on.

If you have done a good job of contracting with your client, of setting out clear and explicit treatment goals, recognizing the appropriate termination point will be easier. Therapy should end when the stated goals have been achieved or when the client is stuck and is no longer moving toward those goals. It is not your job to figure out all of the other possible things he might benefit from working on, and it is certainly not advisable for you to stay stuck with him indefinitely. Rather, you can share with him your assessment of what is happening, invite him to join you in reviewing his progress, suggest other resources that may be available to him, and then say goodbye.

It would be most comfortable for both therapist and client if the actual point of termination were clearly indicated by some unmistakable marker, some event that signals "Now we are done," but it does not usually happen that way. Even in the best-planned terminations, there is an arbitrary quality. The client chooses to stop now, and we help him to do so. He might have stopped earlier, or he might profitably continue longer; he must decide. In deciding, he gains in some ways and loses in others. There will probably be some pain for him in terminating (we will discuss this and other emotional responses to termination in a later section), but there is also gain. "The romance of transference gives way to the realities of time, money, and energy that might be better spent" (Kopp 1977, p. 157).

Often, of course, therapeutic goals shift and change over the course of treatment. We have talked before about making these shifts explicit; recognizing the appropriate termination point is one reason why explicit goal shifts are important. Beware of the client who chooses a new goal or set of goals after you have introduced the idea of termination: he may be fishing for some excuse to keep the relationship going, and this need (rather than the goal he has suggested) may be the underlying theme throughout the rest of his treatment. Beware also of your own inclination to suggest that the successful client now turn to an exploration of this or that new issue: to what degree does your suggestion arise out of your own desire to hang on?

Therapist-hanging-on is not necessarily the most common termination error. In fact, when a termination error occurs, it may involve terminating too soon rather than too late. Premature termination can occur for a variety of reasons, some of which are unavoidable. People move away, time and schedule commitments shift, finances change. Sometimes therapy must end even though both client and therapist would like to continue. Again, one should be cautious about accepting at face value such outside-of-treatment reasons for terminating. Clients (and therapists!) find it very difficult to say that they want to quit because they feel they are not getting anywhere or that they are afraid of moving into what may really be the central issue of treatment. It is much easier and more socially acceptable to use the excuse of running out of money, of no longer having time for therapy, or of objections from a spouse or other family member as a reason for quitting. When a client requests termination for this sort of reason, you will need to explore very carefully all of the feelings connected with the decision. Similarly, you may need to confront yourself with your real reasons and feelings if you find you are thinking of terminating a difficult client. If is often a good plan to discuss such a case with a colleague or supervisor, someone who is not personally involved in the relationship, before moving ahead in termination planning.

It is always useful to frame your discussions of termination—whether you are talking with the client, with yourself, or with a colleague/supervisor—in terms of a set of desired outcomes. After all, there are many levels of success in therapy. Terminating at point X may be premature in terms of some set of long-range possibilities but quite appropriate in terms of more limited goals. This is particularly true in the case of the client who fears his own dependency needs, and who wants to work through some specific issues quickly and then leave before he gets too involved. Balsam and Balsam point out that such a client may have a fantasy of himself as an enormously needy and clinging person who, once enmeshed in a long-range therapeutic relationship, would find it terribly painful and difficult to give up that relationship. "Depending on what the patient wants from therapy, it may be perfectly legitimate to respect such fantasies. One may decide to leave them untouched or to touch upon them only briefly and agree with a rapid termination if this is what the patient wants" (1974, p. 147).

The ultimate criterion for ending treatment is that both client and therapist sense that it should end, either because it has accomplished its purpose or because it would better for the client to stop now even though the stated goals have not been reached or have been only partially accomplished. A good dollop of common sense is useful here; do not get so caught up in theoretical oughts and shoulds that you lose sight of the fact that you and the client are two people, working out ways for the client to get what he needs. He does not have to get it all; he does not have to solve all of his problems. He will continue to live and grow after therapy is over, and he may even enter into another therapeutic relationship some time in the future. Your job as therapist is to help him to explore his reasons for quitting, to understand and appreciate what he has accomplished in his work, and to anticipate what those accomplishments will mean as he goes on about the business of living his life. A clear termination decision made in this context will probably be both appropriate and therapeutic.

Discussing Termination

While the issue of termination becomes a foreground concern in the final phase of therapy, it is really an appropriate subject for discussion throughout the treatment process. Enright (1970) points out that the whole course of therapy is different when termination is a central issue from the beginning. The client is more aware of goals, more likely to evaluate and take responsibility for his own progress. Planning for termination becomes part of the contracting process: client and therapist together specify the goals of therapy and how each will know when the client has achieved those goals. It is appropriate to give the client some sense of how long treatment will probably last, even though this is often an approximation subject to revision as the process unfolds, and to talk about any problem that either of you may anticipate. Planning the therapy during this early stage will include provisions for stopping to evaluate progress and revise treatment goals at regular intervals; again, each of these steps is a logical and appropriate time to reintroduce the idea of termination.

The end of therapy, in other words, begins with the first interview. The whole process points toward its ending, and that fact is an integral aspect of the process. "If we accept our patients' dependent feelings but do not foster these feelings," says Goldman, "it will be possible for the patient to learn both to care for us and to feel appropriately independent. When the work of therapy is done, the person will naturally begin to separate from us." (1976, pp. 80–81).

Goldman is talking about one of the major paradoxes of therapeutic work: the dependency between client and therapist. The client needs permission to become sufficiently dependent on the therapist so that he can use the relationship to do his work. He must accept the protection and safety that the therapist provides if he is to explore and to change in ways that previously had seemed too dangerous or threatening. At the same time, he needs to know that he can grow past that dependent posture, once again becoming autonomous and confident. We tell him that right now he may feel that he needs us, but that part of our work together will be to facilitate his moving through that need into a new way of relating to his environment. His needy feelings are real and may in fact be a positive factor in his treatment, helping him to use the therapist appropriately. He will not always experience the therapist in this way, and some part of him is quite capable at any point of carrying on without us. He might not want to, and it might be quite uncomfortable to do so. However, he could, if he had to.

In order to establish this balance between dependence and autonomy, the client should be given some reassurances. He needs to know what he can count on from his therapist. Kopp tells his clients: "I promise you that I will not put you out of therapy precipitously. If it feels to me like I want to end the work at some point, I will be sure to discuss it with you first. Perhaps we will be able to work out the problem, perhaps not. In any case we are both grown-ups and free agents. We come together because we want to and we can stop when we like" (1977, p. 51). Thus the therapeutic relationship becomes the prototype of any healthy adult relationship in which commitment and freedom to change are two sides of the same coin.

THE WORK OF THE FINAL PHASE

Even though the process of working through the termination phase will vary enormously from client to client, some patterns tend to occur again and again during this phase. Endings, after all, have some universal qualities and tend to call forth some typical responses. As with Phase 2, these responses—thoughts, feelings, and behaviors—become the stuff of therapy. The therapy relationship is a microcosm of the client's entire social existence, and in it he will replay his well-learned reactions to and interactions with his world-out-there. Thus the termination of therapy can become an opportunity to work through his whole way of dealing with goodbyes, with endings, and ultimately with his own death. Many clients may not choose to explore all of these issues, of course, and I will respect their choice not to do so. But I am alert to the possibility of dealing with them. I will understand each client's termination behavior in the context of the reality that, for him as for me, all parts of life eventually come to a close.

Repeating Old Themes

As clients begin to realize at an emotional level that termination is approaching, they typically begin to bring up old themes and issues. This may be done in a defensive way, as an un-straight message that "I'm not okay yet, so please don't leave me." Or it may occur in a spirit of review, integration, and even celebration: I've changed here and here and here; I really am different than I was when we began." With either sort of process, the therapist's job is to support and clarify the work, to help the client make explicit what he is doing. If my client is desperately bringing up old issues in an effort to justify continuing in therapy, I will want to explore with him why it is so important to maintain our relationship. If he is sorting through his old issues for fear there may be something left undone, we talk about these fears. If he is reviewing in order to gain a better perspective on just what has happened over the course of treatment, I help him to do that and also encourage him to attend to his feelings as well as his thinking. In each case, my aim is to assist him to integrate what he has accomplished with what he has yet to do and with what he may not wish to change.

"Termination," say Balsam and Balsam, "will represent a distillation of the themes that have arisen in the therapy, the situation that brought the patient to treatment in the first place, and the positive and negative aspects of transference and countertransference" (1974, p. 145). Whether or not the client brings up these themes explicitly, you may be sure that they are present at some level. He is working through the implications of living his issues with no therapy and no therapist to fall back on, and everything he says can be understood in that context. Every association, every insight, every emotional reaction is an interface between old and new, between the in-treatment position and the no-longer-in-treatment position. Material brought up in the session can, of course, be dealt with on its own terms, but it must also be seen in the context of the separation process. To the question, "what does this mean for a person with this kind of life situation and this kind of developmental history?" you must now add, "and what does it means for a person who is ending a supportive/confrontive growth-producing relationship?" The fact of imminent termination inevitably colors and flavors all the work that is done during each last phase session; there is no way to undo that fact or to change the subject.

Hanging On

For many clients, the notion of terminating therapy invites a feeling of neediness, a sense of wanting to hang onto the relationship. They experience an almost panicky "something terrible will happen to me when I'm alone" feeling. This feeling, in turn, may lead them to act so as to prolong the therapeutic interaction. They may bring up old symptoms, reexperiencing them as if the work they have done in these areas had never happened. Or new issues may emerge with a strangely artificial or phony flavor. The same thing often occurs in microcosm at the end of an individual session when the client brings up an important issue with only a few minutes left in the hour in order to hang on and prolong the contact. Again, the underlying concerns are those of separation and control: Can I exist separately? Can I trust myself and my therapist to find a way to separate? Who will decide (control) when and how the separation will occur? Just as with ending-the-session behavior, hanging on at termination time needs to be confronted and worked through. The specific problem or symptom is less important than the separating; the problem is merely the vehicle by means of which the client plays out his need to control and maintain the relationship. It is important to recognize and respect both the reality and the intensity of those feelings while at the same time helping the client to grow past them. In the next section of this chapter, we will explore some of the more common emotional reactions to termination.

FEELING REACTIONS TO TERMINATION

Balsam and Balsam, in their excellent *Becoming a Psychotherapist* (1974), describe the various affects that clients typically experience during the termination phase of therapy. Much of what I shall say in this section was suggested by their discussion.

Sadness

Not surprisingly, one of the most common feelings associated with termination is that of sadness and grief. Termination is a time of parting, of separation. It marks the end of a relationship which has been very important to the client, a relationship in which he has allowed himself to be touched and known in a way that he may never have experienced before. Transference feelings are real feelings, and the transference attachment of client to therapist is a real attachment. Cutting off such a relationship is painful; that the client experiences some grief is both predictable and appropriate.

A major difference between this therapeutic grief and other experiences of separation and loss is that in therapy the client has the opportunity to talk through the feelings with the person he is losing, and that person is in a position to help him explore and integrate the feelings. The sadness and loss cannot be expected to disappear, but they can at least be made bearable; indeed, working through a separation in this way may help the client to manage future grief experiences in a more adequate and less anguished way.

Another aspect of the sadness of termination is often a feeling of disappointment. "Is that all there is?" the client asks. "There isn't any magic? I'm leaving, and all of my pain and confusion haven't been taken away?" Most clients have entertained, at some level, the hope that through therapy all their problems will be solved, never to return. And as long as they stay in treatment, they can maintain the hope that the miraculous cure is just around the corner. With termination comes the realization that this will not happen, that "they lived happily ever after" is a relative rather than an absolute description. If the therapist is skillful and the client willing, this can be another opportunity for significant growth: ideally, the client will come to accept not only the reality of pain and problems as part of living, but also his own ability to cope and to survive without a lifetime guarantee of happiness. On the other hand, if the disappointment is not worked through, the client may become a therapy-hopper, going from one therapist to the next in search of that marvelous panacea that does not really exist.

Anger

"Anger is an integral part of separation, and many patients have a great deal of trouble recognizing it or tolerating its existence" (Balsam & Balsam 1974, p. 153). Therapists differ in their view of just how separation anger is aroused or maintained, but most agree that it usually occurs. Some, like Balsam and Balsam, say that it always occurs. One of the most obvious sources of anger for a client is his sense of being abandoned. This person whom he trusted so much is dumping him! How can she do that? She has no right to leave him alone, especially when he may not be completely, permanently, and blissfully cured. At another level, the anger over being left may have to do with the sense that termination is too easy for the therapist. It is not fair that the client should suffer while the therapist does not. Closely connected to this latter system is the suspicion that the therapist does not really care, after all. She would not leave so easily, or so soon, if she really loved me and cared about me the way I thought she did. She has been faking all along, and I should never have trusted her....And so the anger builds.

There is another flavor of anger at termination, not so much directed at the therapist as at life in general. To the degree that a client experiences the separation as painful, he will feel frustrated; he wants something, and he cannot have it. Feelings of frustration, in turn, commonly vent themselves in anger. The client may direct his anger at the therapist, but he may also lash out at a spouse, a boss, or any other part of his environment which provides a handy target.

A third kind of anger commonly seen at termination is that which is used to mask or override some other feeling. Clients who have difficulty in dealing with sadness or fear may choose to be angry in order not to feel their grief or their scare. Other clients may be embarrassed by their tender or loving feelings toward the therapist and cover those feelings with an angry outburst. Finally, the anger itself may be experienced as unacceptable and be turned back against the self in feelings of guilt and shame.

In every instance, the job of the therapist is to help the client understand both his reaction—the angry feelings—and the source of the reaction. If the anger is derivative, covering some other feeling, the client needs to move through the anger so as to get to whatever is underneath. Similarly, the guilty client may need help in externalizing his rage, putting it out into his social environment rather than turning it back upon himself. Anger is both energizing and contactful and can be a very useful source of strength and power. If we can help clients to use the positive aspects of their anger, rather than flying out of control or sulking or feeling guilty, we can again provide them with tools to help them through future separation experiences.

Fear

There are many things for the terminating client to be fearful about. Probably the most common fear is that he will not be able to make it on his own, that something terrible will happen as soon as the therapist is no longer there to support him. The something terrible may be a slide back to the misery which brought him to treatment in the first place, some new crisis with which he will be unable to cope, or simply the sense of being alone and not knowing what the future will bring. Leaving one's therapist is not unlike leaving home for the first time, leaving the security of the known, the comfort of having some grownup who is in charge or who can take over if one gets into a tight spot.

The very intensity of the client's feelings about termination may be a source of fear. He did not know he had gotten so attached or that he would feel this angry. It can be scary to discover feelings, strong feelings, that you did not know were there. "Where will it end? How long will I feel this way? Will it get worse?" A part of him feels new and strange and out of control, and he does not know what to do about it.

Along with permission to feel their fear and experience the therapist's support as they do so, frightened clients need reassurance that they can deal with these feelings, that the intensity of the feelings will abate with time, and that such feelings are normal during the termination period. Simply knowing that other people react in the same way ("Oh, then I'm not crazy?") does much to reduce the client's catastrophizing and to turn the fear experience into something which can be examined and moved through. It is particularly important for the therapist not to give too much support, not to create the impression that she doubts the client's ability to deal with his own emotional business. Not only can such overcaring suck some clients right back into a dependent and helpless role, but it can actually increase the fear. The fantasy of a therapist who cares too much, who is over-involved, can be terrifying. The correct therapeutic course, then, is a mixture of support, respect, and clear information: it is okay and normal to feel as you do; many people experience the same thing, and I am here for you to use as you help yourself through this part of your growing and changing.

Guilt

We have already mentioned the guilty feelings which clients may experience as a derivative of anger around termination. There are other sources of guilt feelings as well. Clients may feel guilty about sexual or dependency feelings toward the therapist. They may find themselves glad to be free of therapy and feel guilty about that. Or they may fantasize that they have hurt or disappointed the therapist in some way. Feelings that have to do directly with the therapeutic relationship are paradoxically easier and more difficult to deal with in therapy: more difficult because client (and therapist too) may feel embarrassed to talk about them and so tend to discount or suppress them; easier because, once brought out into the open, they can be explored in the here-and-now of that very relationship. New ways of being together, of relating and responding to the other person, can be tested out immediately rather than waiting until the next session for the client to bring back the results of the work he has done.

One last category of guilty feelings involves the sense of having said too much, exposed oneself too completely. "The patient may want to be rid of the therapist quickly, in an effort to reconstitute his defenses and feel more 'whole,' like his old familiar self" (Balsam & Balsam 1974, p. 156). Here the guilt of "I said too much" may be further complicated by anger at the therapist for having encouraged (or seduced) the client into too much self-revelation and by further guilt that he could be thinking such ungrateful thoughts.

Pleasant Affect

It is a common failing in most writings about therapy and therapists that they tend to over-emphasize problems and pain. Such a focus, I think, is unavoidable. People usually seek therapy because they are in some sort of discomfort, and the easing of discomfort is the most common signal that treatment has succeeded and should be terminated. Yet much of the experience of therapy can be exhilarating and joyful, and it would be foolish to ignore the good in our effort to anticipate and work with the painful. So it is with termination. There can be a great deal of satisfaction for both client and therapist during the termination phase. Ending the therapeutic relationship can mark a job well done, a moving forward into new and exciting possibilities. It can be a time for experiencing a feeling of completeness and competence. The client has indeed achieved something valuable. He emerges from a successful therapy experience with new tools, new skills, new confidence. He feels grounded and in charge of himself, perhaps for the first time in his life.

We know how to work with pain, rage, and fear. We help the client to change those feelings in some way or to use them to achieve some positive end. Some of us (a dwindling number, I hope) greet reports of positive feelings with a determined skepticism, refusing to take them at face value but rather poking and prying to find the bad things we are sure must be lurking underneath. Such an attitude may reflect the therapist's own unfamiliarity with and uncertainty about positive affect; at best it is a discount of both the client's ability to grow and the therapist's skill in facilitating that growth. Rather than discounting positive feelings, the experienced therapist joins in celebrating them. She is not so naive as to ignore the possibility that other, less pleasant feelings may also emerge; but she is open to the reality of health and growth. She is quick to recognize and to reinforce evidence that the client has changed and does experience good feelings. In so doing, she may put herself out of business with this client, and that is what good therapy is all about.

THERAPIST FEELINGS

We have spent a lot of time discussing the affects that clients experience during the termination process, and occasionally we have touched briefly on the feelings of the therapist during this phase. The feelings of the therapist deserves more than just a passing comment, however. They are part and parcel of termination, and failure to recognize them and deal with them is probably responsible for more mismanaged terminations than any other kind of therapist error. We are real people, experiencing real feelings; our very genuineness is one of our most important assets in the practice of our trade. Ending a relationship with a long-term client is appropriately an emotionally laden process for us as well as for the client.

Just as the client often feels sadness at parting, so do we. Separation cuts both ways; we too experience the loss of a meaningful relationship. "Our patient says: 'I'll miss you when we stop. It isn't that I can't do things by myself, because I can. I do right now. But I'll miss talking to you. And I'll miss your understanding.' If the relationship has been successful, we will miss the patient too, and we say so" (Goldman 1976, p. 81). Acknowledging our own sadness and sense of loss is not just acceptable therapist behavior but rather an integral part of the separation process. It allows the client to separate cleanly from a real, whole human being, instead of drifting fuzzily away from a shadowy professional role-facade. And such acknowledgement allows the therapist, too, to let go cleanly and honestly.

Transference feelings are no less real because they spring from the transference; counter-transference feelings are also quite real. A client's rage at his withholding therapist/parent must be worked through as must the other transference-based reactions. The therapist needs to recognize her side of that phenomenon: her fear, perhaps, that her client/child may not be able to get along without her or her anger that the client/child is abandoning her. It is seldom if ever appropriate to work through such counter-transference issues directly with the client, but it is essential to recognize and work them through in some other setting. Especially for beginning therapists, it is a very good idea to set up a case presentation with a supervisor or a colleague whenever a long-term client terminates. This will allow you to explore your own termination issues early while they are still readily accessible and relatively unencrusted with rationalizations and other defenses.

There is one very real termination issue that therapists face but that clients are spared. For the therapist, a terminating client may mean the loss of status, of security, of money. One is often tempted to hang on to a client well past the optimum termination point, simply because one needs business. Therapists wage continual war with worries that no new clients will show up to replace the ones who go away. This is especially true for therapists in private practice. We use our filled appointment book to reassure ourselves that we really are competent, and that others recognize our skills. There is little that I can say about these reactions other than do not dump them on your clients. We all suffer through them (any therapist who denies this probably needs to work out some additional issues!), and there is nothing strange or wrong in your experiencing these feelings. What is wrong is to try to soothe them by keeping your clients around longer than they need to stay. Not only is that not good for clients, but it is also very bad for you. Again, find a supervisor or a colleague you can trust, and deal with such feelings there; you will be much better able to work through termination (and other issues as well) with your clients for having done so.

One final problem that emerges over and over again for therapists is that of the kind of relationship (if any) they are willing to maintain with an ex-client. Clients and therapists both find themselves wanting to restructure the relationship, to continue but in a different way. While some therapists claim to be able to manage this kind of restructuring, to be just friends with an ex-client, I suspect that planning to do so before treatment has actually ended is usually a way to deny or distort what is actually happening in termination. It is another kind of holding-on, an implicit recognition that one or both parties in the relationship are not ready to let go. Says Kopp:

> I find that attempting a social-personal relationship between myself and ex-patients never really works. No transference is ever completely resolved. Attempts to have a new kind of meeting have all the limitations of a parent and a child attempting to 'just be friends.' The shadow of the therapeutic alliance haunts attempts to move beyond it. There is residual doubling of role not unlike the usually disastrous incestuous efforts to have a parallel relationship *during* long-term intensive psychotherapy. (1977, p. 156).

Wait a minute, I really like this client. Does all this mean that I have to give up the possibility of ever having him for a friend? I believe, regretfully, that it does. This brings us back full circle to the real sadness of termination: for the therapist, too, it is an ending.

UNPLANNED TERMINATIONS

Everything we have said thus far about terminations has assumed that the termination will be an orderly process, anticipated by both client and therapist, with ample time to work through all the issues that the separation may involve. Anyone who has done much therapy will realize, however, that this kind of planned termination is not always what happens. Therapeutic relations can terminate in a variety of more or less abrupt ways, and many of these leave both parties feeling distinctly uncomfortable.

The "No-Show"

For less experienced therapists, a common problem is that of the client who simply does not show up for an appointment. He does not call to reschedule or let you know what is happening; there is just a gaping hole in your schedule. Is he coming back, or not? Why didn't he show up? And what should you do about it?

Part of the answer here, of course, has to do with the kind of relationship you have established with the client. If you have been seeing him for some time, and have a sense that you are working well together, the issue of no-show is very different from that with a brand-new client or with an old client who has a history of manipulative behaviors. The established client is less likely to no-show without warning and when he does do so the event is likely to be highly significant in terms of his therapeutic issues. Not coming to a session is a dramatic and forceful way to convey a message to one's therapist. What is this client telling you? What is going on between you and him? What happened during the last session that may have provoked or frightened or disappointed him? Part of the answer to these questions may be found in your own response to his not coming. Did you feel angry? Relieved? Sad? Responsible? It is important to sort these questions out before your next contact with the client so that you can be clear about your own limits when you talk with him again.

And you should definitely talk with him.[1]

For one thing, you need to take care of yourself; you need to know what is happening with him and between him and you. More particularly, you need to know whether he intends to see you again or whether he plans to terminate. Most important of all, the no-show is a therapeutic issue, which the client needs to deal with: it is a form of acting out which has been precipitated by some internal or external event. It's not an isolated incident, an odd but meaningless happenstance.

If a client of mine fails to show up, I call him and ask what happened and when he wants to reschedule his appointment. I also remind him that he will be charged for the missed appointment (see Chapter 13). If he says that he has decided not to return, I tell him that I believe it is important for him to have one more session during which we can discuss his decision to terminate and tie up any remaining loose ends between us. Of course, the final decision is his. I cannot force him to come back, but refusing such a final session is a rare occurrence.

In fact, no-shows without notification are rare among established clients unless you have unwittingly created the impression that such behavior is all right with you. If you have established your ground rules clearly, the great majority of clients will respect them. When a client does not respect them, you may be quite sure that his behavior is a signal that something important is going on, something that should be attended to.

With newer clients, no-shows are less unusual (although, again, setting clear expectations will eliminate most such problems). A client may be shopping, setting up appointments with several therapists and planning to continue with only one. He may not have gotten exactly what he wanted in that first (or second or third) session and therefore decided not to come back. (His failure to notify you of that decision is his way of expressing his disappointment or anger that his needs were not met).

---

[1]The only exception to this statement that I can think of would be the client who has failed to show up on several occasions throughout treatment and with whom you have a contract that you will not initiate a contact should this happen again.

A spouse or other family member may have put pressure on him to discontinue treatment. Whatever the reason, it is still appropriate for you (or your secretary) to make contact with him, and clarify the treatment contract. And again, he should be encouraged to return in order to discuss what happened and what he can do next in order to meet his needs.

The more experience you have as a therapist, the less you will have to deal with the no-show kind of termination. It is as if the client can sense the tentativeness and uncertainty of the beginner, and, if it fits into his system, use that uncertainty to justify hanging on to his old ways of not getting what he wants. As you grow in confidence and learn to stop discounting your own ability, you will stop conveying a covert invitation to the client to join you in your self-discounting. In the meantime, you may have to suffer through the pain of a few no-show dropouts. And they are painful. The best that can be said is that they offer a fine opportunity for the young therapist to learn something about herself.

The "Abrupt Stopper"

You and your client have had a run-of-the-mill session. Nothing awful and nothing wonderful has happened. Toward the end of the hour, the client drops his bomb: "I've decided not to come back after today." You're surprised and off-balance; besides, there is no more time left in the session to deal with this. What to do?

The first rule-of-thumb in this situation is: Do not extend the session in order to talk about continuing. "Doorknob terminations" are a favorite ploy of manipulative clients. Rather, let the client know that you are uncomfortable about accepting that decision without having a chance to discuss it, and invite him back for a termination session. "I'm sorry that you didn't tell me sooner, because I think it's important that we discuss this. I'd like you to come back one more time. Please take a couple of days to think about it; if you do decide to come in, call me and confirm your appointment. I'll hold your time open until Wednesday afternoon." If the client does come back, the focus of the session should be termination; assuming that his decision to terminate still stands, do not work with him on any other issues. If he chooses not to return, you have done what you can. The ultimate responsibility is his.

More commonly, an abrupt stopper will let you know at the beginning of a session that he does not intend to continue. In this case, of course, you can focus on termination issues then and there. There are many reasons for abrupt terminations, and some of them are legitimate: a sudden move, a changed schedule, unexpected financial problems. More often, though, the abrupt decision has to do with therapeutic issues. After all, appointment times can be changed to accommodate schedule changes, and reduced or deferred fees can be negotiated. The client should be given every opportunity to talk about what is really behind the termination. He should not be cornered or bullied into "confessing." If the fiction of unavoidable circumstances is important to him, he should be allowed to keep it. Terminating his therapy with his defenses still working and pride intact may make it easier for him to seek treatment again later on.

THERAPIST-INITIATED TERMINATIONS

Early in this chapter, we commented that the termination decision ideally should be a joint one with both therapist and client in agreement. Occasionally, the therapist will terminate with a client before the client is ready. Usually there is plenty of lead time to work such a termination through before the last session actually arrives. In fact, lead time is a legal and ethical imperative. "Abandonment of a case without sufficient notice or adequate excuse is a dereliction of duty" (Furrow 1980, p. 37), and as such may make the therapist legally liable. Once in a great while, however, the therapist must deal with unforeseen circumstances: a major upheaval in personal or professional life that necessitates abrupt termination of clients. The therapist must make every effort to schedule several sessions with each client during which a coming separation can be discussed. It is not acceptable to suddenly inform a client that this will be his last session; it is even less acceptable that the client arrive for an appointment, only to be told that his case has been transferred to another therapist. Nor is notification of such a change by phone or mail an appropriate substitute for a termination session. If some personal problem makes it impossible for the therapist to be really available for her clients (a death in the family, for example), she may choose to let them know what has happened and reschedule appointments for a future date, providing them with names of other therapists they may see during the interim. In the extremely unlikely circumstance that one would be physically called away from the area without notice, clients should at least be sent a personal letter explaining what has happened and providing them with referral names. It would also be appropriate for the therapist to invite clients to write or call her, so that they have the opportunity to round off their side of the relationship.

CONCLUSIONS

Many, perhaps most, therapists have difficulty handling terminations. Perhaps it is partly due to our culture: as I mentioned at the beginning of this chapter, we Westerners do not deal well with endings. It is certainly odd when you think about it. Most therapists are relatively uncomfortable with terminations long after they have learned to manage initial interviews easily, and yet we end exactly the same number of therapies as we begin.

I suspect that we would all find terminations much easier if we were to fully recognize and accept the fact that we cannot (and are not expected to) finish with our clients. That is, we do not send them away completely problem-free, completely grown-up, completely through with their issues. Just as we must help clients to shed the illusion that perfection and unending bliss are reasonable therapeutic goals, so we must work to dispel that expectation for ourselves. Therapist and client both must recognize, moreover, that even if the stated and agreed-upon goals of treatment have not been completely reached, still "certain types of progress have been made and that the patient is capable of working out his life" (Goldman 1976, p. 82).

The end of therapy and the end of treatment are not synonymous. Though it may seem when we say goodbye to a client that we are ending treatment, we should be aware that the client will continue to work on his issues, using many of the tools and insights of therapy long after that final session. Some clients, in fact, discover their greatest therapeutic gains after therapy has terminated; it is as if breaking free of the therapeutic relationship provides the permission they need to let go of their old ways of being. Some simply need time to integrate, to bring together all that they have learned and experienced, and to make it a natural part of their everyday life. Some rediscover their earlier progress in the new, post-therapy context and are surprised at how differently they react to problems that once would have seemed insoluble; others literally continue the therapeutic process long after formal termination, as if they had actually taken some part of the therapist into their own personality structure. A letter I received from an ex-client more than a year after her therapy ended describes this kind of experience:

> I have grown and changed in many wonderful ways. A lot of the growth I see in me I can relate specifically to areas of work during the time with you....An amazing awareness for me—that really effective therapy is not just immediate in its obvious effects but never stops having positive and lasting effects, allowing us to ever be changing and growing...our work together is always present in me and helping me.

A therapist is a kind of gardener: we plant seeds here and there, tend them carefully, provide care and nurturing, encourage the young and growing plants to shape themselves and develop their natural interaction with their environment. When the plant is strong enough to get along without its gardener, the gardener moves on, knowing that the plant will continue to grow and flower and bear fruit. Our clients may endure some very bad weather; they may experience some long dormant periods; they may even need help from another gardener some day, but they do not stop growing when our time with them is done.

7 THE CLIENT IN CRISIS

INTRODUCTION

This chapter marks a turning point in our discussion of counseling and therapy. Up until now, we have been talking about "generic" therapy, describing concepts and techniques that are appropriate across a wide range of therapeutic situations. While not every technique or approach will work with every client, none can be classified as being more useful in one sort of therapy setting than in another. Indeed, the usefulness (or lack of usefulness) of each of these concepts is more likely to depend upon the therapist—her theoretical stance, her comfort level, her degree of experience—than on the kind of client with whom she is working.

    But now things are going to shift a bit. Crisis work, career counseling, group work, and therapy with couples and families all require some special skills, different from (though often relevant to) general one-on-one therapy. The next five chapters will focus on these sorts of skills. So here we go, beginning with crisis work. What, exactly, does that mean?

In the broadest sense, nearly every client who comes for therapy is in a crisis of one sort or another. Gerald Caplan defines a crisis as occurring "when a person faces an obstacle to important life goals that is, for a time, insurmountable through the utilization of his customary methods of problem-solving" (1961, p. 18). And that is what all therapy is about: helping people to find new ways of coping, of relating, or problem-solving, when the old ways are not working anymore.

Our common-sense understanding, though, tells us that a person in crisis is different. There is a feeling of urgency, of need for action now. A crisis has the quality of a turning point, a time when decisions take on special significance. The therapist feels this quality in her own heightened sense of responsibility: we experience pressure to save the client, to fix things. Everything looms larger than life during a crisis period. The irony is that at the very time when we and our clients most need to think things through, to act wisely, we are under the greatest pressure to move quickly.

Rosenbaum and Beebe (1975) talk about three interrelated factors that can produce a state of crisis. First is a "hazardous event," something out of the ordinary that happens to a person and because of which he feels threatened. Second, that threat is somehow linked to earlier events or learnings so that the client feels especially vulnerable. And finally, as a result of those first two factors, the client is not able to respond adequately. The stresses from the first two factors seem to operate in an additive way: clients in crisis may be relatively normal, well-functioning people, forced to deal with an extraordinarily difficult life situation; or they may be less well-organized folk for whom minor stresses create major problems. It is the interaction of stressful event and personal resources which determines one's reaction and thus one's experience of crisis.

While all clients, then, can in some sense be described as in crisis, it is useful to distinguish a particular kind of emergency situation as suitable for crisis intervention. In this chapter we shall talk about the crisis client, discussing the kinds of approaches and techniques that have been developed specifically to deal with crisis situations. We shall also look in more detail at one particular kind of crisis, that of the suicidal client.

BASIC PRINCIPLES

One of the most notable characteristics of a crisis is its complexity and confusion. Everything seems to be happening at once; demands are coming from all directions; the client feels overwhelmed by the pressure of events. If she is not careful, the therapist too may begin to feel overwhelmed. An important antidote to therapist confusion is a clear grasp of crisis theory: what is a crisis, how does it unfold itself, what are its separate stages and aspects? As we begin to unravel the various threads it becomes possible to think in terms of dealing with one bit at a time—usually much more practical than trying to handle the whole mess at once!

Crisis situations do develop in a more or less predictable pattern, although it often requires hindsight to determine where one actually begins. Phase 1 in a crisis is usually not experienced as such: rather, it is experienced as a rise in tension or stress level, often associated with some external event. The event may or may not be unpleasant, but the person must mobilize some resources in order to deal with it. So far, the system is working well; if the coping strategy is adequate, the crisis may be averted. But if the strategy doesn't work, we move into Phase 2: more tension plus a growing sense of ineffectiveness. Phase 2 signals the beginning of the crisis proper; it is at this point that the person himself is likely to recognize that things are going badly. As the old coping strategies continue to fail and the person feels more and more desperate, he begins to initiate emergency action—often some brand new behavior or one reserved for extreme situations. This is Phase 3, the big push to deal with the problem. If it works, the person must then collect himself and return to his (perhaps somewhat altered) precrisis level of functioning. The crisis was not averted, but it was dealt with and is now past. If the big push does not work, the client moves into Phase 4: still more tension, helplessness, feelings of inadequacy, disorganization, confusion, and high emotionality (Eddy et al. 1983).

Although a therapist may enter this drama at any point, she is most likely to be called in for crisis intervention during Phase 4. Phase 4 is the acute crisis phase marked by the failure of the client's emergency coping system: the mechanisms have broken down, tension has peaked, and disorganization has set in. The time scale can vary tremendously from one situation/client to another. A father, survivor of an automobile crash in which family members were killed, may move into Phase 4 within minutes of the accident itself. At the other extreme is the exhaustion crisis, in which the person may have been functioning for weeks or months at Phase 2 or 3 level but finally has no more energy to maintain the emergency measures. An example here would be the single parent who works for months at two full-time jobs in order to pay medical bills for a child, but who finally collapses: "He no longer has enough strength, and the result is a 'quasi-ungluing' of the total coping structure" (Golan 1978, p. 69).

No matter what the time frame, however, all crisis situations have important common features. First, the final phase (the active crisis) is generally self-limiting, changing in some way within one to five weeks. Second, the nature of that change will depend on present action. It will not be determined by what has gone on in the past. Finally, people in active crisis experience an increased desire to be helped by others and are more willing to accept such help than they are during noncrisis times. All of these characteristics of acute crisis point toward the importance of moving quickly in crisis intervention. There is a relatively short time during which (1) the crisis will continue to be acute; (2) present action will be most decisive and effective; and (3) the client will be most open to being helped.

Moving quickly, in fact, is the common denominator in all crisis intervention approaches. "Quickly" applies to the initial response of the therapist, to the way in which the problem is structured, and to the overall length of treatment. With regard to initial response, it is best if intervention can be made within twenty-four hours of the client's request; a delay of two weeks or more often means entirely missing the period during which the client is most open and available for treatment. Delay may also complicate the client-therapist relationship, as the client becomes angry about or resigned to the lack of response from those who might be able to help.

The need for decisive action carries beyond the immediate response and into the conduct of the therapy hour. Clients in crisis do not want a leisurely, "tell me about whatever you want to talk about" approach. They want action, relief, a sense that something can be done. The therapist needs to work with such a client in a relatively directive way, helping him to focus his attention on the problem area that is to be worked with, and to plan a strategy for making things different. With this kind of problem-solving approach, treatment does not ordinarily develop into long-term, depth therapy. Rather, three to six sessions usually suffice to move the client to a place where he can continue on his own (without the therapist, that is; one of the major goals of crisis work is to help clients develop and use support in their own social and work environments).

FIRST STEPS WITH A CLIENT IN CRISIS

The most important initial task for a crisis therapist is deciding whether to work with this client, and, if not, what alternative plans should be made. The client in crisis is demanding help of some sort, and the therapist's job is to respond to that demand. However, we have a number of options: we can agree to see the client ourselves, we can make a referral to some other individual or agency, or we can help the client mobilize his own resources so that no further formal assistance will be needed.

To Treat or Not to Treat?

Ideally, of course, the sooner the client is back on his feet, taking care of himself and independent of us or other helpers, the better. And the more personal resources he has, the sooner he will be ready to be independent of us. Assessing the client's resources, then, is a major focus of the first session in a crisis intervention. Even as you invite the client to tell his story, to share his perception of the nature of the crisis, you should be aware of his underlying resource structure. Who are the significant people in his world, and which of these provide support for him? What is his economic situation, the state of his financial resources? Does he have a job, regularly scheduled activities, hobbies or other interests? What are his skills? Is he able to think clearly and solve problems? (It should be noted that a client who is using chemicals has, by definition, impaired thinking abilities. The client who is drunk or strung out on drugs needs specialized drug/alcohol treatment and should be referred to an appropriate agency; it is extremely unlikely that he will get the help he needs in a general-purpose setting.) Are his emotional responses appropriate to the situation? If he has a good resource bank, one session of clarifying the situation and planning future action may be all he needs from you. If you do work with him longer, you will need to know which of these resource areas need building up and which ones he should be encouraged to fall back on.

At the other end of the spectrum from the client who has only minimal need for your services is the client who needs more than you are prepared to give. Some clients are so demoralized by their crisis situation that outpatient care is simply not enough. Others may need specialized help that can and should be found elsewhere. And still others may need psychotherapy beyond the present crisis situation. Two factors especially important in assessing a client's appropriateness for traditional crisis work are his verbal ability and his past therapy history. Because the crisis intervention model is primarily a cognitive, problem-solving approach, it is most useful with clients who are able to talk openly about their problems. The client who cannot (or will not) talk clearly and coherently about what is happening in his life is not likely to respond well to the fast verbal pace of crisis intervention; some other strategy may be best for him.

The key factor here is availability: does the client have enough available personal resources so that he can work with the therapist in a joint problem-solving effort? Besides his speech (what he says, and how he says it) there are several other things that will help you make this assessment. First, notice his general appearance and behavior. Is he dressed appropriately, within the context of his normal lifestyle? Is he responsive to his surroundings? People who are in the process of withdrawing from reality often dress and/or act the role, sending an unconscious message that they can no longer manage their lives. How about his overall thought processes: does he answer questions appropriately? Does his story make sense? Is he able to concentrate on a topic or does he jump randomly from one thought to another? Finally, pay attention to his level of affect. Some emotional disturbance is to be expected in a crisis client, but how much do his emotions interfere with his ability to work productively on his problems? How much do they interfere with his ability to take care of himself once he leaves your office? The answers to all of these questions will help you to decide how much this particular client is likely to benefit from the kind of help you are prepared to offer.

Beware, too, of the crisis client who appears to be functioning too well. For most people, the first visit to a "shrink" is quite anxiety-provoking. They do not know what is expected of them, or what they are supposed to talk about. Some confusion and hesitation is normal. When there is none, you may be dealing with a client who has had a lot of practice in this setting, whose pattern is to hop in and out of therapy for any of a variety of reasons. Ewing warns, "In assessing the client with multiple prior psychiatric contacts, the crisis psychologist should carefully enquire as to the circumstances surrounding the initiation and termination of such contacts before committing further time and resources to the client" (1978, p. 102). Our energies as crisis therapists are best used working with people who are needful of and open to making changes and moving on. We do nobody any good by reinforcing the dependent and maladaptive behaviors of the chronic therapy-shopper.

Gathering Information

Assuming now that we have decided to work with a particular client (or, while we are in the process of making such a decision), we will need to gather some very specific information right away. Assessment in crises, say Cohen et al., "involves an understanding of the hazardous event, the client's coping repertoire and previous attempts at mastery, the client's environmental supports, and the client's current stage of crisis" (1983, p. 107). There is no need (and usually no time) to collect a detailed history or to do a precise DSM-3R diagnosis; rather, we need the information that will allow us to make that first, practical, solution-oriented intervention.

We need to know what is and has been happening, as Cohen suggests, and we also need to know who is involved. Who are the actors in this drama? What is happening to each of them? What expectations, hopes, and fears does each of them have? And the final, fundamental question: Why now? Why is help needed today rather than tomorrow or last week? What is special and significant about the present situation that led the client(s) to decide to ask for help now? It is the answer to this "Why now?" in all of its variations and permutations that will give you the clearest pointers for what should be done to begin solving the problem.

Most crisis situations, unfortunately, do not involve single, straightforward problems. People can usually take care of that kind of problem on their own! Crisis therapists are more likely to see multiple problems, layers of stresses and tensions and demands, complex intertwinings in which problem A has grown out of efforts to deal with situation B, which is in turn a result of demand C, and so on. Indeed, the multiple-problem crisis is often so entangled that the client loses track of just what is the most pressing demand, the source of greatest stress or conflict. Simply sorting things out, helping him understand and make sense of all that he is responding to, can be very therapeutic.

Holmes and Rahe (1967) have developed a "Social Readjustment Rating Scale" which lists some common life events together with the "strength" of each event in terms of creating stress. A summary of this scale (taken from Golan 1978, p. 67) is found in Table 7–1. The stressors on this scale are additive: lots of little ones may do more damage than one big one! The authors suggest that a total score of 300 or more signals the likelihood of a major depression or physical illness within a year. Notice, also, that not all of the items on the scale are bad. Any pervasive life change can contribute to the experience of crisis; the crisis therapist needs to be alert to the good changes such as promotions, graduations, or birth of a (wanted) child as well as the negative ones.

While the detailed history-taking of some traditional psychotherapeutic approaches is not necessary or even desirable for most crisis clients, it is important to get some idea of what sorts of problems the client has faced in the past and of how

TABLE 7–1   Social Readjustment Rating Scale

LIFE EVENT	MEAN VALUE
1. Death of spouse	100
2. Divorce	73
3. Marital separation	65
4. Jail term	63
5. Death of close family member	63
6. Personal injury or illness	53
7. Marriage	50
8. Fired at work	47
9. Marital reconciliation	45
10. Retirement	45
11. Change in health of family member	44
12. Pregnancy	40
13. Sex difficulties	39
14. Gain of new family member	39
15. Business readjustment	39
16. Change in financial state	38
17. Death of close friend	37
18. Change to different line of work	36
19. Change in number of arguments with spouse	35
20. Mortgage or loan for major purchase	31
21. Foreclosure of mortgage or loan	30
22. Change in responsibilities at work	29
23. Son or daughter leaving home	29
24. Trouble with in-laws	29
25. Outstanding personal achievement	28
26. Wife begins or stops work	26
27. Begin or end school	26
28. Change in living conditions	25
29. Revision of personal habits	24
30. Trouble with boss	23
31. Change in work hours or conditions	20
32. Change in residence	20
33. Change in schools	20
34. Change in recreation	19
35. Change in church activities	19
36. Change in social activities	18
37. Mortgage or loan less than $10,000	17
38. Change in sleeping habits	16
39. Change in number of family get-togethers	15
40. Change in eating habits	15
41. Vacation	13
42. Christmas	12
43. Minor violations of the law	11

Social Readjustment Rating Scale, by T. H. Holmes and R. H. Rahe, *Journal of Psychosomatic Research.* 1967, pp. 213–218. Summarized and reprinted in N. Golan, *Treatment in Crisis Situations*, Pergamon Press, 1978. Used by permission.

he has dealt with them. This information will help both you and your client to sort out patterns of response, to begin looking at what has worked and what has not worked for him during past periods of stress. It also will give you a sense of his normal state. Since a major goal of crisis intervention is to bring the client back to at least the level of functioning that he maintained before this present crisis, the therapist must have some notion of what that level of functioning was. If the client was not doing well even before the crisis, he may not be a good candidate for a problem-centered, short-term approach and you may need to think about some other kind of intervention.

What we are trying to do in this general crisis assessment is to decide how well the client is likely to respond to a situation-oriented cognitive approach. We want to know if, given a little professional help, he will be able to move ahead on his own, using the resources available within his system, to solve his problems. A good resource for the therapist facing this kind of decision is the *Handbook of Psychiatric Emergencies* (Slaby, Lieb, & Tancredi 1981). This truly encyclopedic volume gives symptoms, signs, typical history, differential diagnosis criteria, and case management guidelines for a wide range of therapeutic emergencies.

While we are carrying out this initial assessment, we are also building a relationship with the client. We are letting him experience us as a person and as a professional. We are giving him a chance to tell his story without being judged or shamed or pressured to take care of it on his own. We are hearing that story calmly, without being overwhelmed by it. Rosenbaum and Beebe suggest that the information-gathering process is itself a kind of treatment: "The patient benefits by watching the emergency therapist bring logical order to what seemed a chaotic situation. The therapist's ability to cope comes through, too; there is a great deal of modeling or *ego borrowing* at this phase of the interview" (1975, p. 6).

Confidentiality

As we shall see later in this chapter, one of the major strategies in crisis intervention is mobilizing the client's resource system. This may mean talking to other people in the client's world, alerting them to what is happening, and enlisting their support. For this reason, it is particularly important not to make early promises about confidentiality that may later have to be broken. Often, a part of the client's crisis involves some family secret (which may, in fact, be no secret at all) that he is worried others may discover. Rather than promising to help keep the secret, the crisis therapist will do better to make it clear that, while she will do her best not to use any information in an embarrassing or hurtful way, she must be free to do whatever needs to be done to protect the client and others with whom he interacts. Beginning therapists are often concerned that refusing to promise confidentiality may prevent the client from sharing important information. In my experience, this is seldom if ever the case. The client may wait a little longer while he checks me out. Generally my very insistence that he understand my own limits and that I will take whatever action I believe necessary (always, of course, informing him of my intentions) tends to make him more trusting of me rather than less so.

The Crisis Contract

The final task of the first crisis interview is the specification of an intervention contract: what is to be done and how. I have discussed contract building at some length in a previous chapter and will therefore deal with the concept here only briefly.

Contracting is especially important early in the crisis intervention process for at least three reasons. First, the client in crisis is seldom aware of all the facets of his problem situation: he is confused and bewildered. Setting up a contract helps him to choose what he most wants to work on and to focus his energies into solving at least that one part of his problem. It provides him with two essential ingredients for success: a sense of direction and a sense of hope that something can be done. A second reason for contract setting is the fast pace needed in crisis intervention. Clear contracting makes it possible to zero in quickly on a plan of action, one in which everyone involved knows what is expected of them. Which brings me to the third point: responsibility. The crisis client needs to take charge, to do something, to begin to resume control in his life. Making a contract underscores the client's responsibility and makes it clear that he is not a passive victim but rather will participate actively in remedying his situation.

In building the crisis intervention contract, make sure that you specify at least the following points: (1) the focus of the problem—exactly what is to be changed or solved; (2) the time limits—how long it will take to bring about change and how long you will be working with the client; (3) who else is to be involved and how; and (4) what are the responsibilities of the client and of the therapist. Once you have spelled out who will do what, with whom, for how long, and to what purpose, you have defined the framework of a good crisis work contract.

In essence, the whole of the first contact with a crisis client is an exercise in building trust in both directions—therapist for client as much as client for therapist. Your whole effort of assessment, evaluation, and contract-building serves to inform you of how much and how far you can trust this client. The more you can trust him, the more effective your work is likely to be, for "the client will probably place as much trust in the caregiver as the latter places in the client" (Hatton et al. 1977, p. 34).

MOVING IN

The client in crisis feels overwhelmed and helpless. So much is happening in his life at such a high level of intensity that he can no longer hold things together. The coping strategies that have worked for him in the past do not work anymore, and he is left with a choice between floundering about doing useless or wrong things (that only seem to enmesh him further in the problem) or becoming immobilized. In order to turn the situation around, he needs to back off and explore possible alternative solutions, to choose the best available strategy among those he has explored, to implement that strategy, and finally to practice and develop the new behaviors until he can function acceptably on his own. As the therapist moves in to help in this process, her first task is to clear a space for the client, to give him some breathing room so that he can begin to think again and can sort out the various resources and courses of action available to him. Listening to his story and helping him to put it into enough order to communicate it to you is the first step in this back-off-and-sort-out process. Deciding on a contract, a specific plan of action, is the second step. The contract need not cover all aspects of the crisis; it centers on one part, one thing over which the client can exercise some control. With the experience of even partial success in this one area, the client feels less demoralized and can start to work through and unravel the rest of his situation.

Cognitive Work

A direct implication of the problem-solving approach is that much of the work will be very cognitive. The client needs to learn—or relearn—to think, to understand what is going on and what options are available to him. As people slide deeper and deeper into crisis, their thinking tends to become confused. They torment themselves with worried catastrophizing or berate themselves for having caused the problem, rather than working for effective solutions. A major task for the therapist is to interrupt these destructive kinds of thinking and to replace them with clear assessment of what is happening and how that might be changed. "I know that you feel very guilty about this situation and wish that you had done something about it sooner. It's normal and natural to feel that way, even though there may have been nothing you could do. What is important now, though, is to look at what is happening *today,* and at what you can do *now* to make things more bearable for you and your family." "Of course you feel angry; most people would. It's okay to feel angry, as long as you don't let your anger get in the way of figuring out what can be done to make things better." Notice that each of these responses contains three elements: acknowledging the client's emotional response, reassuring him that his feelings are normal and acceptable, and then moving the focus from feeling to thinking.

A good way to get from talking about how bad and awful things are (which most crisis clients can do) to exploring possible solutions (which is more difficult) is to discuss what steps the client has already taken to deal with his problems. Every client in crisis has tried some things that have not worked: that is part of the crisis, the experience of old coping strategies failing to do the job. "What are some of the ways you've tried to help yourself deal with this situation?" "You say that nothing helps—will you tell me some of the things, specifically, that haven't helped?" Not only do questions like these shift the client from passive victim to an active (though unsuccessful) problem-solving position, but they also yield information about the client's overall problem-solving skills. "In considering the client's recent, apparently unsuccessful, coping efforts, the crisis therapist will seek to understand not only what attempts have been made but also why these attempts have failed. Not infrequently, this approach reveals that certain coping mechanisms that have apparently failed may, with appropriate modification and/or greater client effort, turn out to be quite effective" (Ewing 1978, p. 113).

In order for the client to come up with a plan of action that will work, he needs to have accurate and complete information about what is happening. The therapist may want to check with others (other professionals, friends of the client, family members) to find out just how accurate and complete the client's story is; at the least, she will confront discrepancies and gaps within the story itself. More particularly, the client needs to be aware of his own impact, both positive and negative, in the crisis situation: what is he doing (or not doing) that is keeping things from getting even worse? A question that often helps clients toward a fresh perspective on their own interaction with their situation is "What would happen to all the other people involved if you were suddenly to vanish?" (Be aware that this question has some special implications for potentially suicidal clients. It may be quite useful with such clients, but the therapist should be ready to address the specific suicide issues that it will bring out.)

Still within the context of understanding what is happening, the client needs to think about his emotional reactions. Thinking about feelings is a new concept for many clients. They know how to think, and they experience feelings, but they do not put the two together. Teach your client to stand back from his feelings and to simply reflect on how he responds to his situation and how that response affects what happens next. Watching himself from outside may provide the shift he needs to move away from his repetitive and unproductive patterns into a more effective way of thinking and reacting.

Affective Work

With all of our emphasis on cognition and problem-solving, we must not forget that all crises have emotional components as well. The client in crisis does experience painful feelings, and these feelings are a part of the crisis. The therapist acknowledges and validates the emotional responses of her client. She may also provide him with an opportunity to experience or vent his feelings. With her, it is safe and okay to be angry or scared or despondent, and to talk about what those feelings are like. Ewing points out that crisis therapists go beyond just offering a safe opportunity to release feelings. "The client is also helped to keep his affects at a conscious level, where they can be clearly identified and managed through direct effort" (1978, p. 27). Again, it is the idea of thinking about feeling. When I can think about how I feel, I am not so much at the mercy of my feelings.

Some emotional responses are so common in crisis clients that we can expect them, be prepared to deal with them, and even probe for them if the client does not talk about them. I have already mentioned guilt as one such response. Clients may feel guilty about past or present behavior, about their (supposed) causal role in bringing about the crisis, about their negative feelings toward themselves or other people. Another common feeling is ambivalence, which is often experienced as confusion. The client wants to hurt and wants to comfort; he wants to run away and he wants to fight; he feels triumphant (his dire predictions came true) and he feels miserable (he does not want those predictions to be true). He does not know what he wants or feels! The correct intervention here involves voicing both sides of the ambivalence and validating both. Rosenbaum and Beebe give an example of a man with a controlling wife, caught between his feelings of dependency and his hostility toward her. The therapist intervenes: "It must be very hard, when your wife has been so good to you, to admit that there are times when, good as she is, you find yourself angry with her" (1975, p. 57). Thus the therapist acknowledges both the dependency and the anger as well as the difficulty of feeling such conflicting responses at the same time.

Clients in crisis feel a loss of self-esteem, a threat to their sense of competence. They have not been able to cope, to handle things on their own. They are seeing a therapist, the ultimate admission of personal failure. They must also cope with the sadness of their position, the loss of what-might-have-been, and the longing for what-is-no-more. Even in crises which do not obviously involve loss and grief, there is usually a sense of loss: loss of possibilities, loss of illusions. Sooner or later, all of us must grieve over the death of Santa Claus; the crisis client faces this loss in a particularly intense and poignant way.

Another common emotional experience in crisis is, of course, anxiety. How will it work out? What will I do? What will become of us? The sooner a plan of action can be worked out and implemented, the sooner this anxiety will begin to dissipate. Doing something about it is the best antidote for anxiety. With the dissipation of anxiety, however, may come frustration. The new plan is not working as well, or as quickly, as the client had hoped. Or he is finding it more difficult and demanding than anticipated. He does not like it; it is not good enough. An important part of the later phases of crisis intervention often involves helping the client to develop new, perhaps lower, standards of well-being, to do without some things he had previously taken for granted, to delay gratification until the situation works itself out. Developing and accepting these standards may take him back again through the gamut of crisis emotions: guilt, anger, ambivalence, loss and grief, the whole package. Hopefully, he will have gained both self-knowledge and coping skills in the earlier crisis work so that this set of feeling responses need not be as intense or as debilitating as his original emotional state, but it is no less real and no less demanding of therapeutic attention.

Some Guidelines

Although crisis intervention techniques may be as varied as the crises themselves, there are nevertheless some common themes which recur again and again. One of these has to do with advice-giving. Typically, the client in crisis is so overwhelmed by internal and/or external pressures that he is no longer thinking very clearly. It may be that the therapist can see solutions or strategies of which the distraught client is not aware. Should she share these? Should she tell the client what, in her opinion, would be good for him to do? If the client is truly confused and open to suggestion, such advice-giving can be appropriate. Crisis intervention is short-term, action-oriented treatment; it is designed to get the client quickly to a place where he can begin to manage his own life again. Advice from someone outside the situation, someone who has experience with similar kinds of problems, can be comforting as well as useful in accomplishing short-term goals.

For other clients, though, advice-giving is generally not helpful. These are the clients who are looking for easy, pat answers to complicated problems, answers that usually involve making somebody else change. Clients who have a long history of therapeutic contacts, or who are glib or hostile in their interactions with the therapist, are not likely to benefit from direct advice.

Another type of client for whom advice-giving is not particularly helpful is the manipulative client. Such clients are adept at misusing advice, at acting on the advice in such a way as to prove that the therapist (and everyone else) is wrong and the problem is truly insoluble. Indeed, the crisis itself may have grown out of this client's unconscious desire to have an insoluble problem, one that will focus everyone's attention on his own needs. Giving advice, punishing, or scolding such a client often pushes him into further escalation of the problem. "When the therapist takes the infantile signal for attention seriously, he interrupts this vicious cycle and allows the 'infant' in the patient to enter treatment along with the bewildered adult" (Rosenbaum & Beebe 1975, p. 23). In other words, the therapist must consider the underlying need for attention to be as valid a concern as the more obvious aspects of the crisis and must help the client find other, less destructive ways for him to meet that need.

In every case, the primary task of the crisis therapist is to help the client to learn to use his own social resources to resolve the crisis and to continue to maintain that resolution. This implies a continuing effort to involve others in the therapeutic process. In a real sense, "the client" includes not only the individual in the therapist's office, but also the whole social network of which that person is the center. Family, friends, and co-workers are all potentially part of the solution, just as they are (overtly or covertly) part of the crisis. Although the identified client must learn to take responsible action to better his situation, that action can and should be supported by the other people in his life. Because crises are often emergencies that involve real danger to the client and others around him, we cannot afford a more leisurely approach in which the client gradually learns to work with and accept support from his significant others through individual work with the therapist. To the extent that these significant others can be involved from the outset, the system itself can be helped to find and maintain a solution, thus freeing the therapist to act as consultant rather than trying to carry the full treatment responsibility herself.

ENDINGS IN CRISIS COUNSELING

In Chapter 6 we discussed the whole issue of termination of therapy. Endings with crisis clients have some special characteristics, however, that should be kept in mind. I am using the word "endings" in a broad sense to include ending the session as well as ending the treatment. Indeed, one of the problems for the crisis therapist is often that of not knowing for sure whether a given session will in fact be the last one with that client. People in crisis are frequently unable to make a strong commitment to therapy. Such a commitment requires energy, and the crisis client has very little energy to spare. His resources are stretched to the limit simply by the effort to survive.

For this reason, every crisis session should be conducted as if it might be the last contact you will have with that client (Butcher & Maudal 1976). This does not mean that you will not plan for future sessions. Indeed, knowing that one is expected to return, and can count on seeing the therapist again at a specific time, is an important lifeline in a crisis. Rather, it is a matter of planning ahead for what if? What will you do if the client does not show up for the next scheduled appointment? Who else knows about this situation? Where and when are the major pressures likely to make themselves felt? What can go wrong, and how can you and your client anticipate these events? You may or may not choose to discuss such questions explicitly during the therapy session, but you should certainly be thinking about them.

On the other side of the coin, you should think about the possibility of between-session contacts. Crisis clients (as well as their friends and relatives) often call for help between scheduled appointments, asking for advice, for specific interventions in the system, or for extra sessions. I know of no hard-and-fast rule for handling such requests; different theoretical orientations as well as different situations call for different kinds of response. It will always be true, though, that you will respond more effectively to the degree that you have thought ahead and have anticipated the kind of request that may be made. The client may call to say that he is feeling desperate and needs to see you right away; he may tell you he has had to stay home from work and needs you to intervene with his boss; a family member may be fearful, fed up, or wanting specific advice. In any of these situations, or in dozens of others, the therapist needs to think. Instead, she is under tremendous pressure to act, to decide, and to do so quickly. A plan of response, even though she may ultimately have to revise or deviate from it, will help her to keep from being stampeded into an intervention which she (and the client) may later regret.

The crisis client, when he leaves the therapist's office, should know what to do next. He needs relief and hope—relief from his sense of helplessness and hope that things can be changed. Much of this relief and hope will be gained from his sense of partnership with the therapist: they are working together now, using a plan of action that he can understand and believe in. Rosenbaum and Beebe advise: "*Never leave the patient in midair*. When you refer him, make sure he knows where he is going, when, and why. Be sure he knows how to contact you if the initial plan proves unworkable." (1975, p. 15). To this I would make one addition; also be sure that you know what you will do if he does contact you with a further problem.

Ultimately, the acute crisis passes; the final job of the therapist is to help her client reintegrate his life. During the crisis, he has probably been relatively dysfunctional. His behavior and his relationships have changed, and both he and others have adjusted to the changes. He must now decide which, if any, of the changes he wants to maintain and which ones he wants to shift back to the way they were before the onset of the crisis. Golan (1978) suggests that there are three major steps in this reintegration process. First, the client's distorted beliefs and perceptions must be corrected. He must learn to see clearly how he (and perhaps others) contribute to his problems, how to anticipate and plan for future events, how to use effective problem-solving strategies. Second, he must learn to manage his affect, to accept his feelings and to release them appropriately. Finally, he must develop and practice new behaviors, behaviors which will help him cope within the framework of his ongoing life situation.

Each of these three tasks requires that the client be able to think, to reflect, to weigh priorities. In psychodynamic terms, they require ego strength. In the middle of his crisis, the client is less able to do these things; his ego strength is seriously impaired. The therapist may need to do things for him, or to enlist others to do what he cannot do for himself. As he begins to respond to this support, and to actual changes in the system that support and/or the passage of time bring about, his ego strength begins to grow, and he can be encouraged to enter the reintegration stage.

Crisis intervention tends to be short-term, quick-and-dirty therapy. There are seldom elegant solutions, seldom cured clients. Rather, people overwhelmed by internal and external pressures are supported and maintained while they and their systems are helped back to their previous level of functioning. With some clients, this level of functioning may seem quite minimal. We ourselves would not want to live in poverty, with little social intimacy, or to support ourselves by working at a job far below our potential. Generally, though, it is not for the crisis worker to make such judgments. That is a luxury she cannot afford. She is the front-line surgeon, the MASH unit. Others may be called upon to do more elegant repairs back in the relative safety of the base hospital. She has no time for this; she must attend to the next casualty.

SUICIDE

Of all persons with whom a crisis therapist must deal, the suicidal client is perhaps the most demanding and the most frightening. You may hope that you won't have to handle this kind of problem, but chances are that you will—it comes with the territory in our profession. In fact, suicide problems are on the increase in our society, at least among young people. Consider the following statistics (quoted in Fairchild 1986):

One out of every 1000 adolescents attempts suicide.

In individuals 10–14 years old, deaths by suicide have increased 32 percent since 1968.

In a study of depression in seventh and eighth graders, 33.3 percent were experiencing moderate to severe depression and 35 percent acknowledged current suicidal thinking.

Suicide ranks as the second leading cause of death in adolescents and college students.

Between 1965 and 1975 the suicide rate for 15–19 year olds had increased 124 percent.

There are an estimated 50–150 attempted suicides for each completed suicide.

Sooner or later, you will work with a client who is or threatens to become suicidal. Suicidal clients tend to push their *therapists* into a kind of crisis. We often feel threatened, responsible, and helpless in the face of a determinedly self-destructive client. And, as with anyone else in crisis, what we need is information, a set of coping strategies, and a way to accept and release our feelings appropriately. In this section we will attend to the first two of these needs; Chapter 13, on the Care and Feeding of Therapists, will contain some discussion of the third.

The therapist's task with a suicidal client has four parts: first, to recognize the client as actually or potentially suicidal; second, to assess the immediate danger (lethality) of the suicidal behavior; third, to understand some of the dynamics underlying the client's desire to kill himself; and fourth, to develop a treatment plan.

Recognizing the Suicidal Client

It should be stated at the outset that many, probably most, people have some suicidal thoughts at one time or another in their lives. Begin by assuming that any client either is thinking or has thought about suicide, just like everybody else in the world. Making this assumption will go a long way toward defusing the suicide issue and allowing you to talk about it more matter-of-factly with your client. "Most people think about killing themselves at some time in their life—have you?" Or, "When was the last time you thought about suicide?" If the client denies any suicidal thinking, you can accept the denial with mild surprise: "That's interesting; most people do think about it at some time or other," and go on with the interview. More likely, he will experience relief that here is someone he can talk with openly about suicide, someone who will not be frightened or angry with him.

The person who says that he has not thought of suicide may or may not be telling the truth. Many people feel guilty or ashamed of suicidal thoughts, fearing that they will be prevented from carrying out such plans if they reveal them. The client who presents himself as hopelessly resigned to his fate or who shows signs of psychomotor retardation (a general slowing down of all responses, common in cases of severe depression), as well as the previously depressed client who now appears inappropriately euphoric, may be signaling suicide potential. If such a client denies any suicide ideas, it is well to return to the topic gently or find other ways to explore it.

Unfortunately, there are a number of beliefs about suicide commonly held in our society that are both untrue and misleading. Table 7–2 lists ten such beliefs.

TABLE 7–2   Ten Common Misconceptions about Suicide

FALSE	TRUE
1. People who talk about suicide rarely commit suicide.	1. People who commit suicide have given some clue or warning of intent. Suicide threats and attempts must be taken seriously.
2. The tendency toward suicide is inherited and passed on from one generation to another.	2. Suicide does not "run in families." It has no characteristic genetic quality.
3. The suicidal person wants to die and feels there is no turning back.	3. Suicidal persons most often reveal ambivalence about living versus dying and frequently call for help immediately following the suicide attempt.
4. Everyone who commits suicide is depressed.	4. Although depression is often associated with suicidal feelings, not all people who kill themselves are obviously depressed: Some are anxious, agitated, psychotic, organically impaired, or wish to escape their life situation.
5. There is very little correlation between alcoholism and suicide.	5. Alcoholism and suicide often go hand in hand; that is, a person who commits suicide is often also an alcoholic.
6. A person who commits suicide is mentally ill.	6. Although persons who commit suicide were often distraught, upset, or depressed, many of them would not have been medically diagnosed as mentally ill.
7. A suicide attempt means that the attempter will always entertain thoughts of suicide.	7. Often, a suicide attempt is made during a particularly stressful period. If the remainder of that period can be appropriately managed, then the attempter can go on with life.
8. If you ask a client directly "Do you feel like killing yourself?" this will lead him to make a suicide attempt.	8. Asking a client directly about suicidal intent will often minimize the anxiety surrounding the feeling and act as a deterrent to the suicidal behavior.
9. Suicide is more common among the lower socioeconomic groups than elsewhere in our society.	9. Suicide crosses all socioeconomic groups and no one group is more susceptible than another.
10. Suicidal persons rarely seek medical help.	10. In retrospective studies of committed suicide, more than half had sought medical help within the 6 months preceding the suicide.

From C. L. Hatton, S. M. Valente, & A. Rink, *Suicide: Assessment and Intervention.* Englewood Cliffs, N.J.: Prentice-Hall, 1977. Reprinted by permission.

Notice that, in many instances, holding the belief would tend to make one less likely to suspect a given client of being suicidal. It is as if we have created a comfortable stereotype to protect us from the painful reality of how common suicide is among normal people. Perhaps the layperson can allow himself the luxury of such inaccurate beliefs; we therapists cannot.

Schneidman (1979) lists several characteristics of suicide crises that are helpful in both identifying and dealing with the situation. First, he points out that the acute suicidal period is likely to be relatively short, lasting hours or days rather than weeks or months. Supervision or even restraint may be necessary over the short term but can generally be shifted to a more traditional or relaxed approach as the crisis passes. Second, the suicidal client is ambivalent. "The prototypical picture of a person on the brink of suicide is one who wants to and does not want to" (p. 150). While recognizing and respecting the part of the client who wants to kill himself, the therapist must ally with the healthier part, the part who wants to live. Finally, Schneidman reminds us, most suicides are two-person events. They involve some significant other person in the suicidal client's life; effective treatment will also involve that other person, either in reality (bringing them into the treatment process) or in fantasy.

Assessment of Suicide Danger

There are four basic questions which must be answered in order to assess the likelihood that the suicidal client will actually carry out his intent. The questions should be put to the client, calmly and matter-of-factly; the answers will help you to decide whether the client can be left to his own devices (in the context of whatever plan you and he will work out together) or whether more stringent measures (ongoing supervision or hospitalization) should be considered. The first of these has to do with method: has the client chosen a method for killing himself? If he knows that he plans to use a gun, take pills, or jump from a high place, he is in more danger than if he has just thought of suicide in a vague and general way. Next, is the chosen method available? Does he actually have the gun or a stockpile of pills? Related to this is the question of specificity. Has he clearly thought out exactly what he will do? "If the method is concrete and detailed, with access to it right at hand, the suicide risk obviously increases" (Hatton et al. 1977, p. 52). Finally, is the chosen method likely to work? Taking half a bottle of aspirin or slashing one's wrists is less likely to result in death than shooting oneself or driving one's car off a cliff. You should be aware, too, of the very real danger of accidental suicide. While no actual figures are available, it is likely that a significant number of successful suicides occur among clients who intended only to call attention to their need for help. As one worried therapist put it: "I don't think my client really intends to kill himself, but he's so dysfunctional that he'll probably mess up his attempt and end up successful in spite of himself."

Suicidal gestures are a clear danger signal. Contrary to folk wisdom (which in this case is not wisdom at all), the history of a past suicide attempt is probably the single best predictor of present suicidal behavior. Many people who succeed in killing themselves do not do so on their first attempt; if your depressed client has made previous tries at suicide, no matter how ineffective they may seem in retrospect, he should be considered in serious jeopardy.

When is a person most likely to make a suicide attempt? There are several ways to answer this question, and one goes back to our previous point about suicide gestures. Statistically, the risk of a repeat attempt is greatest during the three days following an unsuccessful try (Rosenbaum & Beebe 1975, p. 27). In terms of the overall course of treatment, people are more likely to commit suicide when a depression has begun to lift or after having felt better for a short time. We can speculate that this may be related to the amount of energy available. People in the depths of depression have little energy for taking any kind of action. Or it could be related to the dread of slipping back into despair once they have experienced something better. Whatever the reason, suicide danger increases rather than decreases during the initial improvement phase of a depression.

Obviously, external forces also affect suicidal behavior. The outbreak of suicides during the Great Depression may repeat itself in any economically unstable period, when people see their financial security and sense of vocational achievement melting away. Student suicide rates increase dramatically around final exam time. By far the most important external event, in the context of suicidal behavior, is the loss or potential loss of a significant relationship. The popular songs that moan "I can't live without you" reflect a sadly common belief among young people; loss of lover or of parent are among the most common triggers for suicidal behavior.

In short, there are a variety of criteria that can be used to determine the degree of risk for a suicidal client. Some of these are statistical; others are a matter of clinical judgment and assessment. There is no formula, no sure way to decide that this client will while that client will not. Hatton et al. (1977) have put together a set of behavior descriptions, together with ways in which each behavior tends to be manifested among people of high, moderate, and low suicide risk (Table 7–3). While such lists and tables are highly useful, ultimately there is no substitute for clinical experience.

In the meantime, the beginning therapist is well advised to make ample use of supervision and consultation when working with a suicidal client.

The Meaning of Suicide

In order to work successfully with a suicidal client, it is useful to have some idea of what it feels like to be suicidal. What is the frame of reference of someone who wants to kill himself? What is the real meaning behind the suicide message? Many books and articles have been written on this topic, and we will not try to condense all of them into these few paragraphs. Rather, let us look at a few outstanding themes.

Suicide has often been described as an angry or aggressive behavior. It is the final, unanswerable response to an uncaring and unfeeling world, the ultimate revenge against life itself. Yet, more often than not, the suicidal person is not consciously aware of his rage. For him, the overwhelming feeling is one of despair. There are no options left, no hope. There is no way that things could possibly be better or less painful. "Everything possible has been tried that could have resolved the problem, but nothing has succeeded. The person is now at a complete loss, for there is *nothing left to try;* and this is the feeling of despair" (Filstead 1980, p. 59).

TABLE 7–3   Intensity of Suicide Risk as a Function of Common Client Behaviors or Symptoms

BEHAVIOR OR SYMPTOM	INTENSITY OF RISK		
	Low	Moderate	High
Anxiety	Mild	Moderate	High, or panic state
Depression	Mild	Moderate	Severe
Isolation/withdrawal	Vague feelings of depression, no withdrawal	Some feelings of helplessness, hopelessness and withdrawal	Hopeless, helpless, withdrawn, and self-deprecating
Daily functioning	Fairly good in most activities	Moderately good in some activities	Not good in any activities
Resources	Several	Some	Few or none
Coping strategies/devices being utilized	Generally constructive	Some that are constructive	Predominantly destructive
Significant others	Several who are available	Few or only one available	Only one, or none available
Psychiatric help in past	None, or positive attitude toward	Yes, and moderately satisfied with	Negative view of help received
Life style	Stable	Moderately stable or unstable	Unstable
Alcohol/drug use	Infrequently to excess	Frequently to excess	Continual abuse
Previous suicide attempts	None, or of low lethality	None to one or more of moderate lethality	None to multiple attempts of high lethality
Disorientation/ disorganization	None	Some	Marked
Hostility	Little or none	Some	Marked
Suicidal plan	Vague, fleeting thoughts but no plan	Frequent thoughts, occasional ideas about a plan	Frequent or constant thought with a specific plan

From C. L. Hatton, S. M. Valente, & A. Rink, *Suicide: Assessment and Intervention*. Englewood Cliffs, N.J.: Prentice-Hall, 1977. Reprinted by permission.

While the feeling of despair is pervasive, coloring every event and every relationship in the suicidal person's life, there is usually some specific happening that triggers the acute crisis. The event may be one which would seem to anyone tragic or debilitating, or it may be one which appears rather trivial to an outsider but is experienced by the client as overwhelming or as the last straw, the final insult in a series of painful, humiliating, or hopeless situations. It is important, then, to understand not only what has happened but what the meaning of those events may be to the person experiencing them. It is not the bad grade on a test, the reprimand from a boss, the break-up with a lover per se which triggers a suicide; it is that event in the context of the person's emotional world. The client defines his experiences, reframes them so they fit into his map of the world, and then acts and reacts on the basis of those definitions rather than on the basis of the event itself. If your lover leaves, you may begin to make plans to go out and meet new people; the suicidal client may, instead, understand that now he is forever alone, deprived of all companionship. Talking with him about new relationships will at first have little meaning, for within his emotional frame of reference there is no such thing.

For all humans, the prototypical relationship is that between parent and child. It is with our early caretakers that we learn the meaning of relationship. The death of a parent thus carries enormous symbolic meaning in addition to whatever real loss it may entail. Perhaps this is why suicidal people are often preoccupied with the death of parents. It is as if with a parent dead, all possibility of real contact with other humans dies too. The person focuses not forward on growing, living, building new relationships, but backward on his frustrated yearning for that which is irretrievably gone. Irretrievably, that is, so long as he himself still lives. For such a person, the dead parent is "somehow forever pulling him into death, where they can be together" (Rosenbaum & Beebe 1975, p. 21).

The strength of this dead-parent/living-child bond can be seen in the anniversary reaction, in which the client's crisis is triggered by the anniversary of the parent's death. It is wise, in assessing a suicidal crisis, to ask about traumatic events that have occurred around this date (that is, the date of the present crisis) in the client's past. Sometimes the link is not through the date of the parent's death, but that of a spouse or a child; other links may be the client reaching the same age level as the loved one who died or the client's own child reaching the age that the client was when he was bereaved. Whatever the link, identifying it will again give you some sense of the meaning of the event for the client.

What to Do

All the understanding in the world will not help a suicidal client unless it is coupled with a course of action. The overall strategy has several steps that will be utilized with every client. First, you must establish a relationship with the client that will begin to meet his need for help. Second, gather information about what is going on, assess the immediate danger, and decide on a strategy. Third, put that plan into effect. Last, evaluate how well the plan is working and be prepared to cycle back to step two if necessary.

That is all very well, you may be saying, but it still looks pretty vague. What are these strategies that may be employed? Let's start with the most drastic ones and work backwards.

The client who is clearly in danger of harming himself (or others) can be hospitalized. You should be familiar with hospitalization procedures in your area and have a working relationship with at least one physician who has admitting privileges in whatever facilities are available. You should also know the law having to do with involuntary hospitalization (commitment) and how to implement such procedures. Obviously, voluntary hospitalization is always preferable to commitment, but should you find yourself working with a client in acute crisis and clearly at risk, you do not want to have to take time out to read up on what you can or cannot do.

Another option open to you is referral for psychiatric evaluation and possible medication. You should be able to recognize the kinds of symptoms most likely to respond to drugs—anti-depressants, tranquilizers—so that such referral is not just a knee-jerk reaction to any mention of suicide. You should also be familiar with how such medications affect people, so that you can give your client some idea of what to expect from his medication. (Of course, the doctor or psychiatrist prescribing the medication should do this, but it does not always happen that way.) A good rule of thumb is to suggest psychiatric evaluation if you think there is any possibility that the client might benefit from medication in addition to other therapy. It is irresponsible and unethical for you (or anyone else) to treat a client without medical supervision when that client might otherwise have sought and obtained needed medication.

Referral for evaluation has another benefit for both you and the client. It allows you to consult with another professional about the situation. Two heads are often better than one, especially if the consultant is not feeling scared and responsible (as therapists with suicidal clients often do). Use your own colleagues to get advice, discuss options, and talk about your concerns. Not only are you likely to get some new ideas, but also you will feel better and thus be more effective in working with your client.

If you need support, then your client needs it even more. Another set of options open to you is to enlist the help of members of the client's real or potential support network. Various combinations of people from the client's family, friends, work group, church, etc., may be brought together (along with the client himself) to discuss the fact that the client has been having suicidal feelings and is at definite risk. This group can then develop plans for immediate supervision/support as well as help the client to find longer-range solutions.

Whatever else you may or may not do, a key element in the treatment of suicidal persons is talking about suicide. "Suicidal emotion thrives if it is not disclosed. To share his frightening, 'selfish,' or 'immoral' suicidal thinking with someone else is almost always a great relief to the patient, and his gratitude is the beginning of a firm bond with the therapist" (Rosenbaum & Beebe 1975, p. 48).

Talking about suicide, and about death in general, is not often socially acceptable behavior. The therapist does not pussyfoot or use polite euphemisms. She wants to know, and wants her client to know, exactly what will happen if the client carries out his intention. Such an insistence on what it will really be like may help the client to realize that the reality of his death may be very different from what he imagines. One therapist, for instance, insisted that she and her suicidal client compose a letter to his two young sons, to be kept for them until they were eighteen, explaining to them exactly what he was doing and why. (He eventually decided that his suicide would never make sense to them and so was not a reasonable option.)

Be very sensitive to the nonverbal communications of the client and bring them explicitly into the discussion. A deep sigh, a gallows laugh ("Well, I can always drink myself to death, ha-ha…"), leaning away and withdrawing eye contact are all statements about the client's experience and intent. If you are not clear about the meaning of such communications, ask: "I've noticed that whenever I mention your ex-wife, you fold your arms and cross your legs and begin to swing your foot. What does that mean?"

One of the most important presuicidal communications is the missed appointment. Unlike some other clients, with whom missed appointments may be dealt with at a later time or during the following session, the suicidal client's missed appointment should be responded to immediately. Not only may such a response prevent an actual suicide, but it also deters the client from deciding that since the therapist did nothing, she really does not care about him or take him seriously.

Ultimately, the plan of action with a suicidal client will involve a contract to live. Some variant of a no-suicide contract is essential to successful working-through of a suicidal crisis. The final, and most desirable, form of such a contract is a commitment on the part of the client not to kill himself (or anyone else), either accidentally or on purpose, for any reason whatsoever. There are many workable variants. For instance, the client may insert an escape clause having to do with suicide or euthanasia in the case of a painful terminal illness. The client who is unwilling to make a long-term commitment to life may contract to live for some shorter period of time, after which the contract will be renegotiated. (Be sure to follow up on such a contract, even though the person may no longer be your client. Due dates for no-suicide contracts can be anniversary events triggering a fresh crisis.) Another workable variant is the contract to get in touch with the therapist (or some other person who is party to the contract) if the client believes he is about to kill himself. These short-term contracts give you some working space to deal with the crisis. The client who refuses to make such a contract may be genuinely unable to do so, in which case some form of supervised care should be arranged for him. He may also be manipulative. In my private practice, I will not work with a suicidal person who refuses to make some sort of no-suicide contract. Once this is made clear, most clients address quite seriously the task of deciding how long they are willing, right now, to choose to live.

CONCLUSIONS

Crisis intervention is perhaps the most demanding and stressful area in which a therapist can choose to work. Clients in crisis need a lot from their therapist—time, energy, resources, ingenuity—and they often do not give much back. They may return to a level of functioning which seems to us pretty minimal and unsatisfying.

Or they may simply disappear, leaving us wondering if our efforts made any difference at all. The ones that we do know about are likely to be those for whom we were unable to do enough—the hospitalized, the jailed, the broken family, the suicide.

Crisis workers need to develop strong professional support systems. They need people to talk to about clients, to get angry with, to weep with, and to celebrate with. It is very important not to underestimate this need, and we will return to the topic in Chapter 13.

Keeping ourselves alive and effective as crisis workers requires that we get support. It also requires that we know what we are doing, even when we do not! Paradoxically, like so many facets of therapy, even when the crisis worker is confused and frightened for her client, she needs a clear plan of action, a set of specific options for herself. She needs to know as much as she can about how other professionals work with crisis clients; she needs to be aware of all the resources available in the community. In short, she needs to know that she is doing the best that can be done. Secure in this knowledge, her failures will bring sadness rather than guilt; and her successes will be celebrations indeed.

8   CAREER COUNSELING

"In terms of time, work is the single most important thing that I do during my life. During the course of my life, I will probably spend a minimum of 90,000 hours involved in gainful employment. No other activity, except sleep, will occupy so much of my time. No single waking activity will even approach work in the consumption of time" (Harkness 1976, p. 20).

In the decade or so since Harkness wrote those words, we have begun to tune in to the importance of leisure activities as well as work per se (Super 1984). Professionals now are more likely to talk of life planning rather than career planning and to encourage clients to take seriously their off-work activities. Yet there is a curious paradox here: never before in our history has there been a greater pressure to succeed, to work hard, to achieve. Competition and the drive for excellence are having an impact on younger and younger students; high school athletic programs are treated almost as professional sports; getting into a good college requires enormous effort; the forty-hour week has virtually disappeared as a way of life for the career-oriented young person. Work is important, and we cannot afford to ignore it as we help people to find meaning and fulfillment in their lives. And this is true for youngsters as well as for adults; research has shown that the early work experiences of youth are among the most powerful predictors of career/life satisfaction (Raelin 1980).

Most of the people who seek psychotherapy experience some imbalance between their work and the rest of their lives. They may invest so much energy in work that they or their families are slowly starving emotionally and socially. Or they may experience little or no work satisfaction and try, desperately and unsuccessfully, to fill the void with a frantic and somehow pathetic search for identity or happiness. But happiness and identity are seldom acquired directly; they come as a by-product of the process of balancing work and play. As therapists, we need to be aware of the critical importance of this balancing, of the ways in which career patterns affect all of life, of the danger signals that warn of a work situation out-of-joint with the rest of the person, and of some specific tools for dealing with typical career-life disruptions.

Career problems do not always, or even usually, indicate an underlying personal problem. A career problem may be just that: difficulty in choosing, entering, maintaining, or leaving a particular occupational arena. But a career problem, unattended, is very likely to lead to other problems such as emotional or social difficulties which may appear, on the surface, quite unrelated to work or job or profession. Many social and emotional problems that are presented as the focus of therapy may persist until a related career problem is resolved. The psychotherapist cannot afford to ignore career decisions and indecisions as she works with her clients. It is unfortunate that most of us have little formal training in career or occupational planning, that we have little information about how to guide people through the critical decisions that they must make as they respond to the developmental stages and long-term career decisions of their lives.

This chapter will not teach you to be a career counselor, but it will point out some of the career issues that therapists need to be sensitive to, the kinds of information that people need in order to make clear career decisions, and some guidelines and techniques that are particularly useful in working with career-related problems.

The relationship between general psychotherapy and career counseling poses something of a chicken-egg problem. On the one hand, career reevaluation is a natural sequel to successful psychotherapy; the client is now functioning more clearly, free of his old games and garbage, and is able to look at his whole life—career included—in a new way. It is appropriate that he deal with possible career shifts or enhancements at this time. Yet, as Crites asks:

> How many psychotherapists engage their clients in career counseling, either directly or indirectly by referral, after they have completed treatment?...If they have been successful in effecting some personality change, and if personality is related to career choice, as it appears to be, then it would seem to be at least incumbent upon these psychotherapists therapeutically if not ethically, to consider with their clients possible reorientations and new directions in their career development. (1981, p. 14)

Equally plausible is the notion that career decisions have an impact on personality in general. Our jobs help to shape our self-image; they provide opportunities to grow and change. Work influences our social roles and relationships, stimulates feelings of success and failure, gives us an arena in which to experiment with a whole host of behaviors, attitudes, and expectations. As a client sorts through his dreams and fears about the world of work, this process will inevitably have an impact on his away-from-work self. Some career counselors make deliberate and specific use of these connections in a process called yoking, drawing implications about life in general from the client's discussion of career issues. For instance, a counselor might point out how the client looks to her for a career decision and then ask if the client relies on others in this same way when making other life decisions. Previously out-of-awareness patterns can thus be brought into awareness by yoking them to the clearly visible issues and processes of problem-solving about career.

Career counseling and more general counseling or psychotherapy would seem, then, to move in tandem, with each having implications for the other. "Work is conceptualized as a major commitment in life-planning," says Zunker, "which must be integrated into an individual's style of life" (1981, p. 32). People develop careers, and careers develop people. It is not enough for the therapist to acknowledge career concerns as an important concern of the client; she needs to be sensitive to career issues and either work with them directly or refer the client to someone else who will help with that phase of the work.

SPECIALIZED INFORMATION

Careers are not simply chosen, they are developed. Each of us is involved in career decisions throughout our lives. Careers have patterns; just as one's personal life goes through stages, so do one's careers. Notice the plural—careers. Although some clients will choose to stay on a single track, most will work through up to five careers in the course of their working lives. The one-career person has a work pattern that Super (1957) characterized as either "stable" or "conventional." The stable pattern involves going directly from school into a single job which continues through life. In a conventional pattern, the person may change jobs, but these jobs are seen as steps along a single career track, moving toward and through a series of connected goals. In contrast, an unstable pattern is one of moving from trial to trial, settling for a while in one occupation and then shifting to another. The multiple trial pattern is still less settled and less satisfying; here the person does not have even short periods of stability, but never stays with a job long enough to feel established in it. A fifth pattern, which has become more common in recent years, might be called the single-shift: a change in either external circumstances (economic conditions or technological developments, for example) or in the person (a new interest or skill or a change in marital status) may lead to a single, radical career change.

While these five patterns may describe the career life of men or women, other patterns are almost exclusively female. Super described the stable-homemaking pattern as that of a woman who marries during or shortly after school and continues as a homemaker with no other job. Somewhat similar is the conventional-becoming-homemaking, in which the woman holds a job until marriage and then shifts to a homemaking career. The double-track woman pursues both homemaking and career simultaneously, while the interrupted pattern is one of entering work, stopping for several years while children are small, and then returning to an outside-of-home career. Finally, and relatively new to emerge, is the late-career pattern in which the woman who has not held an outside job during the early years of her marriage chooses to enter the work world during middle adulthood.

The point of all this is that careers do not always or even usually follow a simple pattern from education through employment to retirement. Today's society is much more complex—and still is changing rapidly. In the United States only one person in six now lives in the kind of family that we learned about in our old Dick and Jane readers, where Dad goes to work every day while Mom stays home with the kids. Family structure, population demographics (the growing proportion of older and retired people), work force mobility, the transition from a production to a service economy—all of these factors make the late twentieth century the most volatile and variable socio-economic environment the world has ever known. People do still move through career stages, but the sequence is often jagged and interrupted. A common career stage model, for instance, suggests five stages: growth, exploration, establishment, maintenance, and decline. It is not difficult to imagine a person going through all five stages in order several times; or to imagine another who cycles back through various segments of the process before reaching the last stage. To be most useful in helping someone sort through his career, we need to understand what career stage he is in and what he is moving toward; we also need to take into account such variables as his age, sex, education, cultural background, and job history. The kinds of problems, options, and factors that are relevant during the career exploration stage, for a young black woman with two years of high school, for example, are quite different from those to be considered when working with a 40-year-old white Ph.D. who has been working for the same employer for the last twelve years and is in a maintenance stage. Questions such as "What kinds of changes or shifts have you considered?" or "How long do you expect to be doing this same general sort of work?" or "How many different kinds of jobs have you held?" will help client and therapist determine the career stage as well as the overall career pattern that the client has established. Awareness of the importance of the various demographic categories will help in developing a realistic sense of the career opportunities available and barriers to be overcome for that client.

TESTING

Testing has become the trademark of the career counselor. Since the early days of trait-factor counseling, in which the traits of the prospective employee were matched to factors characterizing a particular occupation, tests have been used to classify career-seekers in a variety of ways. Testing is, of course, a specialized skill. Only with extensive training can a therapist know which of a variety of tests will be most useful for a particular client and be able to administer and interpret them correctly. Nevertheless, even those counselors who do not actually do testing themselves should be familiar with the major categories of tests and have some sense of the strengths and limitations of each.

All tests, no matter what kind, have one thing in common: their usefulness is determined by their *validity* and their *reliability*. Anyone who uses tests, or test results, in any way whatsoever (and that includes you!) needs to understand these two concepts. We cannot discuss validity and reliability in depth here, nor can we even begin to deal with a number of other concepts important in the field of test construction and interpretation, but we can give a brief introduction to each.

Validity.   Test validity has to do with whether a test really does measure what it's intended to measure. A test can't be just *valid,* period; it must be valid for some purpose—to assess school achievement, or to measure verbal ability, or to discriminate among those who will or will not do well in a medical career. A test that is valid for one purpose (say, measuring reading skill) may be quite invalid for another (predicting success in mathematics or job satisfaction as a psychologist).

Reliability.   The reliability of a test has to do with whether the test gives the same information every time it is used. A reliable test is not influenced by chance factors; it can be relied upon to be stable and consistent in its measurements. Scores on an unreliable test might be affected by the time of day the test was given, or by the mood of the person taking the test (of course, if the test was intended to measure one's mood, then you'd want the scores to be so affected in order for the test to be valid!), or by the test-taker's luck in guessing at the correct answer. The more reliable a test, the more impervious it is to this kind of variability.

If a test is to be *valid,* it must be *reliable.* If I am going to trust that it measures what I want it to measure, I must know that it is doing so dependably, steadily. On the other hand, a test may be quite reliable and yet invalid for a particular purpose. Using a balance scale to measure someone's weight, for instance, is a quite reliable test, but it does not provide a valid assessment of that person's anxiety level.

Reliability and validity are two of the major concerns that must be addressed as we select and use tests. There are many others: norms, theoretical bases, difficulty level, cultural influences. For more information, read an overview such as Anastasi's *Psychological Testing* or Salvia and Ysseldyke's *Assessment in Special and Remedial Education.* In-depth review of most published tests can be found in Oscar Buros's *Mental Measurements Yearbook,* and the manual accompanying a test is also an invaluable source of information.

Achievement Tests

These are usually the most straightforward type of test. Achievement tests measure just that: achievement. They come in literally hundreds of varieties, from tests of school achievement (either general academic progress or achievement in a specific subject area) to artistic accomplishment to highly specialized, job-related skills. Scores are usually reported in terms of percentile comparisons with national norms and may also be convertible into age or grade equivalents for younger clients. Most tend to correlate rather highly with formal, mainstream academic success, and so should be interpreted cautiously when used with clients who aren't a part of that mainstream.

Aptitude Tests

More ambitious, the aptitude test attempts to measure ability rather than achievement: to predict how well a person may be able to do something in the future, not just what he has done in the past. Unfortunately, most aptitude tests fall short of this goal and are heavily dependent on past achievement. Some, in fact, are little more than disguised achievement tests, and few if any can be shown to be *valid* predictors of future accomplishment.

Interest Tests

These tests help the client to sort out the kinds of things he enjoys doing or might enjoy if he tried them. They are often valuable in calling a client's attention to activities or pursuits that may not have occurred to him before. Some interest inventories categorize the client as falling into one or two of a relatively small number of interest types; others are vocationally linked, yielding a list of occupations or careers whose successful members have interest patterns similar to those displayed by the client. The wider the variety of experiences a client has had, the more useful this kind of test is likely to be for him.

Personality Tests

Most personality tests fall into two broad categories: self-report inventories and projective tests. In self-report inventories, the client answers questions about his ideas, feelings, and past experiences. The questions are straightforward, and it is assumed that the client can and will answer them honestly. Scoring is largely determined by the theoretical orientation of the test-maker. The Sixteen Personality Factor Questionnaire, for example, yields sixteen categories such as reserved vs. outgoing, trusting vs. suspicious, and humble vs. assertive on which the client is ranked (Cattell et al. 1970). Projective tests are also based on a particular theory, but they assume that the client will unconsciously reveal his personality character-istics as he responds to more ambiguous questions, pictures, or designs. Scoring and interpreting projective tests generally requires a great deal of training and experience, and even the experts may disagree as to the meaning of test results.

The Minnesota Multiphasic Personality Inventory (MMPI) is probably the most widely used of all personality tests. Strictly speaking, it is neither a projective nor a self-report test. It consists of more than 500 true-false questions, and the client's pattern of responses is compared to patterns obtained from clinically identified groups—highly anxious people, people with psychosomatic complaints, aggressive or sociopathic individuals, etc. As with the true projective tests, accurate interpretation of MMPI results requires considerable training and practice.

Values Inventories; Career Maturity Inventories

More specifically geared to career decision-making, these inventories attempt to discover the underlying values that may affect a client's ability to function in a particular career or job. Values inventories deal with the values held by a client, values that may have a bearing on the kind of job he will be satisfied with. Career maturity inventories are designed to help the client determine where he is from a developmental perspective; how well he has mastered the kinds of skills, adjust-ments, and orientations that characterize the various stages of career development. Unfortunately, most values and career maturity inventories promise more than they can deliver: they tend to be highly unreliable and therefore, as we pointed out at the beginning of this section, their validity is necessarily low (Crites 1981).

Using Tests

Career counselors differ enormously in the emphasis which they give to testing and test results. Some see tests as the heart of the career counseling process, opening up aspects of the client's functioning which cannot be discovered through simple discussion of problems, options, and aspirations. Zunker takes this position, arguing that "assessment results constitute counseling information which can pro-vide the individual with an awareness of increased options and alternatives and encourage greater individual exploration in the career-decision process" (1981, p. 115). Others, more skeptical of tests (or perhaps more trusting in the power of the therapist-client dialogue), use testing as a means of corroborating and validating what the client already knows; test results are little more than a framework for discussion, to be ignored or discarded if client and therapist find good reason to disagree with them.

However important or true you believe test scores to be, it is essential that their discussion be integrated into the ongoing therapeutic process. The "three sessions and a cloud of dust" approach of the early days of career counseling, in which clients (usually students) took a standard battery of tests, received a batch of results, and were sent away to draw their own conclusions, is not very useful. More effective approaches tend to involve clients in selecting which tests will be helpful to them, as well as discussing the meaning of the results in the context of a particular career development stage or problem situation.

Probably the most critical factor in using tests for career counseling lies in the way test results are provided to the client. Crites quotes an early article by Bixler and Bixler (1945) which gives five ground rules for sharing such information: "(1) give the client simple statistical predictions based upon the test data [but remember to check out the test's reliability and validity, so that you can be appropriately cautious about such predictions]; (2) allow the client to evaluate the prediction as it applies to himself or herself; (3) remain neutral toward test data and the client's reaction; (4) facilitate the client's self-evaluation and subsequent decisions by the use of therapeutic procedures; and (5) avoid persuasive methods—test data should provide motivation, not the counselor" (1981, p. 80). Even though these rules were proposed some forty years ago, they can hardly be improved upon today.

OCCUPATIONAL INFORMATION

One of the most difficult aspects of career counseling, particularly for the general-purpose therapist, is providing the client with accurate, up-to-date occupational information. The world of occupations is so complex, and is changing so rapidly, that keeping up with it is a full-time job in itself. How can we possibly know enough to give the client all the information that might be useful to him? The answer is, of course, that we cannot. Simply by giving herself permission not to know everything, the therapist frees herself to address with the client the problem of figuring out where to go to get what is needed. Are there books, magazines, or journals relevant to the client's interest? Should he check out help-wanted ads? Employment offices? Professional "head-hunter" services? Whom can he talk to about this or that career? What is the demand? The typical entry-level salary? The local/regional/national hiring practices? The training requirements and opportunities? Who knows? Who has been there? Who is there now? When you encourage clients to find out such information on their own, you not only release yourself from an impossible task but you also foster responsibility and initiative on their part. Clients learn that they can move out independently; gathering information provides useful practice in a variety of career-relevant activities, from time management to interviewing. Moreover, information obtained by clients themselves is much more likely to be remembered and used than information simply handed to them by the therapist.

Since the early 1970s, an important new tool for information gathering and sharing has burst upon the career counseling scene. This is the computerized career information system. Most now have such systems; they allow the client to type in his own characteristics (skills, interests, limitations) as well as the kind of work he is seeking. The computer compares this information with stored job data and returns to the client a list of occupations or career areas that fit those characteristics. Often, the client also gets statistics indicating the relative availability of work in each category, sometimes classified according to geographical area. Computer information systems can be updated quickly and efficiently, and the client need not sort through pages of irrelevant information in order to find what he is interested in. Additionally, using the system forces the client to interact at least minimally with a computer, an experience that in itself is work-relevant in an increasing number of jobs.

Knowing the shape of typical career patterns, knowing something of testing and how to use tests, and knowing how to get information about what is actually going on in the world of work are all important in helping clients with career issues. Most critical of all for the general-practice therapist, however, is knowing one's own limitations. When a client needs skills you do not have, or could benefit from career information not available to you, refer him to a specialist! Do not try to use tests that you are not trained to use, even if you have access to the test materials; do not fake qualifications that you have not really acquired. Most career counselors are willing to work cooperatively with other therapists, accepting referrals for specialized career problem-solving with clients who are working through other issues in ongoing therapy, and consulting with the primary therapist (that is you) so as to provide the best possible experience for the client.

Of course, in order to make such a referral, you need to be aware that the client is, in fact, dealing with a career issue. The more you understand the nature of that issue, the better-equipped you will be to decide whether to refer, to whom, and what to tell both the client and the career specialist to whom you refer. The next topic to consider, then, is diagnosis of career problems.

DIAGNOSIS

Diagnosis is categorizing. The kind of diagnosis you make depends, first of all, upon the category system that you use. Predictably, many systems have been used to sort out the wide array of career problems that clients experience. Bordin, for example, has suggested five major areas of career difficulty: (1) dependence—the client cannot or will not assume personal responsibility for solving problems or mastering developmental tasks; (2) lack of information—the client simply does not know what he needs to know in order to solve the problem; (3) self-conflict—the client experiences two or more conflicting views of himself, or a conflict between his self-image and some aspect of his career or desired career; (4) choice anxiety—making a career choice involves conflict between the client and some other significant person, or conflict arises out of positive and negative aspects of the choice options; (5) no problem—the client is essentially satisfied with his ongoing career process, but comes for counseling in order to get support and validation (Bordin 1968, p. 296).

Another more recent category system is that devised by Healy (1982). Healy looks for the kinds of things that typically get in the way of clients reaching goals on their own; identifying the impediment helps the therapist focus her efforts on dealing with that specific difficulty. Healy's list is as follows:

1. unrealistic or unclear goals
2. insufficient knowledge, ability, interest, training or resources
3. does not try hard enough
4. has misconceptions about how the system operates
5. system itself has defects or is obstructive
6. cannot decide or commit to one alternative
7. problem is formulated incompletely or inaccurately
8. interpersonal conflict
9. inappropriate affect

That last category, inappropriate affect, suggests one of the most pervasive of career-related problems: anxiety. Anxiety can interfere with a client's ability to make a career choice, to get the job he has chosen, to keep the job once he gets it, or to advance up the career ladder. The more anxious he becomes, the more the anxiety itself is experienced as a problem, regardless of its effects on his work situation. People differ widely in their ability to cope with anxiety. Good copers seem to be able to use the anxious feelings to energize themselves and perform even better than they would in a nonanxious state while poor copers, on the other hand, are debilitated by their anxiety; they fumble, freeze, or flee the task entirely. Often, such highly anxious individuals can benefit greatly from training in general anxiety management. Only when the level of anxiety is reduced and/or the client has learned to cope with it can he deal effectively with whatever specific career problem (if any) remains. Later in this chapter, when we discuss specific techniques, we shall have more to say about anxiety.

Goodstein (1972) has suggested another important diagnostic distinction. He differentiates between career *indecision* and *indecisiveness.* Indecision involves lack of information about self or work or both because of insufficient experience. People with indecision often feel anxious, but the anxiety is caused by the indecision. In contrast, the indecisive person experiences long-standing anxiety around any decision-making. He cannot make the decision because he is anxious; he has always been anxious in decision-making situations as long as he can remember. Obviously, the latter situation is more difficult to deal with and requires anxiety-management therapy; the former can usually be handled simply by acquiring information and/or experience.

Diagnosis of career problems is most effective if it is arrived at by both client and therapist. "Many persons," says Healy,

> have not learned to appraise their attributes and goals and to relate them to working. They have not acquired the habit of gathering information about career opportunities and changes occurring in themselves; nor have they learned to resolve problems, profit from mistakes, and improve their own confidence. These people feel the frustration of

such deficits, but often they do not relate it to their own ignorance or their erroneous information and beliefs. (1982, p. 166)

As the client comes to understand the nature of his difficulties, as he learns to diagnose himself, he gains in self-confidence. Not only does he know what he needs to do, but he also begins to believe that he can do it. It is appropriate, therefore, to end this section on diagnosis with a set of questions for both client and therapist. They are questions that the therapist needs to answer in order to work most effectively with the client; they are questions that will also help the client to continue solving career problems on into the future. I have worded these questions as the client might ask them of himself.

1.   What sort of person do I believe I am?
2.   What sort of person would I like to be?
3.   What do I need in my life in order to feel good about myself?
4.   What do I like to do?
5.   What would I like to be able to do?
6.   How hard am I willing to work? What risks am I willing to take?
7.   What do I know about myself from past work and school experiences?
8.   What are my accomplishments/achievements?
9.   What skills do I have, enjoy using, find satisfying?
10.   Who are (or have been) the key people in my life, and why are they important?
11.   What things stand in the way of my getting what I want and need?
12.   What resources can I use to get what I want and need?

Although these questions certainly do not exhaust the list of things one might need to know in order to make a good career-problem diagnosis, they do introduce most of the key concerns. As you move into any of these concerns in depth, you have probably left your diagnostic focus and have begun actual treatment or problem-solving.

THE OVERALL PROCESS

Donald Super, one of the early giants of career counseling, suggests that choosing an approach to career decision-making depends on where the client is in the whole career-choice process. At the beginning, he recommends a nondirective approach in which the client is encouraged to explore both the problem and his sense of self in whatever way he chooses. As these begin to take shape, the client is helped to direct his own process by setting specific topics to explore. Self-acceptance and insight are gained through the therapist's reflection and clarification of self-related statements; thus the therapist continues to maintain a client-centered stance. The first major shift occurs when the therapist begins to provide direction and structure for dealing with specific information sources: tests, occupational pamphlets, work experiences, school grades, etc. As feelings are aroused by this information, the work shifts back to the less directive, affect-oriented style. Finally, the client is helped to choose for himself a course of action which will lead to a decision and to make a clear commitment to follow through on that course of action (Super 1957).

One implication of Super's model is shared by most modern career counselors: it is important to let the client tell his own story at the beginning of the process. Often the most important part of the work lies in discovering just what the problem really is. Zeroing in, getting down to business too fast, may result in finding an elegant solution to the wrong problem.

This first, nondirective stage must last long enough so that the client has a chance to tell his story, discover his problem, and establish a good working alliance with the therapist (if such an alliance has not already been formed during work dealing with previous, noncareer issues). It must not go on so long that the process bogs down in a meandering and aimless kind of storytelling. Crites warns that if the therapist

> allows the first stage of the career counseling process (problem exploration) to last too long, then the most likely outcome is increased dependence of the client on the counselor, as manifested in redundant and circuitory recounting of the problem. If (the therapist) moves too quickly to the second or third stages of career counseling, then the client may feel threatened or rejected and 'break contact.' (1981, p. 185)

The second stage that Crites is talking about is a narrowing-down process. The focus intensifies; extraneous issues are dealt with or set aside. The therapist's major tools here are interpositions or open-ended questions, which serve to direct and channel the client's attention to relevant issues, and juxtapositions, in which one part of the client's story is compared or contrasted with another. These contrasts and comparisons serve to focus attention on relevant issues and significant information and to highlight the problem-solving process.

Crites sees the final stage of career counseling as the one in which the therapist is the most directive. In the gentle first stage and the more-focused second stage, the client has developed a sense of self-direction and confidence, so that he can now interact with the therapist in a spirit of collaboration. He is not so likely to be bowled over by confrontation or offended by disagreement now; he can state and defend his own point of view. Nor is he likely to swallow the therapist's suggestions uncritically; the therapist can dare to be more active and directive because the client will, in fact, now stand up for himself clearly and appropriately—exactly as he will need to do in the world of work.

GENERAL GUIDELINES

Although there are some kinds of activities and interventions that are more appropriate for one stage of career counseling than for another, there are also rules that tend to apply throughout the whole process. Although these rules have been formulated by career specialists and are intended to apply specifically to career counseling, they may provide useful guidelines in many other areas of psychotherapy as well.

Talk Ratio

The first such rule is: attend to the client/therapist talk ratio. There are few, if any, times when the therapist should be using more than 50 percent of the air time. This is true even when the focus is on information-gathering or on dealing with test results. The client's reaction to what the therapist says always deserves at least as much attention as the therapist's original statement. The therapist who exceeds the 50 percent ratio is probably preaching, cross-examining, interrupting silences inappropriately, or trying to persuade the client to do something he does not want to do. Any of these may either drive the client away or (paradoxically) draw him too close into an overdependence on the therapist.

Pronouns

Another useful rule has to do with language: eliminate the words I, me, my, and mine from the therapist side of the dialogue. While all uses of first-person pronouns are not wrong or inappropriate—phrases such as "I'd like to understand that more clearly" or "my sense is that you really are wanting..." can be useful and are, indeed, nondirective and client-centered—following the no-first-person rule will help to keep the beginning therapist from straying into statements of her own opinions or experiences. After all, in career counseling the client is the "first person," and he needs to discover what he thinks, wants, and avoids. Anything that gets in the way of that discovery is, in the long run, counterproductive.

Goal Setting

"Social psychology suggests that the actual declaration of a goal increases client commitment to its achievement, and makes clearer the expectations of counseling" (Healy 1982, p. 168). We discussed the notion of contracting for therapeutic goals in Chapter 4; here we see the same idea applied specifically to career issues. As the client learns to state what he wants and how he intends to get it in the world of work, he will clarify his plan of action and the obstacles that stand in his way. Initially, goals may be relatively broad and nonspecific; as the process continues, the client begins to specify and prioritize exactly where he wants to go and how he will get there. Moreover, the very act of verbal commitment to a goal increases the likelihood that he will follow through on the plans he develops during the counseling hour. Reading and homework assignments are useful adjuncts to such goals. Finding information, practicing skills, and trying out new behaviors all lead to significant real-world progress.

Commitment

Clients often make an appropriate decision to acquire job training, to look for a particular kind of work, to change on-the-job behavior in some specific way, but become discouraged and fail to follow through when they leave the therapist's office. Crites lists a number of principles that the therapist should keep in mind when dealing with commitment issues: (1) commitment to any group or individual increases when one believes that others in the group share his personal goals, values, or interests; (2) commitment to an occupation increases as one recognizes that he is able to enter and succeed in that occupation; (3) commitment increases as one feels positively toward something and sees that other significant people share those positive feelings; (4) commitment to a job increases as one is rewarded for one's work in that job; (5) acknowledging the strengths and weaknesses in a job increases one's commitment to it; (6) commitment to a particular course of action increases as one publicly announces that he will pursue it, delineates its benefits to himself or others, and refutes arguments against pursuing it (1981).

In order to inoculate a client against dropping out, giving up, or otherwise failing to follow through, the therapist may help him to anticipate the probable immediate and long-term effects of his behavior. Knowing what is likely to happen and what resources he can call on to deal with each new situation gives the client a sense of power and self-efficacy. If he has predicted a series of events and decided ahead of time what he will do when they occur, he can overcome discouragement much more easily than if he is constantly having to react to a new and unexpected challenge. Anticipating the future can transform the client's feelings of powerlessness and defeat into pride in his ability to foresee and plan for a variety of circumstances.

TECHNIQUES

In addition to general rules that apply to all phases of career work, a number of techniques will be more appropriate at one time than another. Career specialists are trained in the use of these techniques and have a tool kit of exercises, tests, and specific problem-solving approaches. A few of these are described below; they will give you an idea of the variety of approaches used in dealing with clients who are wrestling with career issues.

Role Playing

Much of the career counseling task involves teaching the client something: information about jobs and job requirements or skills needed in order to succeed in the world of work. We have already discussed a number of issues related to the client's responsibility in gathering information. Skill learning is even more dependent on active client participation; skills simply cannot be acquired without practice.

Role playing is one way to involve the client in active practice during the treatment hour. It is particularly effective in teaching new social behaviors. Clients can play themselves in a variety of social situations (a job interview, a group of fellow employees, or a problem with a subordinate) and practice several alternative ways of interacting with others. They can alternate roles, playing themselves first and then the other person(s). This role reversal allows the client to experience the other person's needs and responses as well as to see himself and his own behavior through someone else's eyes. Healy makes six specific recommendations for helping clients to use role-playing in order to practice social skills:

1. Specify the concepts, principles, and skills to be acquired beforehand to ensure that the scenario has elements related to the target skills and concepts.
2. Provide descriptions of the scenario and the roles in sufficient time for clients to study materials and to obtain clarification, but do not use scripts. If some members of a counseling group are to be an audience, describe their function.
3. Have the simulated scenario approximate the real situation as much as possible.
4. As soon as the role playing is completed, let the client share individual reactions about what happened, receive reinforcement feedback about the positive aspects of the performance, and discuss methods for improving the performance. Make sure each important element of the situation is discussed.
5. Give the client the opportunity to repeat the performance after planning corrections in order to receive reinforcements for improvement, especially if role playing occurs in groups.
6. Role play continuously unless the scenario specifically calls for interruptions. The realism of the role-playing situation and consequently its learning impact can be lost if a player steps in and out of the role. This fact is especially true in role reversal (1982, p. 500).

Role plays are powerful tools for gaining both insight and practical skills; they are especially impactful when used in a group setting or enhanced by video recording equipment which allows the client to review his performance.

Journals

More than any other sort of therapy, career counseling is particularly suited to homework assignments that require the client to read and write. Clients can keep a journal in which they record all activities that lead toward problem-solving or meeting career goals. One such journal is the decision diary which details each decision the client makes: what the alternative options were, advantages and disadvantages of each, the final choice that was made, and how the client came to make that choice. Clients should be encouraged to analyze all their decisions, large and small, in the diary; even choices of what to wear or when to eat can yield useful insights about how one makes or fails to make a decision. Career autobiographies are also useful exercises. In such an autobiography, the client describes the major life decisions he has made in the past. A useful addition here is to have the client pay particular attention to the people who have influenced his life choices. Who were they? What did they say or do? What difference did their influence make to the client? Why were they so important? This information, seen in historical perspective, helps the client to understand how he uses his social network either to move ahead or to stay stuck.

Reading

Reading assignments can be used alone or in conjunction with journal-keeping. Clients can read business or technical journals to update their knowledge of a career area or to find out where they need more information or training. Following the help-wanted columns helps one to gain a sense of job patterns in the community. There are many excellent books available on career and occupational choice; they often provide written exercises that can lead to significant insights into one's unique career needs. The psychology section of any large bookstore is likely to have several such books, and most are both inexpensive and easy to read.

Anxiety

As you work with people who are experiencing career problems, you will often find them to be "anxious, bewildered, apathetic, and frustrated. That very distress will make it more difficult for them to build the skills necessary for directing their careers" (Healy 1982, p. 5). We have already mentioned the distinction between undecided clients, for whom the lack of decision creates anxiety, and indecisive clients, whose anxiety gets in the way of making decisions. In either case, the anxiety must be dealt with in order that the decision-making process be clear and appropriate.

Crites (1981) points out that the nonthreatening nature of the therapy relationship may be a significant anxiety-reducer:

> The conditional stimulus (CS) of the relationship with the counselor is paired (contiguous in time) with the talk of the client about decision making. If the relationship is nonthreatening, that is, it fulfills the conditions of acceptance or non-retaliatory permissiveness and unconditional positive regard or warm concern, then it should stimulate in the client feelings of comfort, safety, confidence, and hopefulness, which are the conditioned responses. (p. 149)

Gradually, these comfortable feelings become associated with the discussion of career issues; since anxiety is incompatible with comfort and confidence, the anxiety level necessarily is reduced.

To help the client carry feelings of confidence and comfort out of the therapy session and to avoid being overwhelmed by anxiety in actual job-related situations, he can be taught the cognitive modification techniques developed by Meichenbaum (1972). The client is asked to notice when he makes anxiety-producing self-statements ("I can't do this," "This is scary," "The competition is too tough") either out loud or to himself. Often, he is instructed to congratulate himself for having noticed such a self-statement, thus turning the negative event into a positive one. Having attended to the negative statement, he can now consciously counter it with a positive statement, perhaps one of a set of such statements ("I'm just as good as anybody else") that he and the therapist have constructed during the therapy hour.

Clients can learn other anxiety management techniques such as thought-stopping (shouting, aloud or in fantasy, the word *stop!* whenever he notices an anxiety-related thought), muscle relaxation, or breath control. All of these have in common the notion that the client himself can be in charge of his feelings; that anxiety is something that he creates for himself rather than something that happens to him. With this realization, the client finds himself able to choose whether or not to be anxious. It is up to him.

Future Pacing

The final phase of career counseling should always include some form of future pacing. Future pacing is planning for what is to happen when the series of regular therapy appointments is completed. Client and therapist need to discuss the weeks and months to come in the context of the decisions that have been made. They should anticipate likely banana peels or self-sabotage, plan how to use a variety of resources, devise strategies for continued recognition and reinforcement of appropriate problem-solving behavior. They may also want to schedule some kind of checkback procedure so that the client can utilize the therapist's help during future career stages. If the therapist has succeeded in becoming a collaborator rather than a superior in the client's career development process, such checkbacks need not foster dependency; they may be simply a sensible use of available resources.

Groups

Throughout this chapter, I have talked about career counseling as if it were a one-on-one process. It often is. Many career counselors, however, prefer to work in a group setting. There are many advantages of the group for career counseling purposes: information sharing is more efficiently accomplished; many exercises and role plays are specifically designed for groups; the group can provide important emotional support for positive change. Chapters 9 and 10 deal with the general characteristics and processes of group therapy, and most of the issues that are discussed in these chapters are applicable to the career counseling group.

CONCLUSIONS

Whether in a group or individually, clients do need to deal with career issues. How I spend my working hours is perhaps the most important single component of how I spend my waking hours. Any imaginable presenting problem that a therapist could meet, from anger to zoo-phobia, may be and often is associated with work, either partially caused by work difficulties or having a significant negative impact on work or both.

All therapists need not work with all career issues, and most general practice therapists should probably refer clients to career counseling specialists when the client needs specific career-related information or skill training. All of us, however, need to be sensitive to career issues. We need to recognize the relationship between work and nonwork activities and the fears and hopes that bridge the two. We need to encourage clients to examine how well they are working at their jobs and how well their jobs are working for them. We must support the client's efforts to align career with self-image, to find a way to make work satisfying and productive and ego-enhancing. By noticing and attending to career issues and asking about them when the client fails to bring them up spontaneously, we can be available for the whole person as he moves among the many arenas in which he acts out the drama of his life.

9 GROUPS AND GROUP THERAPY

As long as there have been people, there have been groups. People are social creatures; they form groups naturally and inevitably. Why, then, not make use of this grouping tendency in psychotherapy—why not work with groups of folks, all at once? It's a logical notion, and perhaps the most surprising thing is that group work took so long to gain acceptance in the therapeutic world. Nobody knows exactly when groups were first used in therapy, but the actual term "group therapy" was coined in the early 1930's when J.L. Moreno began experimenting with psychodrama groups. And group work really hit its stride during World War II as psychiatrists looked for ways to treat larger and larger numbers of soldiers needing mental health services.

In this chapter we will first take a look at some of the characteristics of a group, and how these characteristics can be therapeutic to the group members. We'll then turn to the special concerns of the group therapist: how to get started with a group, how to work in a group setting, and how to deal with some of the problems that can occur in a group.

CURATIVE ELEMENTS OF THE GROUP

Group therapists are fond of saying that things go on in groups that cannot happen in individual work. They talk about group energy, support, momentum. Some sound almost mystical as they try to describe the way in which group members use each other in their process of growth and change. This kind of mystique, while it may sound wonderful, is not much help to the beginning group therapist. You need to know what a group does and how it does it in order to capitalize on those effects. Corsini and Rosenberg (1955), Yalom (1985), Berzon et al. (1963), and Block et al. (1979) are among those who have attempted to specify the ways in which a good group is useful to its members, and I have freely borrowed from Yalom's list of curative factors in the following discussion. As we move through the list, it will probably be helpful for you to keep asking yourself two questions: Do I want my group to operate this way? And, if so, what can I do to enhance this particular effect in the group?

Imparting Information

One of the most obvious ways in which a group can be more effective/efficient than individual therapy sessions is in giving information. That is what schools are about; that is why most formal teaching goes on in classes rather than in individual tutorial sessions. If you have information that you want clients to know about, it is common sense to say it once to several people rather than to repeat it again and again to one person at a time.

Even in settings where all of the formal therapy is on an individual basis, groups may be used in this informational way. Some agencies request that clients attend a group class before beginning therapy in order to acquaint themselves with the philosophy of the agency and/or the possible goals which therapy may help them to reach. Others may run classes in assertiveness or relaxation training or communication skills, which clients attend concurrently with their individual therapy.

In the therapy group, information may come from the therapist or from other group members. You may teach some skill—how to paraphrase, for instance, or how to become more aware of body sensations—and encourage members to practice the skill right there in the group. A member may recommend a book that he found helpful or alert the group to a community resource. Through both formal and informal teaching, group members and leader share important information with each other.

Socializing Techniques

Along with information, many clients need to acquire simple social skills. They have been more or less socially isolated (as both cause and consequence of their other difficulties). They do not know how to listen to others, do not know how to share their thoughts and feelings appropriately, do not know how to assess or use the feedback they get. The group setting gives them the opportunity to develop and practice such skills. The therapist may, as I mentioned above, give information about social skills and then involve the group in structured exercises in which they can practice what they have learned. Or she may simply comment on social behaviors as they occur naturally in the group, encouraging members to communicate openly, to give clear feedback, and to begin to notice verbal and nonverbal messages from others.

Even without this kind of formal attention to social skills, group members will learn to communicate with each other in new and usually more open ways. Disclosure fosters disclosure; as one person risks sharing at a more personal level, others will begin to do the same. The communication skills developed in the group will probably help most members to improve social interactions in relationships outside the group as they become more comfortable and confident in their ability to make good contact with other people.

Instillation of Hope

"I did it; you can too!" is a standard advertising pitch used to sell everything from diet plans to carpenters' tools. It works: the audience sees Jane Doe standing there in her size-nothing bathing suit (or in front of her lovely new hand-crafted whatzit) and thinks, "Wow, maybe I could...."

The same phenomenon, though not so blatantly engineered, happens in groups. Through watching and hearing about what others have accomplished, each member is invited to hope that perhaps he, too, can work through his problems and achieve his goals. "If so-and-so, with all of the mess in his life, can end up feeling good about himself, why not me?" "Mary says she was so depressed she wanted to kill herself, and look at her now. Maybe there's a chance that I won't have to feel bad forever, after all."

Hope, the belief that things can be better, is an essential ingredient in therapeutic success. Without hope, there is no energy to do the work, the hard work, of therapy. Why put myself through even more pain and suffering, unless I think some good may come of it? The invitation to hope may be direct and overt as members encourage and support each others' efforts. It may be a more subtle influence, coming simply through the obvious, visible changes that are occurring in one or several members. However it happens, it is an important curative factor.

Closely related to the instillation of hope is the phenomenon of universality. Many clients enter therapy with the conscious or unconscious belief that they are the only one who has ever been in this particular situation. Nobody else has ever felt just this way, has ever had these kinds of problems. Often, there is a sense of shame: "I'm worse (more stupid, more selfish, more angry) than anyone else around." Ashamed to let others see how bad he is, the client sits in a cocoon of secret misery and guilt. Gradually, as he listens to the other group members, he begins to realize that he is not unique, that others feel the same kinds of feelings and experience the same kinds of pain.

Part of the curative aspect of this kind of sharing is expressed in the old saying "misery loves company." There is a great relief simply in knowing that one is not alone: other parents are troubled by their children's behavior; other couples have sexual difficulties; other people feel trapped and helpless in jobs or at school. Beyond the simple relief of sharing, knowing that other people experience the same kinds of shameful feelings or desires makes it easier to break down the barriers, to talk about and work on that which had been too awful to let anyone else know about.

Altruism

As people share what has been kept secret, they also share their needs: the need for love, nurturing, forgiveness, support. Group members can and do meet these needs for each other. Although this is of great help to the needy member, it may be even more helpful to those who give. Clients are often so locked into their own pain and distress that they lose awareness of their ability to be helpful to others and of the satisfaction they get from helping. They lose their sense of social interest, as Adler puts it, the awareness of being bound into the social web, of being part of the stream of human interaction. It is this kind of connectedness, this ability to share in the joy and in the pain of others, which makes us truly human.

As a person's personal problems grow, it is inevitable that his connectedness to others becomes distorted. He may withdraw from those around him as he feels increasingly angry or hurt or ashamed. He may smother his genuine connectedness by desperate attempts to hang on, to keep others around. He may simply stop being aware of what is happening outside of his own painful internal processes. In any of these cases, the group provides a road back. It surrounds and bombards the person with evidence of the presence of others who feel, hurt, laugh, and care. It offers a person the chance to reach out, at first tentatively, and give something of himself to someone else. In so doing he breaks through the shell and begins to feel connected. He is a part rather than apart.

Cohesiveness

The giving and the receiving that occur in groups are really inseparable, like two sides of a coin. One cannot occur without the other, and both are curative. I cannot give unless there is someone who will take from me. In a deeper sense, I cannot give unless I am also willing to take; connectedness flows both ways. Just as people in pain may lose the ability to give to others, they may also lose the ability to receive. They have been hurt so often, or they feel so rotten and unworthy, that they are no longer open to caring contact. Learning to let others in, to be warmed by the warmth and concern of another human being, can be as frightening as it is exhilarating. The group offers the chance to relearn acceptance and closeness. It is a safe place to experiment with trust, with loving and being loved.

As the safety and cohesiveness of the group begins to grow, it builds upon itself. The more I trust, the more I am willing to risk; and as I discover that my risking does not end in disaster, I will risk yet again. Others watch and listen; encouraged by my experience, they too decide to risk. The process is not always an even one: there are setbacks, down times, ruptures in the fabric of cohesiveness. These heal, and with healing comes an even greater sense of the strength and safety of the process. The collection of people becomes a group, and the group becomes *my* group, *our* group. We belong together; we support each other. We care, and in caring we cure.

Transference

It is a given in therapy that whatever the client is doing out there to perpetuate his problems, he will also do in the therapeutic relationship. This is even more apparent in group work where the client has a whole constellation of relationships with which to reenact his maladaptive responses. Clients set up the same kinds of no-win situations with fellow group members as they have set up with teachers, colleagues, relatives. In terms of transference, they now have not only the therapist as a transference target, but also a whole family. Old business with mother, father, siblings, and other significant childhood figures can be played out in the group.

Just as in individual therapy, the group offers a setting for redoing the relationship, finishing the unfinished business, playing out the old trauma to a new and healthier conclusion. Yalom points out that group members need to work through not only the distortions in their relating to therapist/parents, but also—vis-à-vis fellow members—"other interpersonal issues; competitive strivings with their peers; conflicts in the area of assertion, of intimacy, of sexuality, of giving, of greed, of envy" (1985, p. 46). All adult relationships are, in one way or another, derived from early family relationships. After all, that is where we first learn that other people do exist and that we have to discover ways of getting along with them. In a psychoanalytically oriented group, much attention may be paid to early learnings, to exploring the unconscious processes that underlie the here-and-now relationships in the group and that lead back to primary and primitive family experiences.

Even in more present-time-focused groups, there is an assumption that whatever happens in the group reflects, in some way, what is happening elsewhere. (Conversely, what is happening elsewhere socially will be brought into the social structure of the group.) Interactions and transactions between members are not simply taken at face value; the therapist concerns herself with the broader implications of each member's behavior. If a member makes a critical comment, for instance, he may be invited to experiment with a new kind of response to the person he has just criticized; or he may be asked who else in his life he feels critical toward. The leader might suggest that he criticize everyone else in the group, that he tell the group what happened when he expressed criticism as a child, or how he feels (felt) when he is (was) criticized.

The unique contribution of the group setting, then, lies in the client's ability to recreate and reexperience old or troublesome relationship patterns within the group itself. The therapist (and other members, too) provide feedback, confrontation, and encouragement to explore these patterns.

Imitation

In the course of developing new ways of relating to others as well as to oneself, clients often find themselves stuck. Sometimes this stuckness signals an inner conflict, an old belief system or emotional reaction that needs to be worked through. Sometimes it is simply a result of not knowing what else may be possible, of never having seen things done differently. The group provides many examples of different ways of responding, and this can help clients find new options. Simply imitating the behavior of another group member can lead to important and powerful new insights.

Clients not only imitate end-product behaviors ("I could respond to my mother the way you responded to Jack when he said he was angry..."), but also pick up techniques of working through, of doing their own therapeutic work. Seeing a fellow member cry or watching someone ask to be held gives permission and encouragement. The client who would need many individual sessions before he allowed himself to express strong feelings may do so much more readily after several others in the group have dealt with fear or rage. Group members often comment on the common-theme phenomenon: as one person brings up a particular issue, others discover their own version of that issue. The whole session may focus on feelings of loneliness, on dealing with frustration, or on sexual fears or fantasies. It is partly imitation, but something else as well: the work of the person sitting next to me can help me to recognize my own needs and to find new ways of meeting them. The group as a whole, by supporting this kind of creative imitation, helps me to move into new areas more deeply and more meaningfully than I might otherwise have done.

Catharsis

Catharsis is usually understood to refer to the expression or the venting of strong feelings. Once thought to be useful in and of itself as a sort of emotional housecleaning, it has lately come under considerable criticism. Behavioral therapists, in particular, have suggested that catharsis alone, with no corrective follow-up, can serve to reinforce the very maladaptive behaviors that the client needs to change. It might be more appropriate (though more cumbersome) to refer to the curative aspect of catharsis as the "corrective emotional experience" (Yalom 1985). As Yalom describes it, the corrective emotional experience in group therapy has five components:

1. A strong expression of emotion that is interpersonally directed and is a risk taken by the patient;
2. A group supportive enough to permit this risk-taking;
3. Reality testing, which allows the patient to examine the incident with the aid of consensual validation from the other members;
4. A recognition of the inappropriateness of certain interpersonal feelings and behavior or of the inappropriateness of certain avoided interpersonal behavior;
5. The ultimate facilitation of the individual's ability to interact with others more deeply and honestly.

Again, the group setting allows a more intense expression and experience of the kind of emotional learning that is expected to occur in many other therapeutic encounters. Rather than risking, checking out, and getting feedback just from the therapist (who is, after all, expected to respond differently than most of the other people in the client's life), the client can discover how a variety of people react to his behavior. He can experience both positive and negative responses, and he can take in feedback from several people at once. Through the mechanisms of transference, he can begin to examine how he filters and translates those reactions so as to maintain his old patterns which are no longer helpful to him.

BUILDING AND MAINTAINING THE GROUP

Information About Group Members

Few therapists acquire a group ready-made; our first task is usually finding the people who will be in our group. Experts differ as to how much prior information a therapist needs about prospective group members. Fried (that is Edrita Fried, not a typographical error of the psychoanalyst with a similar last name), for instance, maintains that "every patient accepted into a group should be understood as much as possible by the therapist" (1971, p. 50). In other words, the therapist should take a careful history so that she knows the client well before putting him in the group. At the other end of the spectrum is Stoller's position: "Knowledge about a person which does not emerge from the group experience, is not necessarily as helpful as might be believed and may even dilute the impact that the individual makes within the situation" (1968, p. 62). What is a new group therapist supposed to believe?

Obviously, as you gain experience in the kind of group work you are best at, you will develop your own guidelines for what sort of prior information is most helpful to you. In the meantime, the most important concern is the protection of your clients. There are some things that you do need to know in order to provide that protection.

1. Medical status. Is the client on any kind of medication? What is his physical condition? Is he under a doctor's care, and has he had a recent physical examination? Group work can be very intense, and you need to know if there are any potential health complications—asthma, for instance, or a history of heart problems.

2. Reality orientation. Some psychotic clients do reasonably well in groups, and some groups benefit from the presence of a seriously disturbed member. Some do not. This may have more to do with the leader's comfort and skill level than with the actual behavior of the client, so your first task here is to decide how you feel about including a psychotic member. Probably, for beginning therapists, the best rule is to exclude such clients if you are at all uncomfortable about having them in the group.

3. Concurrent treatment. If the client is in treatment with another professional, you must get the client's permission to share information about the client with that professional. Exchange of information is essential in order to ensure that the two treatments are compatible. If the client is unwilling to give such a release, he will have to choose one or the other treatment; to continue him in both would be unethical as well as countertherapeutic.

4. Illegal activities. Although you can (and should) request that the group treat all group discussion as confidential, you cannot guarantee that this will happen. A client who is, or has been, engaged in illegal activities (selling drugs, for instance) may incriminate himself in the group. Moreover, his revelation of such activities can create unnecessary problems for other group members who may be torn between conflicting values: to report a crime to the proper authorities or to maintain the confidentiality of the group. Unless the group is a special-client offenders group, it is probably best to exclude people involved in illegal behavior; to do so, you need to know about such behavior before the group actually meets.

5. Relationships with other members. Ideally (except for couples' groups or family cluster groups), it is best if new group members not be involved in outside-of-group relationships with each other. Practically, this is not always possible. In order for you to do your job, you do need to know if such relationships exist—that Bill and Bob are employer and employee, for instance, or that Carol and Jay used to be lovers. Both client and therapist must be able to veto such group membership. Bob must be told that his boss may be in the group or Carol that her ex-lover may be there. Both may be given the option of excluding themselves. The therapist also may decide that having both parties there would not be in the best interest of the group. Dealing with this kind of situation can be tricky, as it involves potential breach of confidentiality, but it is very important. One way to handle it is to ask each potential member to make a list of anyone now living in the area with whom he would be unwilling to share group membership. Just making such a list, by the way, can produce useful therapeutic material!

The client has a right to know if people who stand in significant relation to him are likely to be in his group. What else do prospective members need to know? What should they be told about the group and about group therapy in general? Gazda

(1982) has developed a set of principles for informing clients about group work. Although many of the points may seem to you to be self-evident, you must not assume that every client will know them all; it is your responsibility to see that each member is informed of each of these points. First, he should be told what will be expected of him in the group and how he is likely to benefit from participating. He should have a general idea of the techniques that will be used and what risks there may be for him. Second, he should know that his participation is voluntary, that he does not have to follow the suggestions of the leader or other members, and that he may leave the group if he wishes. Procedures for leaving should be explained; many groups request that a member who decides to leave the group discuss the decision in the group rather than simply absenting himself without saying goodbye to the other members. Third, he should be informed about what kinds of records (notes, tape recordings) are being kept. In particular, he should know about any research that is being carried out in the group and should give his permission, in writing, for such research. Fourth, he should know what kind of confidentiality there will be in the group. He must be aware that complete confidentiality cannot be guaranteed; and he should be explicitly informed of the areas in which the therapist is required to break confidence. Finally, he should be told that he may be removed from the group if the leader decides that he is harming or being harmed by other members.

Setting the Stage

Most of us want our groups to be self-curing. We want the members to be helpful to each other. We are aware of the danger of becoming too directive, too powerful, of making interventions that would be more therapeutic if they came from another group member. So we make a conscious effort to sit back, to let the group develop at its own pace and in its own way. Yet there are some functions that we cannot relinquish, some responsibilities that cannot be left to the group. "Even the most permissive, nondirective counselor cannot shirk the assigned task of organizing and launching the group. Because the de facto initial leader screens the candidates, sets the meeting times, develops the group contracts, and perhaps specifies the length of the group sessions, he or she is placed in the center of the group interaction" (Dinkmeyer & Muro 1979, p. 63).

Part of what Dinkmeyer and Muro are talking about here is indeed managerial. Someone has to make housekeeping decisions, and the group leader is the obvious person to do so. But not all of these activities are simply housekeeping; again, there is an overlap into more therapeutic responsibilities.

As soon as the group convenes, it begins to establish its norms. It begins to develop implicit and explicit rules for what will and will not go on in the group. The obvious guidelines of time and place and length of meetings are only the tip of the iceberg here. Much more powerful and pervasive are the unstated rules: who will speak first about what; will members address each other directly or only through the leader; are interruptions permitted, by whom, and of whom (in some groups, members will interrupt each other but will not interrupt the leader). Such norms, once established, can be changed only with great difficulty; it is as if they take on a tenacious life of their own. Making sure that the group norms are therapeutic or, at least, do not interfere with the therapeutic process is perhaps the most important early job of the therapist.

Norms may be established either explicitly, by stating them directly as rules or guidelines for the group's operation, or implicitly, by example. If there are some guidelines that are very important, things that you may need to refer back to as the group progresses, it is probably wise to get them out on the table at the first meeting. The leader may request, for instance, that people not leave and return to the group (for a cigarette or a bathroom break), but rather wait until a scheduled break time. Some leaders have a no gossip rule: "We do not talk about people. If you have something to say, say it *to* the other person. If the other person is not in the group, put him here in fantasy and talk to him." Another frequently observed norm is that of the check-in: the session begins with each member making a brief statement about how they are feeling and/or what they want to get out of the group interaction this time.

Members may ask questions about norms: Are we expected to let you know ahead of time if we cannot make it to a session? Is it okay to bring snacks to share with the group? If you are truly neutral about these issues, it is fine to let the group decide; but if you have an investment in one particular outcome (not wanting members to be munching on goodies while the group is working, for instance), it is best to be straight about it. Many an unwary leader has tried to manipulate a group into choosing to do what the leader has already decided, with disastrous results.

There is no way, of course, that you can specify all of the norms that will operate in your group. Fried points out that "explanations given by the therapist are usually not very helpful in alerting the patients to the actual treatment course" (1971, p. 32). Nor are they the most effective norm-establishing technique. Moreover, a member's violation of an implicit group norm has therapeutic potential in the group, for the group as a whole as well as for the violator. Members can learn much about themselves and their ways of interacting with others from the experience of dealing with norm violations.

Even though you do not state many of the desired norms explicitly, you will help to establish them by your own behavior. Remember "imitation" in the list of curative elements in Chapter 9? The leader is a prime target for imitation. New members, uncertain of what is expected of them, will look to you for cues as to how they should behave. If they see you attending to and taking seriously the remarks of every member, they are likely to do the same. If they see you refusing to join in scapegoating or in laughing at jokes that are inappropriate, the scapegoating and the inappropriate joking are likely to diminish. Groups whose leaders are willing to self-disclose, to make physical contact with members, and to express feelings freely, will have members who are willing to self-disclose, to touch each other, and to express their feelings.

THERAPEUTIC GUIDELINES

The therapist, says Yalom, has two basic modes of presentation or roles in a group: he can be a technical expert and he can be a model-setting participant. Everything that you do in your group will be a variation on one of these themes. As a technical expert, you may give information, ask questions, provide direction. As a model-setting participant, you will use your own internal processing and responding to help members to work through their issues, to deal with each other honestly, to discover their own potential for relationship and growth. In both of these modes, you will be honest about yourself, responsible *to* but not *for* the members of the group. "The basic posture of the therapist to a patient must be one of concern, acceptance, genuineness, empathy. Nothing, no technical consideration, takes precedence over this attitude" (Yalom 1985, p. 112).

Noticing Process

As the therapist attends to and shares her own responses to group members, she sets an example for them to do the same. Gradually, the focus begins to shift from a discussion of what has been happening to members outside the group to what *is* happening to them *in* the group. This is the heart of group therapy. As we have noted before, the interpersonal behavior of the client within the group is an extension of his behavior with the other people in his out-of-group activities. As he examines the within-group process (which, occurring here and now, is available for discussion, confrontation, and feedback from therapist and other members), he will begin to make connections, to see those same patterns in his other relationships. Subsequently, both in-group and out-of-group behaviors will begin to change.

Beginning group therapists often find it difficult to shift from focusing on content issues to focusing on the group process. It is easy to get caught up in a problem-solving session around Jerry's wife's over-spending habits or Ellen's seeming inability to finish school assignments on time, and to lose sight of how Jerry or Ellen or the other members are dealing with each other. Is Jerry's pulling his chair into a corner a nonverbal request that someone notice and invite him back into the group? If so, who responds to the request? Is Ellen setting herself up to be criticized or punished, and who in the group is ready to do the criticizing?

Yalom suggests that the therapist begin by simply "thinking here-and-now." As you think in this way—about what is going on for each member, at this moment—your interventions will begin to steer the group members toward noticing their own process. They, in turn, will begin to be more interested in how the group deals with an issue than they are in the issue itself. They will attend to what people are saying about themselves and their relationships through the process of telling their stories and of responding to the stories of others.

Interventions

The more experience you have with groups, the more confidence you will feel in identifying process patterns. You'll almost surely be tempted to share these insights with the group. It is fun to point out what people are doing with and to each other; it is satisfying to score a bulls-eye! Why not, you may ask. After all, people begin to grow and change as they recognize their styles of interacting with others. Isn't it your job to tell them what you see?

The problem with telling them is twofold. First, people will only hear process feedback when they are ready; often you will notice a pattern before the people engaging in the behavior are themselves open to dealing with it. Second, process interventions tend to be much more powerful when they come from group members rather than from the leader. "One of the very serious errors a group leader can make is to consider that the most meaningful kinds of learning emanate from his actions or his technique" (Stoller 1968, p. 85). The hard fact is, though, that part of your job is to help your clients learn to do without you. They do this by learning to trust their own insight, hearing and using feedback from others (who probably are not therapists).

Sometimes, of course, you will and should intervene. To sit and say nothing makes you an observer, not a participant; you are not being paid for just observing! Most of your interventions (at least those in the role of technical expert) will be made so as to focus attention back on the group process. The therapist, from this point of view, is a kind of verbal sheep dog, nipping at the heels of members who stray too far from the appropriate focus. Yalom comments "Many of the observations the therapist makes may be highly inferential. Objective accuracy is not the issue; as long as you persistently direct the group from the nonrelevant, from the 'then-and-there' to the 'here-and-now,' you are operationally correct" (1985, p. 155). You might notice, for instance, that throughout an animated discussion of "how can I ever pay all my bills," one member has been quietly looking at the floor. You intervene: "I notice you haven't said anything, Peter, and you look worried." Peter may respond, "No, I'm not worried. I'm pissed off that these guys are bitching about money when they spend more in a week than I earn in a month." The fact that you mistook Peter's anger for something else is unimportant; you have succeeded in bringing the focus back to the immediate interrelationships within the group.

Confrontations

Simply calling attention to what you see, with or without a tentative label, is a first-level intervention. It is often all that is needed. Sometimes you will be able to put that observation into a framework that will make it more meaningful, make the behavior more understandable or noticeable the next time it occurs. Some common framework descriptions used in groups include displacement (a member attacks someone other than the original target of his anger), indirection (two members relate to each other through a third person or in some other disguised way), mirror reactions (a member responds to a part of himself which he sees in another person), and isolation (responding to a comment or a behavior as if it occurred in a vacuum, ignoring the context). You may point out these patterns directly, or you may use a self-questioning technique: "I wonder how come, Julie, you continue to talk about Phyllis rather than directly to her" or "I'm curious about how Phillip manages to keep the group focused on his problems with his boss." Such implied questions encourage the group members to generate the interpretation rather than waiting for you to provide it.

These kinds of interventions are, essentially, confrontations. Confrontation, according to Egan, is simply an interpretation that "causes another person (the confrontee) to admit to, reflect upon, examine, question, or change some particular aspect of his behavior" (1973, p. 107). Knowing how to confront, though, may be less important than knowing when confrontation is appropriate. Table 9–1 gives a list of rules for confrontation, which will help you to make this kind of decision.

Lest you begin to feel overwhelmed by all of these rules, by the impossibility of remembering everything, and the need to notice what is actually happening in the group, reassure yourself: first, much of what has been said in this section is a review of what you, as a good therapist, already know how to do. You are already behaving in these ways, often without awareness of your own skills and techniques. Second, it is permissible to make mistakes. Not only permissible—it is inevitable! Missing something, doing it wrong (or not doing it as well as you would have liked), and owning up to your own shortcomings is also therapeutic.

TABLE 9–1   Guidelines for Using Confrontation in a Group Setting

1. Confront in order to manifest your concern for the other.
2. Make confrontation a way of becoming involved with the other.
3. Before confronting, become aware of your bias either for or against the confrontee. Don't refrain from confrontation because you are for him or use confrontation as a means of punishment, revenge, or domination because you are against him. Tell him of your bias from the outset.
4. Before confronting the other, try to understand the relationship that exists between you and him, and try to proportion your confrontation to what the relationship will bear.
5. Before confronting, try to take into consideration the possible punitive side effects of your confrontation.
6. Try to be sure that the strength or vehemence of your confrontation and the areas of sensitivity you deal with are proportioned to the needs, sensitivities, and capabilities of the confrontee.
7. Confront behavior primarily; be slow to confront motivation.
8. Confront clearly: indicate what is fact, what is feeling, and what is hypothesis. Don't state interpretations as facts. Don't engage in constant or long-winded interpretations of the behavior of others.
9. Remember that much of your behavior in the group, such as not talking to others, or expressing a particular emotion, can have confrontational effects.
10. Be willing to confront yourself honestly in the group.

From *Face to Face,* by G. Egan. Copyright © 1973 by Wadsworth Publishing Company, Inc. Reprinted by permission of Brooks/Cole Publ. Co., Monterey, CA 93940.

PROBLEMS

Every group has strengths, expected and unexpected curative abilities which emerge with or without the therapist's intervention. Every group also has problems. It is a common pitfall for beginning therapists to be so aware of and worried about the problems that they fail to recognize and capitalize on the strengths of their groups. One way to deal with this tendency is to know ahead of time some of the kinds of problems that are likely to arise in a group, to be aware that they are common problems (not unique to your style of leadership and not your fault), and to have a sense of how to cope with them.

Air Time

In any group, the amount of time available for each person is limited by the number and the talkativeness of the other members. Some groups have air time problems: some or all of the members do not feel they get enough time or attention. People respond to this problem in a variety of ways: some become demanding, some whine or sulk, some withdraw into helpless silence.

Dealing with air time inequities is not just a group therapy task, it is a life task. As with so many group phenomena, the process within the group is a reflection of the members' general coping behavior. The therapist's task, then, is not so much to distribute air time evenly among the members as it is to help them recognize how they themselves address the task of getting attention, of being heard, of making interpersonal contact. "Each individual is responsible for gaining and maintaining the attention of the group. In this sense, the group is not expected to develop an atmosphere of 'fairness,' but rather to reflect the world as it actually is" (Stoller 1968, p. 47).

Confrontations around air time should direct attention to the how and the why of patterns as they develop. If you choose to draw a quiet member into the discussion, do so in a way that will invite both that member and the rest of the group to examine how he and they contributed to his exclusion. If there are one or two people who tend to monopolize the group, it is better to help the group itself deal with them than to use your leader role to give the others more time.

Remember that many people will occasionally want and need to assume a more passive role in the group. It is not always helpful to talk; sometimes listening quietly or even withdrawing into one's internal business is the best strategy for a group member. While it is not good for someone never to talk, it is therapeutic to know that it is possible and permissible to use the group once in a while as a place to hide, as a time out from pressure, or as just a comfortable and supportive and demand-free environment.

Monopolizers

Our discussion of air time has already highlighted two problem roles, the monopolizer and the silent member. The monopolizer takes up group time by monologing, interrupting, continually demanding that the group focus on him. Members may become anxious or resentful or bored, but (especially early in the life of the group) they may be reluctant to address the problem directly. Process comments are most useful here: "I notice that Kathy has been doing most of the talking." "We've spent nearly an hour discussing Mark's situation. How did we decide to give him all our attention today?" "Rose, you've been shifting around in your chair a lot while Judy talks about her job. Will you tell Judy what's going on for you?" Or you may choose to describe your own reaction: "I'm uncomfortable with the group taking so much time with Randy, and I'm wondering why I keep helping us to do it. I think maybe I'm afraid of hurting his feelings. Is anyone else experiencing this kind of reaction?" Comments like this legitimize dealing with the monopolist's behavior and with his response to being confronted openly. They serve not only to address the air-time problem, but also as examples of process focusing, which is the major task of the group.

Rescuers and Victims

Some group members, with the best intentions in the world, can be quite disruptive of others' therapeutic processes. These are the rescuers, folks who leap in too soon with advice, sympathy, or defense. The rescuer may see himself as an assistant therapist (or may, consciously or unconsciously, be competing with the therapist for the role of leader). He may have learned to get a great deal of personal satisfaction from "helping" other people. He may simply not understand the importance of being allowed to work through an issue on one's own, to express strong feelings, to discover one's own solutions. Rescuers, by interrupting these processes, get in the way of therapy; yet other members often find them very hard to confront. After all, they are only trying to help....

Confronting a rescuer is important for both the group and the rescuer himself. In terms of group needs, confronting and limiting the rescuer's activities makes it easier for others to get on with their work; it also sets a permission-giving example. Early confrontations will probably focus on the needs of the person being rescued: "Dan needs to deal with this himself right now, rather than listening to someone else's reactions." "Give Mary a chance to figure out a solution on her own." Later, you may wish to make a process comment that will help the rescuer to examine his own system: "What does it do for you, Gerry, to always be the one who helps people in the group?"

Rescuers often find a natural partner among the group members, someone who delights in being rescued. These people play a helpless victim role, telling endless stories about how badly they have been treated or how unsolvable their problems are. They often invite members to try to rescue them but manage to sabotage the rescue attempt in some way. The result is the classic "Why Don't You...Yes, But" pattern described by Berne (1964) in which one or more members take turns offering advice while the victim maintains his position by explaining why nothing that is offered will work for him.

Probably the best way to deal with this pattern is simply to describe it. Clients usually recognize their roles very quickly and will, with little encouragement, identify the process the next time they see it being played out in the group. When this happens, the helpless victim (like the rescuer) can be encouraged to explore his own payoff in maintaining this role and to find new options for getting what he wants from the other members.

Disruptors

Most of the problem people we have discussed tend to be more or less disruptive of the group's process. Some individuals are even more overtly disruptive: they become aggressive, they interrupt (verbally or nonverbally), they make inappropriate comments. No single solution is available for dealing with disruptive persons. The closest thing to an all-purpose solution is to discuss with the group what the disruptive person is doing, and how the other members are responding. Ultimately, if the disruptor is unable or unwilling to change, you may have to ask him to leave the group. This is an extreme solution and should never be used before the group has dealt with the problem openly. Of course, it is much more desirable that a discussion of everyone's responses may help the disruptor to change his behavior and help the group to find new, constructive ways of supporting him.

One last problem person should be mentioned here, and that is the scapegoat. Occasionally a group will collectively decide to make one member the target for its anger, frustration, or disappointment. Nothing that person does is right, and everything that goes badly in the group is his fault. The scapegoat does not consciously choose to disrupt the group process though he is often someone for whom the kick-me position is a familiar, though painful, way of interacting with others. "Since scapegoating is obviously a growth-hindering aspect of group life, the counselor must be alert for signs that some member is being singled out for this purpose" (Dinkmeyer & Muro 1979, p. 234). Scapegoating is as bad for the rest of the group as it is for the victim; it allows them to avoid their own role in creating and maintaining the problem. Again, the best tactic is to call the group's attention to what is happening. "Everyone is criticizing Jim today." "We all seem to have agreed that Lucy is to blame for this situation. How did we do that?"

The behavior of problem people in the group can provide useful material for the group to focus on. Looking at such behavior as material to work with, material that is highly relevant to the very things that brought each person to the group in the first place, will help you not to become frustrated and impatient. When problem behaviors do not respond to the process approach, the leader's response must be one of setting limits, of framing the interaction so as to keep one or two individuals from sabotaging the work of the group. Usually, members will respond positively to process comments and will gradually replace their disruptive or maladaptive behaviors with new and more appropriate ones. When this does not happen, you will have to provide protection for the group by setting more explicit limits. Dinkmeyer and Muro suggest a four-step process by which this can be accomplished: (1) recognize the feelings that underlie the problem behavior, and help the person to talk about those feelings; (2) state the limits clearly in terms of what specific behavior is not acceptable; (3) point out other ways in which the person can express his feelings and meet his needs; and (4) help him to deal with his resentment or embarrassment over having been restricted.

CONCLUSIONS

Working with groups provides the therapist with a wealth of possibilities. There are so many things to notice, so much going on, so many different places to intervene. In fact, working in a group setting almost guarantees stimulus overload; there is no way that a single person can take in and deal with all of the information available at any given moment.

Since you cannot deal with it all, you will have to make choices. You will have to ignore some things in order to respond to others. In this chapter, I have introduced some high priority guidelines for the sorts of things that experienced group leaders have found to be important.

In order to further condense this list, let me end with my own set of basic priorities. You may not always want to follow them, but they will be a useful set of rules for you to check in with occasionally. First, attend to the group dynamics: what is the process? Focus underneath the content on who talks to whom, when, in what tone, and with what consequences. Second, review the explicit and implicit contracts. Are people getting what they came for? If not, how is the group failing to help them meet their goals? Third, step back and examine your own role in the group. How do you feel about what is happening? Whom are you angry with, scared of, disappointed in, protective of? What do you want to get out of leading the group, and how are you getting in your own way? Consultation can be invaluable here; it is extraordinarily difficult to back off far enough from our groups to be really objective about how we ourselves are contributing to the process.

The biggest mistake that beginners tend to make with groups is that of trying too hard. It is better to do too little than to try to do too much. Groups do, in and of themselves, have enormous curative potential. If your only function as leader is to create a framework within which members can come together regularly, this alone will be therapeutic for most of those members. Again there is a paradox: the more leadership skills you acquire, the less you will need to use them. Lean back, relax, trust the group to teach you at least as much as you teach them, and enjoy yourself! And your group will prosper.

10 COUPLE THERAPY

"The American marriage ideal is one of the most conspicuous examples of our insistence on hitching our wagons to a star. It is one of the most difficult marriage forms that the human race has ever attempted, and the casualties are surprisingly few considering the complexities of the task" (Mead 1949, p. 342). We Americans want a lot from our marriages, and it takes an anthropologist like Margaret Mead to make us pull back, take a second look, and realize just how difficult a task we set for ourselves. We expect our marriage partner to be our lover, our best friend, our major source of social and economic support. Marriage is the context in which most of us hope to raise our children, manage our dreams and our disappointments, and learn to grow old. Having achieved independence from our parents (often with great difficulty), we scarcely pause to enjoy our autonomy before we plunge into a new and even more demanding kind of relatedness. We push ourselves to learn almost overnight to give and to take, to be strong and to be weak, to trust and yet protect ourselves. We hope and promise to maintain this relationship for decades to come, into a future in which we cannot even imagine what kind of people we, or our partners, will become. Mead is right; the surprising thing is that it works as well as it does.

Even when it does not work out so well, when frictions develop, and the rosy ideals of first love crash on the rocks of reality, we do not want to give up. Couples try to work things out. They talk to each other and to friends, they plan secret strategies of their own; they look for advice in sex manuals, at communication workshops, and from inspirational articles. Sometimes they seek professional help, a third-party expert who will turn things around and make them better.

The couple therapist, of course, cannot make things better. What she can do is help the couple themselves to find new ways of working and living together. She can encourage them to listen, to think, to experiment, to risk. From her standpoint outside the relationship, she can see patterns that the couple themselves are unaware of and can invite the couple to step back and look in a different way. Hiebert and Stahmann characterize all of couple therapy as this sort of invitation: "an invitation to see, experience, and become aware of what the partners do to each other, a searching for links to their mutual involvement and responsibilities" (1977, p. 19).

The couple therapist does not know the answers; she is not a grab-bag of ready solutions. Should she sense what a couple ought to be doing differently, she is often wise not to share that information. The most successful solutions must come from the partners themselves. The therapeutic function in couple work is that of observing and directing process, of protecting the clients by insisting that each observe the ground rules of fair fighting, and of supporting the whole endeavor with a confident certainty that new options are possible.

Stuart (1980) has suggested four conditions that provide a useful framework for couple therapy. First, he insists, treatment must be goal-directed. Whatever happens between therapist and the client couple must be done in the service of some agreed-on goals. Second, the therapist should define her role (at least implicitly and often explicitly) in a way that is consistent with what she is willing to do with and for the clients. Third, the clients need help in defining *their* roles in learning what they are expected to do in therapy. Finally, the course of treatment should be seen as a series of stages, related yet different from each other. The couple will change as therapy proceeds and so will their relationship; the therapist must be sensitive to these changes, fostering a cumulative building of skills.

PATTERNS OF RELATIONSHIP

Most experts agree that there are a number of relationship types that can be recognized. In this section, we will describe some of these familiar patterns; recognizing and understanding them will help you to plan effective intervention strategies for each couple you work with.

Attaching-Detaching

One of the most common relationship patterns among couples is what Hiebert and Stahmann have called the "attaching-detaching marriage." In this marriage,[1] one of the partners is constantly struggling to get closer, to share, to bond with the other. The other partner does the reverse: struggling for distance, pulling away, needing space. Most typically, it is the wife who wants closeness while the husband wants more distance. The more demanding the wife becomes, the more she looks for proof of her partner's love and caring, the farther away he moves. Martin (1976) described this pattern as one of a lovesick wife with a cold-sick husband but notes that the roles can be reversed, that the wife may be the one who needs distance while the husband seeks assurances of love and belonging.

The attaching partner may try a variety of ploys to satisfy her need for closeness. She may be aggressively demanding, or she may present herself as weak and helpless. She may become provocative, teasing, flirtatious. No matter what the technique, though, it is doomed to failure: as soon as she begins to break through, the husband is threatened and automatically pulls back. "Often it appears as though the husband is some kind of great sphinx sitting on the sands of Egypt. The wife appears to be an exotic dancer dancing around and around the great stone sphinx, convinced that somehow if she can only dance creatively and exotically enough the great stone sphinx might at least wink...." (Hiebert & Stahmann 1977, p. 25). If she does manage to startle a wink out of him, he will immediately retreat again into the safety of his stony detachment.

A variation of this pattern has been termed by Martin as the "in search of a

---

[1]Throughout this chapter, I have used the term "marriage" as a shorthand word for the more cumbersome "committed relationship." The patterns and principles which we will be exploring are not unique to couples who are formally married, but rather appear to hold for any pair of individuals who have decided to spend a significant portion of their lives in a couple relationship.

mother" marriage. Here it is more often the husband who unconsciously presents himself as needy and dependent, while the wife takes on the role of caretaker and emotional provider. The roles in this kind of relationship may appear on the surface to be reversed. The man may look like the strong provider while the woman gratefully accepts his caretaking; he earns the money, fixes the family car, thunders at the children. Yet on a deeper level, it is she who provides the emotional stability, the love supplies, for the family.

Double Dependent

In the dependent-dependent marriage—Hiebert and Stahmann call it the "half marriage"—each partner wants to be held up by the other. "Both of these people could be described as having marked dependency needs. Both of them want very much to lean on the other person, both want to be taken care of, and both want the other to be strong" (Hiebert & Stahman 1977, p. 21). Needing both to lean and to stand alone, each partner is in conflict; no matter what they get from their spouse (caretaking or dependency), it feels wrong. The result is an ongoing struggle, a sense of simultaneously wanting, needing, and not wanting to be in the relationship.

The dependent-dependent relationship may continue for years in a locked struggle, like the Pushme-Pullyou of the Dr. Dolittle stories. The balance may shift, as one partner moves out of the dependent position, into an attaching-detaching pattern. Another kind of shift can occur if the partners come to accept their mutual dependency needs: the couple becomes more and more symbiotic, more and more fused, until they lose the sense of their own boundaries. "Neither one is able to be aware of or to take a separate individualistic 'I position' on any significant thought or issue which involves both of them" (Williamson 1977, p. 53).

Interestingly, in both the attaching-detaching and the double dependent patterns, partners who experience strong dependency feelings are rarely able to talk about such feelings. They may present themselves as generous, giving, loving mates; or they may cover their dependency needs with irritation and anger. Or they may appear silent and aloof, unable to allow themselves to feel anything at all. The neediness, with no sure guarantee of satisfaction, is simply too threatening to be experienced directly, much less shared with another person.

Paranoid

In the "paranoid marriage," one or both partners use the relationship to maintain a distorted belief about reality. They may distort the qualities of their partner, using him or her as a scapegoat, an enforcer-of-good-behavior, or whatever else their personal system needs. Alternatively, they may collude with their spouse to maintain a belief about people or the world outside their marriage relationship. This "us against the world" stance may be narrowly focused and relatively harmless, as with couples who see themselves as socially superior to their neighbors; or it may be as highly pathological and generalized as a Manson family system.

Sado-Masochistic

Couples who use each other as scapegoats, continually battling and sparring and competing over who will be victim and who will be persecutor, may also be involved in a "sado-masochistic" marriage. Here each partner uses the other to meet their needs to hurt or to be hurt, and neither is ready at an unconscious level to give up the pain of relating in this way. The therapy session becomes a courtroom "where they each want to hire the counselor to help them in their attack against the other person" (Hiebert & Stahmann 1977, p. 28). Since assigning blame or responsibility to one person only perpetuates the pattern, the therapist must be especially careful not to be seduced into the role of judge and jury, but rather insist on focusing on the process in which each partner keeps the battle going, round after round after round.

Therapeutic

Finally, Hiebert and Stahmann describe the "therapeutic marriage." This relationship is similar to the attaching-detaching marriage in that one partner appears strong and the other weak. In the therapeutic marriage, the strong partner in fact needs the spouse to be weak in order to continue to be a rescuer. Partners may alternate roles, rescuing their spouse one day and being rescued the next. Usually, whoever is at a given moment doing the rescuing feels righteous, but also resentful and uncared-for, while the current rescuee feels both guilty (over needing help) and resentful of the stronger spouse. Only when they are ready to give up the idea of saving each other, willing to take the risk of being autonomous individuals, can they disengage from this pattern.

ASSESSMENT

Being alert to these common patterns of disturbed relationships can help the therapist stay out of the couple's pathology as well as sensitize her to the ways in which they keep themselves stuck. How much time, though, should be spent in formal assessment procedures as opposed to beginning to work with the couple immediately and assessing as we go along?

History-Taking

Ables (1977) is opposed to a lengthy history-taking procedure. "We focus on what is going on between the couple as we begin the first session and encourage them to begin talking and negotiating with each other," she says. "As treatment proceeds, the gestalt of the couple and the necessary information for treatment usually emerge" (p. 17).

At the other end of the spectrum is the technique recommended by Hiebert and Gillespie, who reserve up to three full sessions for history-taking. Hiebert and Gillespie believe that taking this time not only allows the therapist to plan her interventions more effectively, but also serves a therapeutic function by reducing the anxiety of the couple and postponing their need to decide just how dysfunctional or healthy their relationship may be.

A compromise between (or extension of) these two points of view is the use of a relationship questionnaire. Couples can fill out the questionnaire either individually or as a team. The information gathered may simply go into the therapist's ongoing assessment of the partnership, or it may be discussed in subsequent therapy sessions. Figure 10–1 presents one such questionnaire; obviously there are many possible variations.

However you choose to gather information about the couple, it will be useful for you to organize it in terms of a number of basic principles. First, all marriages involve at least two sets of contracts, one conscious and one unconscious. People usually agree on the conscious contract when they get married (though the terms may change and conflicts develop over the years); but the expectations of the unconscious contract often collide. Lorrie and Larry, for instance, married with the expectation that Larry would work at a nine-to-five job while Lorrie would stay home and take care of three lovely children. Now, ten years later, Lorrie is tired of diapers and peanut butter, bored with daytime TV, and wants a career; Larry is confused and resentful over her increasing demands that he share in the child-rearing responsibilities. Unconsciously, Larry's contract read that Lorrie was to pick up where Mom left off, providing a safe and comfortable haven for him and admiring him for his accomplishments. Lorrie's unconscious contract was that Larry would support her growing up and would encourage her to take her place as a full-fledged adult. The therapist, alert to evidence about conscious and unconscious contracts, can help both Lorrie and Larry become aware of what their expectations have been and help them negotiate new contracts that will allow each to function within the structure of the marriage.

Another kind of contract has been pointed out by Sager. This is the interactional contract, and it specifies not what will be done by each but rather how the couple will operate. "The interactional contract is the operational one in which the two mates are trying to achieve the needs expressed in their separate contracts. It is the set of conventions and rules of behavior, of maneuvers, strategy, and tactics that have developed in their dealings with each other" (1976, p. 28). Interactional contracts are rarely made explicit; usually they are out of awareness, and the couple may have no conscious idea that there is any other possible way for them to do things. When Don gets angry with Donna, he storms out of the house; he does not know of any acceptable alternative. Mary asks Mike for help with the dishes when she is feeling frustrated and in need of coddling; both understand the code, though neither is consciously aware of using it. By helping couples to notice the terms of their interactional contracts, the therapist suggests that there are indeed alternative options. What is done consciously can be done differently or can be kept the same, if both partners agree that they want it that way.

A second principle to keep in mind in assessing a relationship is that the

MARRIAGE AND MARITAL THERAPY

Couple Relationship

1. What attracted you most to your spouse?_____
   Is that still present as you see him/her today?_____
2. Did you experience any "second thoughts" after marriage? Explain:_____
   _____
   _____
   _____
3. Do you spend spare time together or separately?_____
4. Do you confide in one another?_____
5. What do you enjoy doing as a couple or family? (e.g., TV, movies, theater, concerts, socializing, sports, etc.)_____
   _____
6. Who decides on the activity? How do you decide on activities, vacations, etc.?_____
   _____
   _____

Current Problems

1. What is the problem you come with? (Try to describe details: length of time, any specifics you consider important, why you came now)_____
   _____
2. What other marital problems have you had?_____
   _____
3. Do you have some idea how they developed?_____
4. Do you feel that your sexual relationship is a problem? Explain:_____
   _____
5. Have you shared any of these concerns about your relationship with your partner? If not, why?_____
   _____
6. What have you done about your problems (any professional help?)?_____
   _____
7. How do you think therapy could be helpful?_____
   _____
8. Do you think your partner would answer these questions differently?_____

FIGURE 10–1   A Form for Assessing Quality of Relationship. From C. Nadelson, "Marital Therapy from a Psychoanalytic Perspective." In T. Paolino and B. McCrady (eds.), *Marriage and Marital Therapy* (New York: Brunner/Mazel, 1978), p. 158. Reprinted by permission.

partners' motivation to achieve their goals is the single most important determinant of success. Implicit in this statement is the notion that the goals of each partner must coincide, or at least not conflict. The therapist must frequently reassess the goals toward which the clients are working: they may shift over the course of treatment and new ones, previously not admitted, may emerge. Most couples come to marriage therapy with at least some goals that they are not willing to share. The most common one is that the partner be "fixed" in some way. (One of my colleagues refers to this as the "this damn thing doesn't work any more" syndrome.) Other hidden goals may include finding a caretaker for one spouse so that the other will be free to leave, or proving that the marriage cannot work and/or that nobody can ever help. The sooner the hidden goals are out on the table, the sooner the couple will be ready to get down to work. Even when the goals are incompatible (she wants to heal the marriage; he wants to leave), it is better to deal with these conflicting motivations openly than to pretend they do not exist.

In assessing a couple's readiness for marriage therapy, it is also important to be alert for the special strengths in the relationship. As therapists, we are often quite good at analyzing weaknesses, at diagnosing pathology, but we can forget to notice the particularly healthy qualities that a couple may present. These healthy qualities are essential. They not only have kept the relationship going thus far, but they are also the raw material for healing the hurts that have developed over the years. "Identification of the behaviors that would enhance the relationship quality can be of great help particularly after the initial presenting problems are altered in the treatment or have lost their sense of immediacy and urgency. Therefore, the identification of desirable behaviors should be made at the outset of the treatment" (Sholevar 1985, p. 290).

Finally, throughout all of your early interactions with a couple, you will need to be thinking about an intervention package, a therapy plan. Couples who seek therapy are likely to be experts (usually at an unconscious level) at enmeshing and confusing a relationship, muddying the waters so that, no matter how hard everyone tries, they both go away hurt and disappointed and angry. The therapist who leaps into this arena armed only with good intentions stands a fair chance of getting snarled in the same kind of relationship. "Counselors who get too involved with a couple and become part of their marriage often do so because they jump immediately into the dynamics and interaction without holding back enough to gain some perspective on the nature of the marital system and then deciding where in fact they are going to intervene in that system in order to change it" (Hiebert & Gillespie 1977, p. 40). Stand back far enough to see the overall pattern of the relationship; carefully assess the nature of each partner's conscious and unconscious contracts; continually reevaluate the couple's motivations for change; and consistently build on the strengths of the relationship.

A most useful mind-set, proposed by Pittman, is to ask yourself, "What, above all, is the change this couple must prevent? What is there in this couple's structure that is so precious that it must, at all costs, be protected?" (1987, p. 19). Keeping in mind that both members of the couple are (probably, but not necessarily, out of awareness) protecting something that feels very valuable to them will help keep you from getting hooked on the same snag that has hung them up. You can steer them in the direction of replacing the threatened "possession," or of finding new and healthier ways of protecting it, rather than blundering in and adding to the sense of danger and threat and the need to protect at all costs that already exists.

THE FIRST STEPS

Beginnings are often awkward with couples as well as with individual clients. The couple does not know what to expect, and each partner may be vacillating between a hope for vindication ("therapy will make my spouse change") and a fear of new demands ("they'll decide it's my fault and I'll have to change"). Anxiety is high, and trust is low. The therapist, especially if she is inexperienced, may be dealing with anxieties of her own: Will I be able to work with these people? How do I teach them to use therapy appropriately? Will I get trapped into their system? Having a clear sense of how to get organized for therapy will help everyone to get past the initial awkwardness and into the treatment process.

It is probably best to begin by settling the administrative details of your working together. Clearly state your expectations about appointment times, fees (who will pay, how much, and when, plus any arrangements for insurance payments), missed sessions, etc. Problems that come up in dealing with these arrangements will be valuable indicators of communication issues between the partners, so this early part of your session has important therapeutic implications as well.

"The first order of business after initial introductions," says Ables, "is to inform both spouses of what one knows about them and how this is known" (1977, p. 37). Since one partner will probably have made the first appointment, it is essential to balance the ledger by sharing with the other spouse just what was said. This brings the second spouse up to date and may allay some suspicions about how much tattling or blaming has already taken place; it also allows the spouse who made the initial contact to clear up any misunderstandings about what was communicated.

Reviewing the original contact, letting both partners know what you think they are asking for, is a natural way to lead into a discussion of the therapy contract. You may want to move directly to history-taking, with an explanation of your usual style of working with such information, or you may choose to invite the couple to talk about what each one hopes to accomplish through therapy.

Part of your responsibility as a therapist is to teach your clients how to work in therapy. While it is impossible (and probably not even desirable) to spell out everything that may happen over the course of treatment, you can and should provide some guidelines for their behavior. Ables suggests the following list of client responsibilities: "to be willing to voice one's complaints and needs, to use one's assertiveness and anger for the protection of self-interests, to be willing to listen to and try to understand the spouse's position, needs, and feelings, as well as one's own, and, ultimately, to negotiate differences" (1977, p. 75). As an astute therapist, you will recognize these not only as guidelines for working in therapy, but also for maintaining a healthy ongoing relationship: they are simultaneously means to an end and the end itself.

THE ART OF COUPLE THERAPY

In the previous pages we have concentrated on the goals of couple therapy and on the activities leading into the heart of the therapy process. Now we turn to the process itself: the actual tasks of the therapist as she works with a couple. We will look first at some general guidelines, and then turn to some techniques specifically relevant to the problem-solving process. We will identify some of the more common problem behaviors that couples need to learn to change. Finally, we will briefly discuss some special situations that frequently arise during the course of couple work.

General Guidelines

One of the first tasks of the couple therapist is that of joining each partner. This joining essentially involves forming a therapeutic alliance; it requires that the client experience the therapist as trustworthy and competent. In individual therapy we talk of establishing rapport, and this is usually accomplished with relative ease. Couple therapy is more complicated because joining with one partner may create distrust in the other. The goal is to join with both, to be seen as caring about each one while taking sides with neither.

The therapist's own attitude is a key factor here: if you do not secretly take sides, favoring one partner over the other, you are more likely to create a balanced relationship with them. That is easier said than done, however; it seems to be a natural social characteristic to make judgments, to choose a favorite, to assess rightness and wrongness whenever we notice disagreement between two people. Williamson makes an observation that I have found helpful in maintaining my perspective. He talks of both partners' desire to find some relief from the pain, "since two parties to the same marriage cannot in honesty be experiencing it very differently" (1977, p. 51). No matter how different the stories, no matter how entrenched the roles or the defenses, it is a safe assumption that, at some level, both partners want (and fear) change.

Joining can be accomplished in a variety of ways. Most obvious are the verbal ones: listening carefully to each partner's story, making sure that each has a chance to speak, choosing your comments and questions so that each will know you have understood what they are saying. More powerful, though, are the nonverbal behaviors: your facial expression as you listen to each, your movements and gestures, the amount of air time you give to one or the other. One of the greatest dangers is that of accepting the couple's initial definition of one spouse as the problem or the sick person in the relationship. Sluzki suggests that "if A is consistently defined as the 'victimizer' (or the 'identified patient') by B, then (a) reduce physical distance with A, and/or (b) mirror A's body position" (1978, p. 376). This will create a nonverbal bonding with A, while allowing you to avoid a premature verbal challenge of the roles the couple is presenting.

In order to join with both partners, we must avoid joining with one at the expense of the other. One way to avoid this kind of imbalance is by encouraging the partners not to talk to you at all, but rather to talk with each other.

Getting the partners to talk to each other is an important therapeutic goal for its own sake, too. Talking to each other is the appropriate mode for problem-solving; talking to the therapist is more likely to involve destructive behaviors like blaming or criticizing the spouse. As partners talk to each other, the therapist can observe the communication patterns in vivo. Rather than describing what did happen, they show the therapist what is happening. Thus they present both diagnostic information and material for immediate working-through.

Often, asked to talk to each other about it, spouses will object: we have talked about it so often already, there is nothing more to say. An appropriate answer is to agree that they have, indeed, talked about things a lot, but that this will be different because there is a third person with them now; the therapist will be there to help them learn more about the nature of their talking together and to help them develop some new skills in dealing with each other.

Typically, spouses will respond to this sort of intervention by beginning to talk to each other, but will turn back to the therapist after only one or two transactions. They can be redirected to the task by an encouraging "Tell her/him about it" or "Good, now tell your partner the same thing." Occasionally it will be very important to one partner that the therapist know or understand some part of the overall situation, and telling the partner (so that the therapist can hear indirectly) will feel frustrating and uncomfortable. It is often useful to listen to the story and then respond by inviting the storyteller to tell the spouse how they felt when that happened.

> Talking with the therapist should be discouraged primarily when it is used to avoid talking with the partner. If a spouse needs to tell the therapist of some pain or hurt, this is appropriate and deserves attention; usually one can then redirect the comment to the spouse by saying, 'Were you aware that your mate felt so badly about that?' (Ables 1977, p. 58)

Nonverbally, continuing to look at A while A talks about B rather than looking back and forth between the two helps to prevent the formation of a two-against-one coalition. Finally, if all else fails and one partner insists on talking to you rather than to his spouse, you may choose to direct a comment about him to the (often silently colluding) partner: "John seems very upset about this," or "I notice that Sally finds it more comfortable to tell me what she feels than to tell you about it."

"It is the therapist's task to slow down the interchange and to help the couple focus on a particular issue. With experienced therapists, often half or even all of a session may center on one or two major issues" (Ables 1977, p. 138). Couples often find it very hard to stay on track with an issue. They side-step, change the subject, switch to a safer topic when they feel threatened. The therapist brings them back to the issue at hand: "Stan, I didn't hear you answer Laura's question." "Betty, Carl just told you how he feels when he gets called in as referee between you and the kids. Will you let him know you heard what he said?"

Some couples need even more than this kind of gentle guidance. They literally do not know how to listen to each other, nor do they know how to let the other person know when they have been listening. In such situations, a technique known as "therapist processing" is useful: the therapist listens for the partner and interprets to the partner what the spouse has said. This way the speaker hears the message reworded (thus getting proof that someone has heard), perhaps picking up pointers on how to express ideas and feelings more clearly and getting an opportunity to correct any errors the therapist may have made in her paraphrase. In the meantime, the listening spouse hears the message twice and can respond to either the original or the therapist's rephrasing of it.

Another generally useful technique with couples is the assigning of homework. Couples may work issues through in the therapy session only to go home and fall back into the same old nonfunctional patterns. Giving them a specific assignment helps them to solidify the gains made during the session and to translate those gains to the home environment.

It is usually a good idea to insist that the homework assignment be written down by both partners before they leave the session. "No matter how intense the involvement and how difficult the battle, agreements finally developed in the triadic sessions have a mysterious way of fading once the couple have left the therapist's office" (Ables 1977, p. 74). Even if you choose not to assign specific homework, you may want to ask the couple to write down toward the end of the hour the main things they got out of that session. Differences and similarities between their perceptions, or between theirs and yours, will give useful information for them to discuss and for you to consider in your ongoing treatment planning.

PROBLEM SOLVING

Couple therapy, whatever else it may involve, is a problem-solving process. Problems are what bring the couple to treatment in the first place: something is not going well, and the couple has not been able to find a solution on their own. Although the therapist cannot, and should not, solve the problems for the couple, it is imperative that she believe solutions are possible. She helps them to identify what they have tried to do to solve the problems, thus shifting the focus from blame and criticism, and consistently operates from the premise that there are always new and unexplored options.

Primary and Secondary Goals

A basic problem-solving principle is that the solution must involve doing something rather than not doing something. Nobody can stop a behavior without putting some other behavior in its place; conversely, when you start the replacement behavior, the old behavior has to stop. Getting rid of an undesirable behavior, then, becomes a secondary goal while starting a desirable behavior is the primary goal. Many (perhaps most) couples come to therapy with a good idea of the secondary goals: "I want him/her to stop nagging, spending too much money, going out with other men/women, ignoring my needs, etc." The first step in problem solving is identifying what the complaining spouse would like the partner to do instead.

Once the couple understands and accepts the idea of primary (doing) and secondary (not doing) goals and has articulated some of their wants in primary goal terms, they are in a position to begin negotiating. In order for my behavior to change,

I must get something out of changing. Either the new behavior is pleasurable in itself, or something else is happening that makes the change worthwhile. Negotiating at the "what's in it for me" level is at the heart of couple problem solving. It requires that each partner be clear about his or her wants, needs, and likes. Obviously, this kind of honesty can be quite threatening, and many sessions may be spent working toward the point at which honest negotiating can take place.

Finding Antecedents

"Early in treatment, a significant issue is the inability of each partner to predict the inevitable result of certain behaviors or interactions despite their repetitive nature" (Nadelson 1978, p. 141). Learning to predict what will happen as a result of doing X or Y is an important treatment goal. When I understand that my doing X typically results in something that I experience as unpleasant, I will be able to decide whether X-ing is really worth the unpleasantness.

A common reason why partners do not understand these cause-and-effect patterns is that they do not recognize the beginning moves as part of the sequence. Marvin and Martha relate a blowup: after dinner, Marvin sat down to read the paper, only vaguely aware that Martha was banging dishes and cupboard doors in the kitchen. A few minutes later she stood in the door, crying, and accused him of being inconsiderate and lazy. He responded angrily; the drama ended with Martha sobbing in the bedroom and Marvin slamming out of the house to spend the evening with the boys.

For both Marvin and Martha, this sequence began at the end of the evening meal; and each found the other's behavior unreasonable and inexplicable. In order for them (and the therapist) to understand what happened, the antecedents must be identified. There are always antecedents. Nothing can occur that has not been preceded by something else. If neither the therapist nor the couple is able to specify an antecedent, its existence can nevertheless be asserted. Moreover, the antecedent itself has antecedents; the roots of a pattern can be traced back. When this kind of search has been done a few times, a pattern will begin to emerge. Marvin may have been late for dinner, or Martha may have been thinking resentfully about the evening out he had scheduled that night; or Martha may have been fighting the budget and feeling some anxieties that she did not share openly. The possibilities are endless. The content is usually not particularly important in determining the pattern. What usually emerges is a sequence of feelings and responses to feelings. When these feeling patterns are recognized and the couple is willing to deal with them as such, the actual content issues become much less important and the problem begins to be solvable.

Vulnerability

Dealing with feelings honestly means being vulnerable. I can maintain my behavior and attack the behavior of my spouse for weeks; I can even weep or scream at him or at the therapist and still stay safe behind my defenses. However, once I start letting people in on how I really feel, what really makes me sad or glad or mad or scared, my defenses are shattered. Before I do that, I need to be quite sure that both therapist and spouse will respect my feelings and not use my weaknesses against me. It is the therapist's job to protect partners against attack or blackmail, providing a forum for discussing such behaviors if they occur (or if someone fears they may occur), and occasionally helping a partner to develop new and more constructive defenses if the spouse continues the attack. Balancing the vulnerability by encouraging both partners to share feelings will help each to feel supported by and supportive of each other. With this kind of support, new options will begin to appear.

The New Solution

Problem solutions, like new clothes, need to be tried on to find out whether they fit. Not infrequently, a bargain or agreement or compromise will turn out to fit well for one partner, but to be less than satisfying for the other. Ables points out that both spouses must be asked how the new agreement is working, but special attention should be paid to the spouse who has made the major behavior change:

> The spouse who modified his or her behavior should have all this fully acknowledged and receive positive reinforcement. However, to determine how satisfactory the solution is, it is extremely important to ask this spouse about the change. What was the degree of struggle? What was the personal cost? A solution that works well for one spouse but not the other, even though he or she complies, is no real solution." (1977, p. 113)

As the couple learns to listen to each other, to attend to and respect feelings, they will discover a whole new arena for communicating and problem solving. This is a very exciting time, and there is often a kind of euphoria, a sense of "everything is wonderful and we'll never have troubles again." The belief that it is all solved forever is a comforting one; couples may deny the existence of other, related problem areas in their desire to maintain the belief that their relationship is now perfect and problem-free. Again, they must be cautioned to expect setbacks. New areas of conflict can and will appear; the real value in the therapy process lies not so much in solving the present problem as providing the couple with tools to use in future problem situations.

COMMON PATTERNS

The guidelines we have been discussing thus far are useful in most if not all couple therapy situations. We now turn to some more specific areas of concern in working with spouses.

Blaming and Complaining

As has been mentioned, many couples come to therapy with a great need to blame and complain about each other. It may be useful to allow a certain amount of tattling to go on: just as a child may need to tell his side of a story and know he's been listened to before settling down to find a new way of dealing with a situation, so spouses may need to know that the therapist understands how things seem from their point of view. The therapist must learn how to listen for and empathize with the feelings underlying the complaint, without taking sides or deciding that one person's viewpoint is either right or wrong.

Complaining can be used as a springboard to problem solving, if the therapist consistently redirects attention to the specifics of what is happening and what is the net result. "The important issue to focus on is not how bad a spouse is, or how much a given spouse's objectionable behavior has occurred, but what behaviors occurred and how do they affect the partner—what specifically does the spouse have trouble accepting and what is the cost?" (Ables 1977, p. 91). Repeatedly asking the complaining spouse to identify exactly what the partner does that is bothersome, and exactly what alternative behavior would be preferable, shifts the process from helpless whining or angry blaming to a search for new ways to get needs met.

Terminal Language

Stuart (1980) uses the expression "terminal language" to describe adjectives or nouns that place a partner into a category, as opposed to "instrumental language" which describes modifiable events. Terminal language defeats the purpose of therapy in that it suggests that the partner *is* some way and thus cannot change. The husband whose wife is a neurotic, for example, has little choice but to learn to live with the neurotic or to leave the relationship.

Spouses who use terminal language need to learn to describe the behavior that the partner engages in, and then begin to identify ways in which their own actions contribute to that behavior. Once such patterns are recognized, each can then look for ways in which changing his or her own behavior will help the other to change. Again, the focus shifts from assessing who is bad or sick or at fault to finding new patterns that will be more satisfying for both partners.

Red Flags

Over months and years of living together, fighting the same battles over and over on a series of changing battlefields, couples develop tender spots. They know each others' weaknesses, know just what word or gesture will pierce the armor and get to the partner. Often this knowledge is out of awareness, so that the hurtful words will seem to just pop out in the heat of the moment. The therapist needs to bring this behavior into awareness, to red flag it, so that the spouses can agree to avoid low blows which only serve to escalate their conflict.

While some red-flag behaviors are idiosyncratic to a particular couple, others are common to many marriages. One such category is the negative noun or adjective which we have already characterized as terminal language. Another is the sentence that begins with "You always" or "You never." Besides being inaccurate, always and never statements also have a quality of unchangeability, of hopelessness. They invite furious arguments about the truth or falsehood of the "always," replete with examples and counter-examples which totally avoid the task of detailing the specific behavior, the specific feeling response, and the possible alternatives at each point in the sequence.

Double Binding

The phenomenon of double-binding was originally described in the context of parent-child interactions, but it also appears in chronically unhealthy marriages. The three characteristics of the double-binding situation are: (1) a message is delivered which will call forth a "wrong response," no matter what the response may be; (2) the receiver is not allowed to question the meaning of the message or comment on its double-binding quality; and (3) the receiver is not allowed to leave the interaction. A typical double bind is the "go away closer" transaction, in which one (usually verbal) component of the message is a request for closeness while another (often nonverbal) component is a demand for distance. Nora may tell Nathan, for example, that he never wants to cuddle with her anymore; when he responds by putting his arm around her, she pulls away and complains that he has bad breath. If he tries to point out what has happened, her response is, "That's right, blame it on me again!" and if he moves away she can use this as additional evidence that he does not want to be close.

Double-binders beget double-binders; often the only defense against double-binding is to double-bind in return. Nathan, after a few exchanges like the one described above, may begin (perhaps without full awareness) to approach Nora only when he has not brushed his teeth or when he has just worked up a good sweat. This can create an interlocking double-bind pattern, which is virtually impossible for the participants to sort out without help from a noninvolved observer.

Dealing with double-binding requires that the therapist insist on unraveling the pattern without getting tangled in details. The technique of looking for what happened before is useful, in that it may uncover a preceding double-binding transaction that is interlocked with the one already identified. "What did you feel?" and "What did you want?" are key questions for both partners; the feelings can be accepted and the wants understood quite apart from the unanswerable question of who actually started the whole thing.

Mind Reading

Many of the marriage patterns described in the early section of this chapter invite a kind of fusion, an inability of the partners to think of themselves as individuals apart from their spouse. Such fusion, in turn, invites a whole host of troublesome consequences: inability to tolerate differences, fear of abandonment, a feeling of being smothered (to name but a few). For such couples, a major therapeutic goal is that they experience their separateness. "We" statements are among the best indicators of the fused relationship. The partner who frequently talks about what we wanted or how we felt is signaling his inability to think of himself as separate from his spouse. He is also demonstrating his belief in mind-reading, as if he, through the closeness of the relationship, actually does know what his partner thinks and feels.

Changing the "we" language is the first step in dispelling the mind-reading myth and separating the fused couple. "To establish separateness," says Ables, "we make an active effort for each spouse to speak for the self only and not to make assumptions about what the other thinks or feels. We stress that none of us are mind readers and encourage spouses to ask directly how the partner feels or thinks" (1977, p. 176). Simply pointing out the process and the false assumption underlying it, and reminding the partners to change their language whenever inappropriate "we" statements occur, can go a surprisingly long way toward moving couples into nonfused ways of thinking and behaving.

Responsibility

A final relationship phenomenon to be commented on here is that of over-responsibility. Spouses who are over-responsible tend to see their mate as faultless and to blame themselves for all the bad feelings in the relationship. They know that they should do better and that they "make" their partners unhappy (note the mind-reading here). The partner may helplessly protest that this is not so or may be quick to acquiesce in this uneven assignment of blame. Whichever way the pattern goes, the therapist's job is to help each person take the responsibility for his or her own feelings and behaviors, while giving up responsibility for the partner's feelings and behaviors. Nearly all the tools and techniques we have described in this chapter may be needed to accomplish this task; surprisingly, partners are often even more reluctant to give up blaming themselves than they are to stop blaming their spouse.

SOME SPECIAL SITUATIONS

Sexual Dysfunction

The treatment of sexual dysfunction has become an area of therapeutic specialty, requiring specific training in techniques not used in other kinds of therapy. It is my position that sexual dysfunction therapy should not be attempted by therapists who have not received this advanced training.

In working with couples, however, it is important to know whether their sex life (or lack of it) is an important part of the problem. This requires some amount of sexual history-taking, and the couple therapist must be able to gather sexual information accurately and with a minimum of embarrassment for the couple. Dealing matter-of-factly with sexual matters can, in and of itself, be therapeutic. "Beginning counselors will find that simple, uncomplicated procedures, such as giving permission to enjoy erotic pleasure and reviving sensual satisfactions of the courtship days, are often effective, as is reassuring couples that fantasies, whatever their nature, are normal and indeed useful in obtaining sexual pleasure" (Freeman 1982, p. 50).

It is particularly important that the therapist be sensitive to her own comfort level when discussing sexual issues. Feelings of constraint or embarrassment will quickly convey themselves to the clients and may heighten their sense of shame, anger, or guilt. Freeman continues, "It should be recognized that beginning counselors or practitioners should use only those techniques with which they are comfortable, and about which they have conviction. It is quite in order for the counselor to limit himself or herself in this way."

If careful questioning reveals that the problem is primarily one of sexual dysfunction, the couple may be referred to a physician or to a qualified sex therapist. If, as is more likely, sexual dysfunction is only a part of the overall relationship problem, you may make some initial suggestions and observe the couple's response; if these first interventions are not helpful, it is probably wise to recommend concurrent treatment by a sex therapist. Although some therapists have been concerned about possible interference between two kinds of couple therapy going on simultaneously, there seems to be no evidence in opposition of such an arrangement; other experts firmly support the practice (Stuart 1980, p. 304).

The Extramarital Affair

Either spouse's involvement in an extramarital affair during the couple therapy process vastly reduces the likelihood that therapy will improve the relationship. The partner involved in an affair has already established an escape hatch, another person to be with in case the marriage does not work out, and thus need not have the same level of commitment to the marriage as does the other spouse. The marriage may have already assumed second-best status, and therapy may be a kind of ritual that must be performed in order to separate without guilt.

Should you know that an extramarital relationship exists at the time the couple requests therapy, or discover it during the course of therapy, you have a number of options. One possibility is to refuse to see the couple as a couple unless the outside relationship is ended. Therapists who take this stand maintain that couple therapy cannot succeed unless both partners are committed to the relationship, and that an extramarital affair is clear evidence that, for at least one partner, such a commitment does not exist.

Another approach is to share your concern and your reasons with the couple, to state your preferences, and then to let the couple decide what they want to do. This is the position taken by Ables: "We discourage extramarital affairs for couples who want to improve their relationship, not on a moralistic basis, but because it decreases the likelihood of resolving existing problems. We try to help spouses determine what the price of an extramarital relationship will be, without telling them what they should do with regard to continuing the affair" (1977, p. 226).

If a partner is unwilling to discontinue his or her affair, you may offer to see one or both spouses individually. Most often, the spouse who has no outside involvement will be the one who will agree to this arrangement; and he or she is quite likely to end up working out a way to end the marriage and say goodbye to the other spouse. It is appropriate for the therapist to warn such a client that this may happen before entering into individual therapy, and to determine whether the client sees such an outcome as acceptable or even bearable.

Divorce Therapy

I mentioned that the spouse who is involved in another relationship may be using marriage therapy as a way to move out of the marriage relationship. It is also possible that one or both spouses, even though not extramaritally involved, may be overtly or covertly wanting to end the marriage. People may have many reasons for seeking couple therapy when they have already decided to separate: they may want to find someone to take care of the partner after they leave, to prove that they did everything possible to save the marriage, or to deal with their own feelings of grief and loss over the separation.

The couple considering divorce or separation will need help in moving through their decision-making stages. According to Turner and Strine, there are five major steps in the process of making any major decision, and these are quite relevant to the decision of a couple to separate:

1. Appraising the challenge (what are the risks if I don't change?).
2. Surveying alternatives (have I surveyed all possible alternatives?).
3. Weighing alternatives (which alternative will best meet my goals?).
4. Deliberating about commitment (will I act on the best alternative?).
5. Adhering to decisions despite negative feedback. (1985, p. 487; adapted from Janis & Mann)

The decision to separate affects not only the couple themselves, but other family members as well. Separation therapy often expands into family therapy, as the children (in or out of the home) are helped to deal with the implications of their parents' new relationship. Even when children are not physically included in the therapy, the separating couple will usually need help in working through both practical and emotional issues having to do with the family as a whole—everything from finances to holiday visits.

Deciding to end a marriage does not necessarily mean that couple therapy has failed. Sometimes a separation or a divorce is the best possible outcome for both partners; some relationships are simply too painful or too pathological to be worth maintaining. The couple who decides to separate can use help in dealing with the pain of parting and the sense of defeat that often accompanies such a decision.

In divorce therapy, the emphasis is on change and risk and loss: "how one feels about loss; how one replaces the loss; an awareness of the need to mourn the loss; realization that the loss must become finished business" (Cassius & Koonce

1974, p. 16). Ideally, the end product of divorce therapy is two individuals who are able to respect each other, to appreciate what was positive in their marriage, and to move out into the remainder of their lives as whole and unentangled individuals.

CONCLUSIONS

Whether the therapy process ultimately ends in strengthening or dissolving the couple relationship, one thing is certain: the therapist's role and behavior must change over the course of treatment. At first, she will be an active intervener in the partners' interactions. She will instruct, interpret, and interrupt; she will determine the pace of the therapy process and will often prescribe activities to be carried out between sessions. Having deliberately placed herself in the center of the relationship in order to bring about changes, she must then find a way to extricate herself, for her job will end only when she is no longer needed. From directing the first efforts of the couple, she will shift to coaching them, and from coaching she will move to simply giving feedback about what they are doing (Stuart 1980, p. 159). Finally, she must separate from them entirely.

The separation need not be an abrupt one, however. It is often useful to invite couples to return for a reporting session several months after they have terminated therapy. This allows them to review the changes they have made, to get a booster shot of therapy to strengthen their new behaviors, and to receive well-earned recognition from the therapist (who knows better than anyone else what they have overcome) for their accomplishments. Couples may also be reassured that they can return for further help at a later date should the need arise: like so many kinds of contingency planning, just knowing that they can go back often helps the partners to avoid having to do so.

Couple therapy can be exciting and fun. There is always something going on; the difficulty is in deciding what to focus on and what to let go by. The couple therapist really has three clients: the two spouses and the relationship itself. In dealing with one of these three, she must necessarily miss something that is occurring in the other two. As with all other kinds of therapy, mistakes are inevitable. Yet there is a resiliency about couples, an ability to bounce back from errors of omission or commission, that is reassuring. On the other hand, couples can seize upon a therapeutic error and use it to confuse and confound the process to an incredible degree. Perhaps in no other kind of therapy (with the possible exception of family therapy, which also involves couples) is a small intervention likely to have such far-reaching and ongoing consequences. It is a roller coaster ride and, like other roller coasters, it is not to everyone's taste. But if you do like it and choose to continue with it, you can count on having an interesting career. You may be excited, disappointed, triumphant, or apprehensive, but you definitely will not be bored!

11 FAMILY THERAPY

Families, and the ways in which we work with them, are changing. First, the families themselves are changing. The 1970s and 1980s have seen the emergence and growth of a bewildering variety of family structures. While the Mom-and-Dad-and-two-kids family has not disappeared, it certainly is no longer the rule. Single-parent families, blended families, his-hers-ours families are far more common; even multi-parent families, communal families, and gay and lesbian families are seen with some frequency.

    Second, the kinds of problems that families bring to counseling have changed. A few decades ago families seen in counseling almost invariably fell into one (or both) of two categories: (1) the family with a severely disturbed or damaged child: these children were schizophrenic, autistic, developmentally disabled—they were clearly and obviously sick; (2) the family in which one or both parents were neglectful, abusive, and/or incompetent: these families were chaotic, disorganized, usually multi-problem families, and the children were the victims of the parents' inadequacies. These kinds of families can still be found in therapists' offices, of course. But a growing acceptance of psychotherapy as a means of achieving health and harmony in the family, as well as a whole new set of family stressors brought on by cultural changes, have brought a variety of other patterns to our attention.

Chief among these patterns—and deserving of special attention—is the abused parent family. As our youth-oriented culture has flourished, many parents have become increasingly confused about the limits of their authority: their right to make and maintain family rules and to discipline their children. In such families "obedience" is a questionable virtue, if not a downright character flaw. Parental rule is replaced by a kind of quasi-democracy, and parents, by trying too hard, allow themselves to be verbally and sometimes physically abused.

As families have changed our ways of understanding and intervening in them have changed as well. We are unlikely to think in terms of a single "sick" family member, of "good" or "bad" parents and their effects on the children. The work of such seminal thinkers as Minuchin, Bateson, Watzlawick, Weakland, and Jackson have led us to look at the family as a dynamic system in which each person responds to and is responded to by every other person. "We cannot simply decipher which event causes a second; rather, experiences in the family continuously and simultaneously reinforce each other" (Massey 1983, p. 34).

In tightly interacting systems like this, patterns become well-established and are maintained by interlocking layers of perceptions, expectations, and habit. Communications are redundant, so that cutting through one maladaptive message path may have little or no effect since there are so many others leading toward the same outcome. Each member feels powerless to change, because whatever he does must (in order for him to feel safe) be matched or validated by changes in someone else—and he's quite sure, based on past experience, that those someones aren't going to change.

Trying to understand a family system in terms of a linear, causal model leads only to frustration. The family therapist must learn to think circularly, in terms of ongoing, interactive loops. She is alert to the ripple effect: the reverberations that a change in one family member will set up in all the others. She is sensitive to the feeling of stuckness, of helpless impotence, that members of an entrenched and malfunctioning system experience, and she attempts to enter that system in such a way that its self-reinforcing patterns will be disrupted and it will be forced to find a new and healthier equilibrium.

Watzlawick uses a vivid metaphor to describe what has to happen if an unhealthy family is to change. He asks us to imagine

> two sailors hanging out of either side of a sailboat in order to steady it; the more one leans overboard, the more the other has to hang out to compensate for the instability created by the other's attempts at stabilizing the boat, while the boat itself would be quite steady if not for their acrobatic efforts at steadying it. It is not difficult to see that in order to change this absurd situation at least one of them has to do something seemingly quite unreasonable, namely to "steady" less and not more, since this will immediately force the other to also do less of the same (unless he wants to finish up in the water), and they may eventually find themselves comfortably back inside a steady boat. (1978, p. 36)

As soon as either of the sailors stops doing what he has been doing, and starts doing almost anything else, the situation will change. Yet to do anything different feels terribly risky, if not downright destructive. When a family is in this kind of a fix (and most of the families seen by therapists are), the therapist's job is to help someone—anyone—to make a change, thus enabling the others to change too.

GETTING STARTED

Family therapy, like any other sort of therapy, moves through beginning, middle, and ending phases. The beginning phase is a getting-to-know-each-other process in which therapist and family check each other out, decide if they can (or want to) work together, and come to some initial agreement on what problems are to be solved. So far, no different from individual therapy. The big difference, of course, has to do with the fact that in family therapy the client is several people. A major task for the first few sessions is what is known as "joining." Therapy proceeds most efficiently when each person in the family feels "joined" by the therapist: listened to, cared about, and taken seriously. Failure to join one or more family members almost always leads to the therapist being seen as taking sides "for" this person and "against" that one. Taking sides, in turn, almost guarantees that the therapy will be at best inefficient and at worst quite ineffective.

How do you "join" a family? The definition says it all: you listen to, care about, and take seriously each family member. You want to hear each person's beliefs about why they are here, with you; you want to know where it hurts for each of them and what they have done or are doing about it. You most definitely are *not* interested in playing judge or jury, elevating one member at the expense of another, or even—at this early stage—finding a solution to their problem. You want to know what is happening, but even more important is *who* is happening, how, and from each person's point of view. If you are genuinely invested in learning about these things and give yourself permission to find out, then the joining will more or less take care of itself.

Finding out about a family is both easier and harder than finding out about a single person client. Harder, obviously, because there are more people to know about and more data to collect. Easier because the family will act it all out before your very eyes if you allow them to do so. Notice what people say with their nonverbal behavior as well as with their words. Who sits next to whom? Who talks for whom? Who obeys? Who looks away? Who is attentive? There will be much more going on than you can possibly hope to take in, so just sample that which catches your attention—and ask about it! Part of your job is to bring into the open what has been hinted at and skirted around; this can best be done by calling attention to the nonverbal messages and requesting a translation.

Sometimes family members will be able to provide the translation—the "meaning" of the behavior—and sometimes they won't. All families operate according to three sets of rules: (1) the ones everybody knows about and can state to the therapist; (2) the ones they seem to be unaware of but will agree about once someone else points them out; and (3) the ones they don't or won't recognize, but that still shape their behavior. Asking person A what person B meant when she/he did X ("I notice that Suzie slumped down in her chair while you were talking, Dad. What do you think she is trying to tell us?") is a way for you to find out about all three kinds of rules.

Most family therapists advocate a particular kind of questioning process, known as "circular questioning," at some time during the joining phase. In circular questioning, every member of the family is asked about something that happens between two other family members. "As long as the therapist invites one member to comment upon the relationship of two other members, he appears at that time to be allied to that person. However, this alliance shifts the moment he asks another family member and yet another to do the same. The end result of the successive alliances is that the therapist is allied with everyone and no one at the same time" (Selvini-Palazzoli et al. 1978, p. 11). When you are allied with everyone and no one, you have in fact joined with the family.

Not only does circular questioning help you to join with the family, but it also begins to break down one of the most common rules that govern dysfunctional families: the rule of nonsecret secrets. Nearly all distressed families have "secrets" that everyone knows but that nobody is allowed to acknowledge. Sometimes several people know the secret but believe that nobody else knows it; sometimes family members know but think that they're not supposed to know and that nobody else knows that they know. Such nonsecret secrets gum up communication, interfere with trust, and create feelings of confusion and resentment and guilt. Getting the secrets out into the open is one of the first steps in bringing families back to health.

Another task for the early sessions of family therapy, also quite compatible with the joining process, is that of giving information. Family members have lots of questions. How bad is my family? Can things get better? Is it really my fault? What will you, the therapist, do with us? Some of these will be answered explicitly and some implicitly. One point that needs to be made clearly and explicitly has to do with protection: it is not acceptable for any member of the family to hurt himself or anyone else. Abuse of any sort—physical or sexual or psychological—will not be tolerated. If it has been occurring, it is now over with; it will not start again under any circumstances. You, the therapist, will take whatever steps are necessary to ensure the safety of every family member.

Questions about how bad off the family is and whether it can be helped to change usually are best answered implicitly (which is how they most often are asked). The family is hurting, or it wouldn't be here. You think they can be helped, or *you* wouldn't be here. Trying to reassure them that things can change is likely to have the opposite effect, making them wonder if you are perhaps just trying to reassure yourself.

On the other hand, it may be quite helpful to predict some of the less comfortable things that may occur during treatment. I often talk about the way that family members learn to protect themselves and each other; how those learned protections get to be so habitual that they seem like the only way to act; and how later, as people grow and change, the learned protections can get in the way of folks getting what they want. I say that part of our job in therapy will be to get those old habits out and look at them again, and that this may be uncomfortable, embarrassing, or even painful at times. I expect that I will make mistakes, and that one or more people in the family may get angry at or disappointed with me, and that is what I tell them. Predicting the negative makes it acceptable, part of the treatment plan; it gives me more leverage and flexibility as a therapist. It also gives the family permission to act naturally—to get mad or be upset with or scared of me. Finally, it models "telling it like it is," which is precisely what most families need to learn to do.

TREATMENT PLANNING

In order to get somewhere with a family, you need to have some idea either of where you want to be or where you want not to be. Sometimes the dysfunction will be clear and the remediation obvious: the children have been given too much power and the parents need to reclaim their authority. Or, the father has abdicated his responsibility as an adult and joined the children, so that the mother is functioning as a single parent; Dad needs to be Dad again. Or, a tyrannical grandparent is running the family while the parents feel enraged and act helpless; the parents need to take control of their own household.

Beware, though, of placing too much confidence in your own hypotheses. After all, that's all that they are: hypotheses. It's not at all unusual for a family to surprise and startle a therapist by finding a solution of their own that works for them and looks quite different from what the therapist thought was needed. It's probably a lot more sensible to base your change hypothesis on an analysis of what needs to be different than to aim at some particular end product. In other words you can help a family get somewhere other than where they are without specifying where you think that somewhere is. Choosing which new way is the family's job.

Knowing "where they are," though, also requires a hypothesis about the process a family system uses to maintain a set of behaviors that cause them pain. As you begin to understand how the system keeps itself balanced (in a painful way), you can begin to upset that balance. Creating disequilibrium in a family system invites—indeed, often demands—change in the system. Without a hypothesis you are likely to mire the family even more deeply in their dysfunctional patterns and increase their distress and confusion rather than alleviate it.

In general, family system hypotheses have to do with the structure of the family, the communication process of the family, or both. Structural hypotheses focus on such things as family hierarchies, alliances, and boundaries. Communication process hypotheses focus on the way in which information flows among members. Communication process therapists are most particularly interested in the meanings of behavior and understand behavior (particularly symptomatic behavior) as a way of communicating nonverbally.

In developing hypotheses about change, it is important to remember that no family operates in a vacuum. Extended family members, friends, neighbors, and outside authorities may exert important influences on family process. "Ask about the power that other professionals and social agents may have in relation to the family," warns Madanes (1984). "The therapist needs to plan how to influence these sources of power so that they will collaborate instead of interfering with his endeavors" (p. 119).

Finally, remember that hypothesizing about change works best when it is done step-wise. It is not necessary and often not even desirable to try to predict *all* of the changes a family can benefit from; you don't need to plan for everything all at once. Making one single change and making it solidly will prepare the way for the next one and frequently will make planning for the next one relatively easy. Here's another aspect of the "you don't need to know exactly where you're going" rule: sometimes neither you nor the family can know where they need to go until all have experienced some in-between places.

THEORETICAL APPROACHES

Historically, we can identify three major theoretical approaches to doing therapy with families. Each approach has its own typical strategies and is based on a particular set of assumptions. Practically speaking, in the therapeutic climate of the 1980s and 1990s, these three approaches often seem to blend together, and most therapists borrow from them all. In terms of your understanding of where the different strategies and conceptualizations come from, though, it's helpful to put them in their individual contexts.

Early family therapies were more or less straightforward educational experiences. One family member (usually a child) was creating a problem for himself and other family members and the family came to treatment in order to learn how to make the problem member change. Family therapy often involved teaching more appropriate parenting skills, helping family members utilize all their potential resources, and improving communication. While it was recognized that the most obvious problem in a family was not necessarily the most troublesome one in the long run and that the family was an entity in itself—rather than just a collection of individuals—therapists tended to approach problems fairly directly and to take at face value the consensus of family reporting about the problems. Gradually, therapists began to suspect that more was going on in these dysfunctional families than met the eye and to look beside, or under, or away from the identified problem. Bowen, for instance, brought in extended family members—especially grandparents—in order to deal with the unquestioned rule structure that is handed down from generation to generation.

The first major break from a generally logical approach came with the advent of structural family therapy as developed by Minuchin. Minuchin became very interested in the ways in which families divide themselves into subgroups, how membership and nonmembership in those subgroups is determined, how the subgroups communicate with each other—in short, how the family is structured and how that structure affects the family's ability to function healthily. Out of this interest came a system of family therapy that manipulated and shifted the substructures and the membership within the substructures in order to re-balance an out-of-balance family. Commonly occurring maladaptive substructures were identified (the family in which one member of the parent substructure has joined the sibling substructure, for instance), and techniques were created to help families reorganize themselves.

Systems theory and the study of paradox gave rise to the third major approach to family therapy: the systemic approach. In this approach the family is viewed as a semi-permeable system with all of the mathematical characteristics of a system. Therapists such as Haley, Watzlawick, and the Italian group spearheaded by Selvini-Palazzoli use concepts like feedback loop, runaway, homeostasis, and second-order change to describe how the family system functions so as to maintain its members' maladaptive behaviors or to grow and change. Double-binding is seen as a major cause of pain and confusion, and the therapeutic paradox is a major tool in breaking through the impasses of a self-reinforcing, homeostatic system.

Modern family therapists tend to be quite eclectic, recognizing that each of the major approaches to families captures a part of the truth and that each offers useful guidelines. In general, the therapist will begin with a fairly direct approach, taking the problem at face value and helping the family to come up with a solution. The child who acts younger than his age will be encouraged to grow up; his parents will be helped to provide the kind of environment in which growing up is best accomplished. The parent who acts more like one of the siblings will be invited to function in a more role-appropriate way. Parents who are confused about whether it is right to insist that their children behave well (and who thus have misbehaving children) will be encouraged to set and enforce clear limits and, if necessary, taught how to do so.

If the family does not respond to a straightforward approach, it is assumed that more is going on than meets the eye: the underlying system is out of kilter and has acquired homeostatic properties. In other words the family now is reinforcing itself so that the problems are self-sustaining. In families that have acquired this kind of stable dysfunction, efforts to change tend to further intensify and entrench the problem. In fact, by the time the family reaches the therapist's office, the major ongoing problems often are caused by the ways in which the family is trying to solve their original problem. The therapist will go about unbalancing and/or rebalancing the system by means of shifting subsystems, opening or closing communication channels, redefining behaviors, or doing whatever else is needed to allow the family to change its perspective, its way of experiencing itself. "The family will have to be maneuvered into stepping out of the old pattern, and the skillful therapist manages this by couching his intervention in terms designed to coincide with this particular family's assumptions and expectations" (deShazer, 1974). Using language that coincides with the family's assumptions, but doing so in such a way as to change those assumptions, is the essence of the family therapist's art.

TOOLS AND TECHNIQUES

Family therapy has a history even shorter than individual therapy, and that history is quite fragmented. It has not developed in an organized way, one step leading to another, but rather out of bits and pieces contributed by many theorists and practitioners working relatively independently. One result of this helter-skelter growth is that the literature is full of techniques, "chunks" that can be used to accomplish this or that effect, but the techniques do not fall into a neat pattern. The tool box has many tools, but they are in a disorderly heap. To order and organize the heap would be a theoretical task of no small magnitude, one which is well beyond the scope of this chapter. Yet the tools and techniques are valuable and, taken together, help us to get a sense of what actually goes on in working with families. Let's take a few pages to examine some of these tools, these ways of conceptualizing and moving in and upsetting the pain-producing balance of a dysfunctional family.

Level Shifting

Families in which the solution itself has become the problem have worked hard to make things better. They have probably tried everything they could think of to deal with their problems, or at least everything that seemed to have any possibility of working. In the process they probably also have tried everything the therapist could think of, as well. Or, they have compelling reasons why the things they haven't tried won't work. As long as the therapist stays at the same level of problem solving, accepting the family's view of what is wrong and attempting to right it, nothing much is likely to get better.

The experienced family therapist is very interested in the family's view, very interested in what each family member thinks is wrong and what should be done. Her interest, however, goes well beyond the content of the problem. In fact, talking about the actual problem (as seen by the family) is often just a vehicle for exploring the family's process. How do they go about *thinking* about what's happening to them? What are they *not* talking about or dealing with? What are the unspoken rules that guide their interactions? In setting up a level-shifting intervention, the family therapist doesn't voice these questions out loud; she asks them of herself and uses the answers to formulate a question or a suggestion that redirects the family's attention. The family that has been wrestling with son Roger's poor school performance may, for instance, find the therapist suddenly interested in the ways in which secrets are kept, or the possibility that Dad is afraid of hurting Mom's feelings, or who in the family is most like Grandpa. While these interests are based on real hypotheses about the way in which the family system operates, they also have major value in re-focusing the family's concern—on helping the family to stop trying to solve the "problem" in whatever way they have been doing so that the pathological balance that has been established can try to right itself. If Mom and Dad stop being so invested in Roger's schoolwork, Roger may discover that he no longer is able to distract them from their own fundamental communication difficulties. Once Roger is relieved of his job as family lightning rod, he may find that he really doesn't enjoy doing poor schoolwork.

"People are most influenced," says Selvini-Palazzoli, "when they expect a certain message and receive instead a message at a totally different level." The level shift technique not only can cut through the unproductive stuckness that the family is mired in, but it also gets the family's attention. It surprises, startles, takes them off guard. In so doing, it can get past the habitual defenses and thus prepare the ground for change.

Reframing

Language is a powerful influence, both for making changes and for maintaining the status quo. Families often find themselves prisoners of their own language. Because of the words they use to describe and understand what is happening, they create a situation that they cannot change. By changing the definition and description of the family's behavior, new possibilities for change can emerge. Such a change of definition is known as reframing.

There are many ways of reframing a given situation. One can shift the role of "patient" onto another person, re-define misbehavior as "helpfulness," or insist that a "helpless" person is really quite powerful. In fact, any adjective describing a family member can be turned into its opposite. Amazingly, such reframing nearly always can be defended as a logical and reasonable way of understanding the family dynamic.

Consider a family consisting of Mom, Dad, and three kids as an example. The two older children are Mom's from a prior marriage, and the third is a product of the present marriage. The second-oldest child, eight-year-old Ellie, is school-phobic, and it is her problem that brings the family to treatment. Ellie cries frantically if forced to go to school, and if the parents persist in taking her she invariably throws up before she has been there an hour. Needless to say, her behavior is disrupting not only the family but the school as well, and the parents are at their wit's end. One way of reframing this family is to talk about the power that Ellie has: she is able to command the attention and concern of so many people whenever she chooses to do so. Or, Ellie could be framed as a highly generous and loyal person, willing to sacrifice herself in order to keep Mom from having to be alone during the day. Gordon, the oldest child, could be made the patient. The therapist is very concerned that he is too conforming and has not learned to express his individuality or to say "no" to his parents (as Ellie obviously has learned to do). The possibilities go on and on; the therapist's choice is determined by the actual dynamics of the family and by her own creative ingenuity.

Many students, when first introduced to this sort of approach, experience a kind of indignation. How could a therapist say such things to a family? Isn't it lying? Disrespectful? Would any family be taken in by it? What good could it possibly do, anyhow? My answer to the first criticism is that if the reframe *is* a lie then it should not be used. Reframes which cannot be logically justified are indeed disrespectful. Most families won't accept a reframe that the therapist, at some level, cannot herself believe. But if the reframe is valid, if it is *both* "true" and "not true," then it can have tremendous power. To check this out imagine yourself in turn to be each family member in Ellie and Gordon's family. Think about how you would feel and react if a believable, knowledgeable therapist, whom you had learned to trust, described your family in these ways.

Positive Connotation

The most effective reframing techniques nearly always involve describing in positive terms a behavior that the family has considered to be negative. In some instances each family member's part in the problem must be positively connoted; at other times, only one behavior is focused on, or an interaction between two members will be defined positively.

Positive connotation tends to weaken or bypass resistance. It allows family members to change without losing face. L'Abate points out that

> it is important for therapists to achieve control so that, and to the extent that, they can help others learn to control themselves. The family is not going to carry out instructions that are contrary to its world view....However, when symptomatic behavior is positively connoted, it is easier for the family to accept control over the symptom and to carry out assignments." (1984, p. 13)

It is somehow easier to stop being a nag or an autocrat or insensitive or lazy if you believe that you have really been "over-concerned" or "too generous with your time" or "protecting yourself from pain" or "expressing your playfulness." And it is easier for all other family members to assist you in changing, in a way that feels good to you, if they too believe in the benign intent of your behavior.

Giving Directives

Reframing and positive connotation help to catch the family's attention and to shift their perspective so that they can see other options for themselves. But talk and insight are cheap; actual behavior change is the ultimate goal for family therapy. To lever the family into trying out changes, the family therapist will use directives: she will tell family members what they are to do outside the therapy session. These directives are generally described as "experiments" rather than "this is how your family ought to operate," and they are set up so that no matter what the family does with them, the result can be framed as a success.

Ideally, the family will listen to the directive and then go home and carry it out, thus learning whatever the therapist intended for them to learn. Mom will praise Dad rather than criticize him, or Dad will cook dinner while Mom goes bowling, or son will take ten minutes a day to brag about his schoolwork, or daughter will clean her room in exchange for driving lessons. If it is a well-constructed directive, however, it will provide useful information even if one or more members sabotage it. There are, in fact, whole groups of paradoxical interventions that can be given with the expectation that someone *will* sabotage them and the family will end up not following the directive—and *not* following it is exactly what the therapist really wanted. These interventions are designed to break families out of the self-reinforcing, stuck-in-a-rut patterns that result when dysfunction has been present over a relatively long period of time.

Paradoxical strategies, however, definitely fall into the category of advanced techniques—not to be attempted without specific training and to be used only under the supervision of an experienced family therapist.

Family Tasks

One of the most common tasks assigned to families is that of "writing it down." Family members can be instructed to write down what happened, with whom, when, what led up to it, what happened next, what one wishes would happen instead—the possibilities are nearly endless. One family member can be the reporter or can act as scribe and write what another family member tells him to write. Each can describe an incident from his own point of view—or each can describe it from someone else's point of view. Writing it down is doable; it takes very little time, can be fitted into a busy schedule, and costs virtually nothing. Therefore, it is ideal as a check on whether the family will be compliant. If carried out, it has significant benefits: not only does it provide the therapist with information about how the family functions, but it gives the family information as well. It also creates a sense of competence, a feeling of we-are-doing-something-about-it. "It is very important for families to keep running accounts of contracts, of conferences, of when they are depressed, of sibling rivalry, of temper tantrums, and so forth. By putting it in writing the family learns to be in charge of itself" (Williams & Weeks 1984, p. 20).

Another frequently used instruction is that of the family ritual. The family members are given a very specific set of behaviors to follow, in a ritualized pattern. Everything that is to be done and said is prescribed; each member has a part to play. The ritual may be straightforward or paradoxical; it may (much later in treatment) be a forum for apologies and forgiveness; it may involve the sharing of information. Sometimes a diagnosis/description of the family's behavior is written in a letter to the family, and a ritual may be prescribed in which one member of the family reads the letter to the others. Or a playful or fantasy ritual may be devised which acts out, symbolically, either some aspect of the family's deviant behavior or the underlying purpose of that deviant behavior. Thus the ritual, like writing, serves a joint function: it is easily doable and thus is a test of the family's compliance. It also is a therapeutic intervention in its own right.

A third kind of directive is the family contract. Family contracts take the form of "if she (or he) does this, then you do that." If Junior gets himself up before 7:10 on school days, Dad will cook breakfast for him. If Dad carries out the garbage, Mom will watch the baseball game with him. Or, they can deal with what happens when a family member does *not* do something: for every five minutes that Junior is late getting up, he will do five minutes worth of work for Mom; and for every morning that Mom forgets and reminds him to get up, he gets to stay up five minutes past his regular bedtime.

CHOOSING A STRATEGY

There are so many strategies available to the family therapist that one may be tempted to throw up one's hands and choose randomly what to do with a particular family. The literature often doesn't help here. An intervention may be described in detail, together with the results of that intervention, but seldom do the authors discuss their thinking in choosing that strategy. There are, however, some guidelines for what to do and when to do it.

When the therapist is in a position of power—when she is clearly seen as the expert and trusted by the family (or at least by the family member toward whom the intervention is directed), then a direct, compliance-based strategy is indicated. Straightforward, rather than paradoxical, interventions should be used when possible; there's no need to get fancy when the family is ready and willing to work cooperatively. Families in an acute crisis generally fall into this category. Such families likely will comply with a therapist's directive since they usually are frightened and looking for something that will give them immediate relief. Moreover, the crisis is new, fresh; the family hasn't had time to settle into the kind of homeostatic pattern that the paradoxical intervention is designed to break up.

Even when cooperation is unlikely or reluctant, though, there still are some families for which paradoxical interventions are inappropriate. One such family is the childlike family, in which "all members, including adults, tend to function on an immature level seeking parenting from the therapist. Such systems are...too loose and lack sufficient cohesiveness and unity of purpose for a paradoxical ploy to be effective" (Fisher et al. 1981, p. 33). Fisher also recommends that paradoxical strategies not be used in chaotic or poorly organized families. The defiance-based intervention works to break up collusions and alliances within the family, and families that are poorly organized don't have enough such alliances in the first place.

The general rule of thumb, then, is first to assess how the family patterns—the process—are getting in the way or creating problems. More often than not, this process will have developed out of an attempt to solve some earlier problem situation; the solution will have become the problem. When the assessment has been made, assign the family some task that will require a change in the process, something they must do that will be incompatible with their current way of operating. In other words, redirect their behaviors into more constructive channels. If they follow through, well and good. If they don't, the way in which they undermine or sabotage or defeat the instructions will give you a clue as to the kind of strategic approach which is likely to be most effective with them. Reframing, which is probably the gentlest of the strategic armamentarium, is most useful with families who exhibit moderate resistance, who are able to reflect on and think about what they are doing, who can handle frustration and uncertainty, who aren't actively hostile and are not involved in severe impulsive or acting-out behaviors, and who aren't in the middle of an acute crisis (Weeks & L'Abate, 1982). Restraining (warning them not to change too fast, or too much) and symptom-prescription (telling them to do the very thing they came to treatment in order to stop doing) are more powerful tools and are more appropriate with families in which resistance is firmly entrenched. For families in which one or more members are cooperative but others are highly resistant, combinations of strategic interventions may be required. Again, remember that such interventions are complicated and can backfire badly if misused. They should not be lightly or casually undertaken.

At some point in this discussion, we need to say a word about the ethics of directive and strategic interventions, and this probably is as good a place as any. When first introduced to these approaches to family work, students will almost invariably ask, "But isn't this manipulative?" My answer is that of course it is—so what's the problem? People come to therapy in order to be changed. If they could change themselves, therapists would be out of business. Manipulation or non-manipulation isn't the issue. The issue is who is to benefit from the manipulation being carried out, and whether it is being done with respect and with skill. Watzlawick puts it well:

> One cannot *not* influence. It is, therefore, absurd to ask how influence and manipulation can be avoided, and we are left with the inescapable responsibility of deciding for ourselves how this basic law of human communication may be obeyed in the most humane, ethical, and effective manner. (1978, p. 11)

Part of being humane, ethical, and effective is not to experiment with paradoxical (or any other) methodology until one has been trained in its use; another part is to ensure that one has available *and uses* consultation whenever a family is being dealt with paradoxically. Using consultation and supervision is the best preventive I know for becoming too impressed with our own cleverness—an occupational hazard which seems particularly virulent among some paradoxically oriented therapists.

PITFALLS AND HOOKS

Being too impressed with one's own cleverness is but one of the hidden pitfalls that lay in wait for the unwary family therapist. On the assumption that to know one's enemy is to be prepared to do battle, let's take a look at some of the others. Do recognize, by the way, that these dangers are by no means unique to working with families. We need to be on guard against them in any kind of therapy we do, but it does seem that they may lurk more insidiously in the family arena than in one-to-one therapy.

We talked at the beginning of this chapter about the need to think circularly in terms of interaction patterns and processes rather than in a more simplistic cause-and-effect way. Yet, because we have been taught all our lives to look for causes and effects and to expect that A leads to B leads to C in an orderly way, it's easy for us to slip back into that kind of thinking. Jackson, one of the pioneers of modern family therapy, comments: "Despite our best intentions, clear observations of interactional process fade into the old, individual vocabulary, there to be lost, indistinguishable and heuristically useless" (1965, p. 4). In families there almost never is a single "cause" of a problem, a single starting point, a single culprit or innocent victim. All members interact to create a pattern, and it is the pattern—the interacting system—that is at once the problem, the solution, the villain, and the victim. The therapist who forgets this will soon be lured into a quest for a mythical starting point or focal person—a quest which, should the family join it, is almost sure to harm rather than help them.

Therapists are, by and large, a well-intentioned lot. We really do want to help people; we feel good when our clients improve and feel bad when they don't. This need to be "helpful" is both a blessing and a curse to our clients. It's a blessing because, when controlled and used in their benefit, it helps us to do our best work. It's a curse because, when not controlled, it lures us into being overconcerned, into "helping" too much. Family members are not likely to learn to take care of themselves when their therapist provides them with ready-made answers, patches up their quarrels for them, pours oil on their troubled waters and sends them on their way. Any time we find ourselves working harder than our clients are working, we need to stop and reexamine what is happening; any time we do more than 50 percent of the work in a session, we are not doing good therapy.

Being overconcerned is first cousin to being overly responsible. The overly responsible therapist really believes that she can "cure" a dysfunctional family system and that it is her job to do so. As Haley and Hoffman warn, "if you accept the sole responsibility, even implicitly, for treating them, in sense of curing them, then they are going to foist it off on you at every opportunity, in ways that can be highly unpleasant because you won't know what to do" (1967, p. 18). The family therapist's job is to provide a structure within which the family can cure itself; it is up to the family to decide whether or not to use that structure, just as it is up to the would-be body builder to decide whether or not to use the weight training equipment. To suggest otherwise is to invite the family to lean back and wait for you rather than engage themselves in the hard work of making things different—and if you *believe* that you can or should or ought to be able to do it for them, you will indeed suggest it whether you intend to or not.

All of the above pitfalls—searching for the "cause," working too hard, feeling too responsible—are forms of therapist induction. Induction occurs when a therapist loses her objectivity and begins to think like a member of the family she is treating rather than like a therapist. She may be inducted into taking sides with one member or faction against another, or with (or against) the whole family in a battle with some outsider. She may be inducted into believing a family mythology: that Dad is unable to deal with feelings, or that Suzie's physical appearance makes all the other kids pick on her, or that Mom just can't help being high-strung and nervous. Worst of all, she may be inducted into thinking of the family as helpless and of herself as their only hope for salvation and health. Pity the poor therapist in that trap, and pity the poor family with whom she works.

What are the antidotes? How can we family therapists avoid the pitfalls and hooks? The first and most obvious answer is: consult. Meet regularly with colleagues and make a point of talking more about the families you are stuck with and the times when you really aren't sure of what you are doing than about your triumphs. If you use your consultation or supervision time well, you often will find yourself wondering if the others in your group think you are quite incompetent, because you will spend so much of your time describing your worst, rather than your best, work. But that's all right, because you will be able to sound so very brilliant when discussing *their* mistakes and uncertainties!

Another major guideline for family (and other) therapists: maintain a position of firm respect for your clients. No matter what sort of nonsense they are involved in or how unhealthy their behavior, they are at bottom human beings doing the best they can to survive. I have yet to meet a person who gets up in the morning and tries to figure out how much damage he can do during that day. We might argue the theology of evil, or whether there are people who are truly "bad." As a therapist, however, you will do best to believe that people would rather be good. This will allow you to function as an advocate for rather than an adversary of the families with whom you work. It also, by the way, helps to inoculate you against that "too clever" problem that I mentioned earlier: for who would want to cleverly outwit people who are working with you, striving for the best outcome of which they can conceive?

Things are often other than they seem at first. As Madanes says,

> In human relations, nothing is ever all black or all white; where there is love there is hate, power is always associated with dependence, behavior is never totally voluntary or involuntary. As soon as one seems to have defined the situation and understood it without ambiguities, the opposite definition comes to mind and appears equally feasible. It may be that what is characteristic of a good therapist's thought processes is a particular tolerance for ambiguity. (1984, p. 140)

As we learn to tolerate not knowing, we free ourselves from the responsibility of having to know. Simplistic, right? But ever so important in the list of antidotes to those toxic family therapy errors. Being willing to work with what presents itself in the family process, not knowing its cause or its result or even if it will continue long enough to find out much more about it; being willing to be seen by the family as fallible and only partly (rather than all-) knowing; keeping firmly in mind that what will *work* for this family is much more important than what is really going on, and that you may never find out much about the latter—all of these seem alien at first to our scientifically trained minds, but all are enormously important in our kit of family therapy tools.

Along with tolerance of ambiguity comes a kind of therapeutic detachment, a willingness to play with ideas and possibilities rather than to hang on to them with grim seriousness. It's not that the family therapist loses sight of the very real distress of the family, but rather that she refuses to let herself get sucked into that distress. She must insulate herself from it or she won't be able to work with it—just as linemen must insulate themselves from the current that flows along the wires on their towers and poles. Thus insulated, she is free to imagine options and alternatives that are not available to the family members themselves. Moreover, she can leave the family behind at the end of a session and return to the healing pleasures of her own private life.

What might on the surface seem a cavalier position (don't take too much responsibility, stay detached and playful, make the family do the work) is balanced in the good family therapist by a commitment to learn from each family with whom she works. Everything the family does is important; moreover, everything they do can be considered as (partially) an output of the therapist's own behavior. The family, then, can never respond "wrong"; it is the therapist's intervention that was ill-chosen or ill-timed for that family. It's a paradox, right? The family is responsible for their behavior, their cure; and the therapist is responsible for their responsibility. X and not-X are both equally true and both must be believed.

When it doesn't work—when the family remains stubbornly stuck or terminates treatment in the same or worse shape than when they arrived—what then? Then at least we can review and use our errors for the benefit of our next clients. Did I use the family's language rather than expecting them to learn mine? Did I base my interventions on what actually happened in the sessions rather than on my fantasies about what happened outside of sessions? Did I attend to everyone present rather than focus prematurely on one or two? Did I frame the assignment of new behaviors as permissions rather than punishments? Did I consistently respect and give credit to the family's motivation and hard work rather than my own cleverness? Finally, one last line of self-questioning that often leads to surprising insights: had I deliberately set out to keep this family stuck/sick/unchanging, what would I have done and how is that similar to what actually happened?

FAMILY THERAPY GOALS

The overriding goal in family therapy is that the family take charge of itself; that its members solve their problems cooperatively and at the same time experience their individual autonomy—and all of this in the context of the behaviors appropriate to each member's developmental level. That's a lot to chew on, and probably too big and too general to give much specific guidance. It serves as an ideal, though, a model against which we can measure our overall success with each family.

There are, within that ideal, some specific rules of thumb for healthy family functioning. While not invariable (all the rules I can think of have exceptions) they are nearly always useful in assessing how far a family has come and what may need to be done next. One of the first of these is that whichever person has been the first to show a change or shift in behavior needs to be helped to maintain that new behavior until the rest of the family catch up. People don't grow at the same rate, and someone will have to lead the way. If we aren't careful to support and nurture the change, that leader may give up in despair because it "isn't working"—i.e., the others haven't done their share.

A second rule or goal is that, in a healthy family, children are not equal to their parents. Parents make family decisions, sometimes after consulting with their children; the children live with these decisions. Healthy parents don't let their children make decisions for them. A major function of family therapy is to reinstate the parents to a position of leadership and decision-making and to dethrone a rebellious or power-drunk sibling or sibling subsystem. Children are not in charge of the well-being of their parents. As they grow and mature, children need to move from positions of dependence on parents into positions of autonomy; parents can be respected and cared about, but are not determinants of lifestyle or happiness. The therapist must

> behave in a manner as to destroy this false belief that the parents must be changed before the child can grow....This message must succeed in stating that it is not the task of the children to improve the relationship between their parents or to substitute for them in their functions, that an adolescent can successfully grow up and become mature regardless of the type of relationship between his parents." (Selvini-Palazzoli et al., 1978, p. 111)

Reinstating the parents as parents means helping them to continue to do the things they are doing well, giving them permission to change the things they are doing badly (and always assuming that the parents will of course want to change these things since they are invested in being good parents), and giving them credit for both. When the family improves, it is primarily due to the efforts of the parents and secondarily due to the efforts of the children; the therapist is a pleased or satisfied or surprised or confused coach and cheering section. Criticizing the parents will only reinforce their sense of helplessness and inadequacy, which will in turn render the therapist helpless and inadequate. Taking credit for the family's changes will likewise undermine the parent's authority and competence. Believing that the parents can and do make the positive difference will allow that belief to be true—and true it must be if the family is to be well.

CONCLUSIONS

We have been exploring a strange world in these pages, a landscape sometimes startlingly different from, and sometimes remarkably similar to, the landscape of individual counseling and therapy. Perhaps the most important difference and the one most difficult to master for those well-schooled in individual work, has to do with indirection. Indirection is the art of seeing where you are not looking, of talking to one person by addressing someone else, of acting upon one process by intervening in another. It is slippery—it's hard not to get caught up in what is happening on the surface and to lose track of the underlying structure, to find yourself focusing on a particular person or interaction and ignoring everything else!

Because this sort of lapse, this therapeutic tunnel vision, is so easy to fall into, perhaps the best way of dealing with it is to expect it to happen. Recognize it, forgive yourself for it, and go back to what you need to be doing with this family. Perhaps even learn from it—it probably is no accident that you chose to lose your perspective just at this moment rather than at some other—so what is there about what the family as a whole is doing right now that invited you to tune it out?

On the other side of the ledger, when it does go well—when you work with a family and the family begins to change—many things will begin to happen all at once. Not infrequently, one or more members will complain that the situation is getting worse, not better. Nearly always, some members will respond (usually without conscious awareness) to changes by behaving so as to bring back the old, stuck symptoms. Each time one person in the system makes a shift, the others also must shift to accommodate the new behavior; not all of these shifts will be comfortable for themselves or for the other family members. Lasting change in one person often requires a shakedown cruise during which everyone else adjusts to the new patterns of communication, the new subsystem alliances, and the new reward and punishment patterns.

When this is accomplished and the family is well and truly launched into a new way of being and growing, what then? Be prepared to hear that nobody did anything different, that change "just happened," or that although the original problem no longer exists there are new ones that are equally troubling. If the family does understand and enjoy its changes, be prepared to get no credit yourself for what has been accomplished. It is not that the family is ungrateful, but rather that they literally cannot see what you have done—especially if your work is elegant. Being parts of a system, the individual members cannot stand back and be objective about their overall process; changes at the system level are likely to seem somewhat mysterious and inexplicable. That is okay; the important thing is that change has happened, that the family is different now, and that each person must willy-nilly be a part of that difference.

12 THE CARE AND FEEDING OF THERAPISTS

In all these many pages we have discussed various topics having to do with the welfare of clients, how to do what is most helpful to the client in managing his growth and happiness. Now, in this last chapter, we change our focus. Instead of looking at what the client needs, we will look at what the therapist needs. The two are not so very different, for one of the most basic needs of any client is to have a therapist who is competent, confident, and handling her own life well. Only when she is in this kind of personal space can the therapist be fully present and available to her clients.

But how difficult it is for therapists to maintain that kind of personal serenity! The peculiar demands of our profession seem almost designed to keep us off-balance and uncertain. Stress is our daily fare; we spend our hours dealing with pain and anxiety. "Practicing psychotherapy is a difficult—if also rewarding—way to earn a living," says Wachtel.

> It is no profession for the individual who likes certainty, predictability, or a fairly constant sense that one knows what one is doing. There are few professions in which feeling stupid or stymied is as likely to be a part of one's ordinary professional day, even for those at the pinnacle of the field. Indeed, I would be loath to refer a patient to

any therapist who declared that he almost always felt effective and clear about what was going on. Such a feeling can be maintained, I believe, only by an inordinate amount of bravado and lack of critical self-reflection. (1982, p. xiii).

Yet, with the built-in dissatisfaction there is also an enormous possibility of reward, challenge, and joy in the practice of psychotherapy. This chapter is all about ways to maximize the joy, excitement, and satisfaction while minimizing the frustration and pain. I must say at the outset that it will be a very personal chapter. I shall speak of issues that are and have been real for me; I may neglect issues that are equally important to others. Each of us has our own tender spots, our areas of special vulnerability, just as each of us develops our own unique ways of coping with these problems. Still, underlying the individuality of each particular therapist with each particular client, there is a common base: the strengths and limitations of psychotherapy as a tool for change and the accumulated wisdom of colleagues and predecessors who have weathered their own storms and have been willing to share what they have learned. It is upon this wisdom, as well as my own experience, that I shall base the following pages.

Proper care and feeding of a therapist, as of any other living creature, involves much more than providing for basic physical needs. It includes maintaining a safe environment, education for growth and expansion, and loving support and encouragement. Therapists need to know how to help themselves and how to get help from others. We need to know what to do to avoid painful situations before they occur, as well as how to deal with them when they happen. We need to learn to recognize and correct our errors when they are correctable and to let go of them when no correction is possible. In fact, we need to do for ourselves the very things we try to teach our clients to do!

In order to give some structure to this mass of need-to's, I have arbitrarily divided the whole into three sections: professionalism, legal and ethical issues, and emotional health and growth. In the first section, we will discuss what it means to be a professional, the attitudes and behaviors that are appropriate and useful in maintaining one's professional role. The second section, dealing with legal and ethical issues, is a logical extension of the first; as professionals, we are bound by somewhat different and more stringent rules of conduct than a friendly neighborhood helper. The third section, which focuses on emotional health, explores some of the particular stresses and demands placed on therapists and suggests a number of strategies for coping with such demands. Finally, we shall talk about how to keep ourselves alive, growing, and excited about our work and our selves.

PROFESSIONALISM

If you, the reader, are newly arrived to the field of therapy, you are probably still turning the corner between amateur and professional. Throughout your student years, you were only too eager and grateful for people willing to share their concerns with you, willing for you to practice your skills with them. You may have found yourself playing therapist with friends, family members, and colleagues. Most of us did that when we were learning, and many of us still occasionally do—usually to our sorrow. You took practicum courses, did volunteer work or completed internships in which you were paid meagerly if at all (and often you did the paying) for working with clients. All in all, you had a long and intensive training period in which you learned through experience that your services were worth very little in terms of hard cash. You also learned to accept whatever working conditions were set up for you: you saw clients in uncomfortable offices, at hours that fit someone else's convenience. You took the clients who were assigned (or available) to you. You made relatively few decisions on your own, and those were subject to revision should a supervisor insist.

Now all that has quite suddenly changed. You are expected to charge money for your work ("All that? Just for talking to someone for an hour!" I heard one newly licensed therapist remark in an unguarded moment). You may be maintaining your own office and setting your own hours. You can decide what kinds of clients you will and will not work with. You set your own therapeutic course, and you are responsible for everything you do. It is an extraordinary transition, and one that most new therapists are ill-equipped to make, mainly because nobody has prepared them for it.

Old hands, too, may have some trouble with maintaining an appropriate professional stance, but for different reasons. Here, the "I've always done it this way and always will" syndrome may creep into our attitudes and behaviors. No matter how long we have been practicing our art (and being paid to do so), it is a good idea to pause now and then to reexamine the rules and guidelines that we normally take for granted. Just as the best-organized closet needs an occasional clearing, so the clearest guidelines can stand inspection and possible revision at regular intervals.

The Setting

The first real introduction between a client and therapist often comes, not through words, but through visual impressions of the therapeutic setting. The client usually arrives in a state of anxious expectation: what will this experience be like? What kind of person will my therapist be? How am I supposed to behave? Consciously or unconsciously, he uses all sorts of information to begin to answer these questions. He notices the location of the office, the kind of furniture, the color scheme, the activity level, the sounds and the smells. He experiences this place as comfortable or uncomfortable, scary or reassuring. Before you say a word to him, he has usually formed some sort of expectation about how helpful or difficult or demanding the therapy experience is likely to be for him.

By creating a setting that matches our own personal style, that is comfortable and congruent for us, we can minimize false expectations in our clients. This certainly makes our job easier, and we do not have to wait for the client to figure out that we really are not the formal/sloppy/stiff/hurried/careless sort of person that some settings suggest. Even beyond the effect of the setting on the client, our physical surroundings have an effect on us. Twenty years ago, Chessick pointed out that "through his personality and office setting and routines the therapist demonstrates to the patient his integrity, sincere therapeutic intent, willingness to work hard and seriously for the patient's benefit, and perhaps above all his genuine respect for the patient as a human being" (1969, p. 79). It still is a valid observation. We also remind *ourselves* of those qualities. Our physical surroundings can help us in maintaining our professionalism, simply through reminding us of who we are and what we are about.

The place where I work should fit me, my beliefs, attitudes, and esthetics. It should, first and foremost, be a place where I can be comfortable. The colors, the furniture, the pictures on the walls should not jar or distract me from the work I am doing. It should be neither stark and sterile nor cluttered. I put a few books and objects in my office that have special meaning to me: they help me to remember ideas and experiences that have been markers on my personal journey into competence, or remind me of people who have given me important gifts along the way. My office becomes, for both me and my clients, an extension of myself. All of the elements—the people, the work, and the setting—are coordinate parts of this whole that we call therapy.

One's dress, too, contributes to the therapeutic whole. Again, the clothing I wear should fit my own personal style, while reflecting and reminding me of my professional role. I am seeing clients now, not going to the opera or mowing the yard. Zaro (1977) recommends that therapists dress fairly conservatively as a way of underscoring both the seriousness of their purpose and their respect for the client. No matter how right you may feel in tennis shoes, cutoffs, and an old T-shirt, a forty-year-old business executive is unlikely to be favorably impressed by such a costume. On the other hand, a suit and tie (or high heels and a tailored dress) may feel constricting and artificial. If so, do not wear them. Clothing that is comfortable, clean, and appropriate to your setting and lifestyle is another important part of your therapeutic self.

The Exchange

The essence of professionalism is that the practitioner receives tangible rewards for what she does. This means, for the great majority of therapists, that we expect to be paid money for our work with clients. If we are salaried employees of an agency or some other institution or corporation, the transition from unpaid student to paid staff member is not particularly difficult. We do not have to take money directly from the client; there is an intervening structure which disguises the exchange.

When we move into private practice, the disguise disappears. Suddenly we are asking that the client pay us for what we do. We even have to decide how much and whether or not to make exceptions! There is a great temptation for beginners in private practice to see some people for little or no money, to be over-flexible about being paid on time, and to be apologetic about fees. The sooner you can get past this stage, the better. If you convey to the client that you are not worth what he is paying you, he is very likely to believe it, and the work will suffer.

"If I do not take good care of myself by seeing to it that I am paid for the time I have contracted to the patient, my resentment will take its toll later in the work" (Kopp 1977, p. 49). Not only will the client come to value me less, but I may also come to value myself less. Or I may value the client less and do poorer work with him than with another who pays me more. It is important to make a clear and straightforward statement of your charges and your expectations about how they will be met at the outset of treatment, coming to an agreement about money before proceeding with therapy.

Many therapists use a sliding fee scale in which clients who have few resources are charged less than others. Each practitioner must, of course, make his own decisions about fees. I have found that discussion about sliding my fees generally results in an arrangement that is unsatisfactory to both myself and my client: the decision of how much can/should he pay is difficult for me to be objective about, and it seems unrealistic to expect more objectivity from him than from myself.

"The fee," says Chessick, "should be set at the general going rate in the community, like that of any other medical specialist, and left there. For the majority of patients this is satisfactory; they come to their sessions and pay regularly. The subject [of money] becomes irrelevant" (1969, p. 120). Except in very unusual situations, fees should not change once they have been set. The idea of accelerating treatment by charging a very high fee, or of allowing a client to continue long term work by lowering the fee, is not a good one. Once the charge is seen as variable, this becomes another therapeutic issue and can muddy up the professional relationship between therapist and client, to the great detriment of the overall process.

Similarly, a clear agreement should be reached and held to with regard to missed sessions. Fromm-Reichmann (1950) suggests that the first missed session should be used as a warning; thereafter, the regular session charge is made whether or not the client keeps the appointment. Again, the principle is one of a professional exchange: the client has contracted for an hour of your time, you have reserved that hour for him and should be reimbursed for it. To do otherwise is to discount both your own value and the client's ability to be responsible.

Before we leave the subject of payment, one other issue should be touched on: gifts from client to therapist. What should be done about the client who brings you a potted plant, a hand-knit sweater, a book that "I know you'd enjoy reading"? There is no hard and fast rule here; depending on the particular client, it may be therapeutically important either to refuse the gift or to accept it. It is essential, though, that the therapist be clear about the reasons for her decision. She needs to ask herself why this client is choosing to bring a gift at this point, and what will be the implication of her accepting or refusing it. Is the client making a subtle bid for specialness, for friendship beyond the therapist-client relationship? Is this the first of a series of manipulative moves? Is the client genuinely appreciative and simply wanting to demonstrate that appreciation? Has the therapist conveyed in some way that she needs or wants reassurance from this client? "Whether one accepts or refuses the gift, the important idea is that the therapist recognizes its transference-resistance motivation and introduces an examination of this behavior into the interview discussions. Therapists who frequently receive gifts from all sorts of patients can profitably explore in themselves the unconscious equation, gifts = love" (Colby 1951, p. 37).

The principle of the exchange is simple. The therapist offers a unit of time and skills; the patient pays a set amount for each unit. Even though the two parties agree to involve themselves in a close relationship in which intangible and emotional factors play an important part, this simple structure must be maintained. Indeed, it is precisely because of the nonmeasurables on both sides of the relationship that a clear understanding of and adherence to the principle is so important; it provides structure and protection within a climate of growth and change.

The Attitude of a Professional

A central aspect of my professionalism is my attitude toward my client and toward myself. Do I see my clients as somehow inferior to myself, as potential payers-of-the-rent, as critics whom I must manage to please, as children, students, threats to my sense of competence? Yes, sometimes I will respond to them in these ways, but, hopefully, not often. Do I see myself as a purveyor-of-wisdom, a scared kid pretending confidence, a healer, a magician, responsible for solving each client's problems? Again, I may feel all of these ways at times, and again I must not do so often.

Chessick suggests that the only reasonable attitude for a therapist to maintain is "that of a nonanxious, investigative, concerned human being, based on a 'physicianly vocation,' with all that implies" (1969, p. 102). For me there are two major components to this physicianly vocation: caring and curiosity. I must genuinely care for my clients, care for them as fellow humans, as people whose joy and pain is important to me. I must be curious, interested in what they say and how they say it, in how they came to be who they are, in how the strands of their lives weave together to create this exact happening at this precise moment. My caring makes me real for them, makes the relationship work as a curative factor. My curiosity allows me to pull back, to be involved without being too vulnerable, to formulate and hypothesize and plan.

As I try to balance these two attitudes, caring and curiosity, I find that what I am feeling toward a particular client from moment to moment gives me important feedback. Am I feeling bored, wondering why the time is passing so slowly? I am probably not giving free rein to my curiosity. Am I annoyed or indifferent? Perhaps I need to allow myself to care more for this person. Am I impatient with a rambling account of day-to-day happenings or working hard to get answers to my questions? Then I am being too involved in my own agenda, and not curious enough about the client's. Or am I feeling overburdened, responsible for solving the unsolvable, stuck in the mire of my client's despair? Then there is too much caring; pull back and let curiosity have its way.

Of course, to see all therapeutic attitudes as based on just these two concerns is an oversimplification. There are many other possibilities, many ways of being with self and clients. Some are helpful, some are not. Some are more familiar than others, depending on our own personal style. We can learn much about what to avoid in relating to clients simply by noticing how we are with people in our personal lives: the patterns we play out with parents, spouse, friends, and children will tend to be repeated with our clients.

One particularly dangerous attitude that the unwitting therapist may fall prey to is the love of power. It can feel wonderful to be influential in someone's life, to be privy to their inmost secrets, to have an important part in their decisions and choices. The client's wish to be cured by a magician, as Feinchel has noted, may be equalled by the therapist's wish to *be* a magician. "There is in every healing profession the temptation to play God, and an all-wise, all-powerful-acting therapist may soon run into unpleasant difficulties, just as new-found powers proved heady for the sorcerer's apprentice. A psychotherapist is really not God, nor even a close relative of his" (Colby 1951, p. 21).

I have often found it useful to remind myself and my clients that I am really a tool for their use. I put my skills at their disposal, but they must decide what to do with those skills. Just like a computer that needs to be programmed in order to solve problems, or an exercise machine that will only help you lose weight if you work with it, the therapist makes herself available. We do not really cure or heal people any more than we grow them. People cure and heal themselves, with our help and encouragement, using our knowledge and expertise, benefitting from our curiosity and caring. We can and must be responsible *to* our clients, but we are not (and should not try to be) responsible *for* them. For me, this is the essence of the physicianly vocation.

LEGAL AND ETHICAL ISSUES

As a therapist, you are bound not only by the laws of the state in which you practice, but also by a professional code of ethics. Most of the time, the legal and ethical guidelines form a comfortable and consistent framework within which to work. Occasionally, they may conflict or appear to conflict. Ultimately, each individual therapist must decide what she will and will not do in a given situation. The guidelines are just that: guiding principles. They cannot provide specific directions for dealing with individual clients.

The first step in making legal and ethical decisions is to know the laws governing practice in your own state or area. Although all states have similar laws, the details will differ. It is the responsibility of each of us to know what is required and what is forbidden: when, for instance, must we report dangerous or criminal behavior to the appropriate authorities? Under what conditions can a client be hospitalized against his will? What are the rules governing treatment of minors or other people who cannot give informed consent for their therapy? For what client behaviors can therapists be held liable? What are your legal responsibilities to your client in terms of availability, recordkeeping, contracting for services? Some state governments will provide, on request, a compendium of the laws pertaining to therapy; in other states these laws have not been gathered together but must be pulled out of general codes and statutes. It is unfortunate that the education of many therapists does not include an introduction to the laws governing the practice of therapy, how they have been interpreted in the courts, and how they can be used to help both client and practitioner. If you are among those who have not received such formal training, you should find a good lawyer, one experienced in the area of psychological practice, and arrange for ongoing consultation and updating. There are several books on the subject, and reading one of these (such as Benjamin Schutz's *Legal Liability in Psychotherapy*) will acquaint you with the general areas of concern.

Knowing and adhering to the bare legal requirements is important, but it is not enough. The ethical guidelines for each of the professional groups involved in therapy and/or counseling go beyond legal technicalities; they attempt to define good practice as it is understood by therapists, counselors, social workers, and psychiatric nurses. One of the most complete sets of guidelines is provided by the American Psychological Association. Their *Standards for Providers of Psychological Services,* together with the more generic *Ethical Principles of Psychologists,* are reviewed and updated regularly, and supplemented by case histories that illustrate how the *Standards* have been applied in specific cases. A less detailed (and more easily remembered) set of guidelines is provided by Redlich and Pope (1980). They suggest seven principles:

1. above all, do no harm;
2. practice only with competence;
3. do not exploit;
4. treat people with respect for their dignity as human beings;
5. protect confidentiality;
6. act, except in the most extreme instances, only after obtaining informed consent; and
7. practice, insofar as possible, within the framework of social equity and justice. (quoted by Pope et al. 1987, p. 999)

What exists beyond formal codes of ethics? We move inevitably into the area of personal values and decisions. Singer points out: "What one deems ethically lofty another may deem reprehensible and wicked" (1965, p. 9). Even such a simple and obvious principle as that of putting the client's best interests first can become cloudy and uncertain in the face of questions such as "When does the welfare of society become more important than the welfare of the individual client?" or "To what degree am I obliged to sacrifice my own needs (for time, money, personal freedom) in the interest of meeting the needs of a client?" The integrity of our profession, as Pope et al. point out, is "contingent to a great degree on the extent to which we—both as a discipline and as individuals—can regulate our own behavior" (p. 1004). Ultimately, each of us must decide what we believe, what we stand for, what we will and will not do regardless of consequences. Knowing the law and the standards of our profession is essential, but such knowledge cannot substitute for a clear examination and understanding of our own personal values and commitments.

Legal requirements, ethical standards, personal values: these form the threads out of which we weave our professional behavior. Let us examine a few of the major areas of concern, areas on which legal and ethical issues have traditionally focused. As we do so, I invite you to continue to question: "Do I, myself, agree with this? Am I willing to be bound by it? Are there any circumstances under which I would feel morally obliged to act otherwise?" For here, as in every other aspect of our profession, knowing myself is as important as knowing the rules.

Responsibility to the Client

The therapist's first duty toward her client is that she be professionally competent and exercise that competence for the benefit of her clients. Competence is, of course, hard to define in any broad or general way. The following is a typical legal description of what is required: the therapist must "(1) possess the degree of learning, skill, and ability that others similarly situated ordinarily possess; (2) exercise reasonable care and diligence in the application of his knowledge and skill to the patient's case; and (3) use his best judgment in the treatment and care of his patient" (*Stone v. Procter* 1963; quoted in Furrow 1980, p. 23). A responsible therapist will only accept a client when she believes that she has the training and skill necessary to help that particular person with that particular problem. No matter how tempted we may be to see a client because he is interesting or because we could learn from working with him, we must not do so unless we are qualified by training and experience. Clients seek therapy in order to get help for themselves, not to entertain or to educate their therapists. If I feel unsure of my ability to work with someone, I am legally and ethically obliged to send that person elsewhere.

Having decided that I am willing to treat a client, I must next help that client to decide whether or not to accept my treatment. Clients must agree to be treated, and it is the responsibility of the therapist to ensure that the client knows what he is agreeing to. The principle of informed consent is one of the cornerstones of therapeutic ethics. However, how can someone know what psychotherapy will be like before he has actually experienced it? How can he give informed consent if he cannot really be informed of what he is getting into? The only answer is the common-sense one: we do the best we can. We tell the client as clearly as possible what sorts of things he can expect during treatment, how long we think it may take, how much it may cost. We tell him in language he can understand; we do not throw jargon or technical language at him, and we give him a chance to ask questions and get answers. When we do not know, we tell him that.

"Conservatively," says Schutz, "a therapist should inform the patient of the nature of his disorder and should describe the therapeutic program recommended, indicating also the anticipated benefits of the program, the foreseeable material risks of the treatment, and the likely results of no treatment. The therapist should also describe alternative methods of treatment" (1982, p. 24).

Notice that you are not required to guarantee the results of treatment. Buying psychotherapy is not like buying a toaster or a clothes dryer. It is more like buying a textbook; a satisfactory outcome depends both on the book being adequate and on the user doing his job. If you guarantee that a client will be cured, you may be held legally responsible for his failure to improve, even though such a failure may be due to his refusal to cooperate. You owe it to him to tell him the likelihood of success, given his full participation in the program; but he also needs to know that improvement depends as much on his own input as it does on yours.

The general public, or at least a large segment of it, still tends to regard the psychotherapist as a kind of latter-day witch doctor, with magical and mysterious power to reach into a client's psyche and bring forth a miracle. Beyond dispelling this notion with individual clients, it may be that our ethical code should be expanded to include some corrective public relations work to let the general public know what we can and cannot do. Again quoting Schutz: "Therapists should attempt to create reasonable expectations for the public about what psychotherapy can and cannot do. Perhaps a return to Freud's goal of ordinary human misery is called for, rather than our current pursuit of wrinkle-free, drip-dry, perfectible man" (p. 95).

Once informed consent has been given and treatment begun, the therapist enters into a new kind of responsibility relationship with her client. She must not only provide appropriate treatment and protection during the therapy hour, but she must also be reasonably available should the client need her between sessions. Of course, "reasonably available" is a very elastic term. What does it really mean? For most noncrisis clients, returning a call within twenty-four hours is generally sufficient availability. The crisis client may need closer monitoring; and many clients will neither need nor request between-session contact at all. The key here is to make clear to the client exactly what you are willing to provide. Will you accept between-session phone calls? How often and of what duration? Will you charge for such calls? If you have an answering service or machine, how often do you check for messages? Spelling all this out for your client, and notifying him explicitly should the situation change, lets both you and him know what to expect of each other.

Therapists need time off, just like everyone else. But sometimes clients do not want their therapists to take time off, or indeed may actually need the therapist during a vacation period. Part of the therapist's responsibility is to provide backup for her clients when she herself is unavailable. Give your client the names of one or two colleagues whose work you respect and who have agreed to serve on stand-by during your absence. This should be done whenever you will be unavailable for more than twenty-four hours at a time.

For absences that will involve missing scheduled appointments with a client, your responsibility extends beyond providing a backup option. You must let the client know ahead of time that you will be gone and help him to decide how he will handle your absence. If you will be away for some time, and if the client has developed a dependency relationship with you, then your leaving will be a therapeutic as well as a practical issue, and you should provide plenty of advance warning so that the client will have time to work this issue through. A good rule of thumb is to let the lead time equal the time you will actually be gone: for a single missed weekly session, a week's warning is sufficient; if you plan to be gone a month, let the client know at least a month ahead of time.

Speaking of dependency leads me to another aspect of therapist responsibility, one that is not generally spelled out in formal codes of ethics but which is of fundamental importance. Therapists differ in the degree to which they allow or encourage clients to become dependent upon them. Some deny that any dependency is necessary or even desirable. A strict behavior therapist, for instance, or an Adlerian or Dreikursian might well see dependency on the part of the client as impeding rather than furthering progress. Others, more psychoanalytically oriented, view dependence (transference) as an essential ingredient of therapy. Most, I suspect, fall between these two extremes, seeing dependency as common but not inevitable, more useful for some clients and less so for others. Whatever your theoretical stance on this issue, however, your ethical responsibility is clear: client dependency should never be encouraged beyond the point of therapeutic usefulness, and the client should be helped in recovering his independence and autonomy as soon as it is therapeutically advisable to do so. Under no conditions may a therapist ever encourage client dependency in order to meet her own needs for ego gratification or professional status, or prolong such dependency for similar reasons. Our job as therapists must be eventually to become unnecessary, rather than necessary, to each client.

Confidentiality

In order to deal openly and honestly with all of his issues, the client needs to know that his privacy will be respected; that the therapist will keep to herself whatever the client tells her. This principle of confidentiality has long been an explicit requirement in all medical treatment. It is a part of the Hippocratic Oath: "Whatsoever I shall see or hear in the course of my profession in my intercourse with men, if it be what should not be noised abroad, I will never divulge, holding such things to be holy secrets." Traditionally, only a few professions have had the legal right to claim privileged communication. Lawyers, physicians, ministers, and psychotherapists are among those few. The doctrine of privilege, however, is not the same in every state. It is applied differently to different specialties within the mental health field (psychiatrists, psychologists, counselors, social workers, psychiatric nurses) and does not always cover every possible communication a client may make. In a few states, for example, most but not all mental health providers are required to report instances of child abuse to the appropriate authorities. You may be required to report other instances of known or potentially illegal behavior, or of behavior which threatens the right of safety for the client or his associates. Again, the place to start in determining your own personal guidelines is the law. "It is imperative," say Hatton et al., "to know the law, the agency, and the rights of the client in any given situation" (1977, p. 36).

Unfortunately, it is in the area of confidentiality that the laws governing clinical practice are perhaps at their murkiest. Actual statutes are less likely to be relevant than case law—that is, courtroom decisions that set precedents on which future decisions will be made. The best known of such recent cases is that of *Tarasoff vs. Regents of the University of California.* A client told his therapist, who worked at the University, that he intended to kill Tatiana Tarasoff, a woman with whom he had been in love. The therapist, taking the threat seriously, informed the police as a first step in having the client legally committed. The police, however, believed that the client was lucid, accepted his promise to leave Ms. Tarasoff alone, and took no further action. The client was enraged at what he experienced as his therapist's betrayal and did not return for treatment. Two months later, he killed Tatiana Tarasoff. Her parents thereupon sued the therapist (and also the police and the University of California) because nobody had warned them that their daughter was in danger; the California Supreme Court, reversing a lower court decision, upheld their suit.

In the state of New Jersey, a court handed down a similar decision to that of the Tarasoff case (*McIntosh vs. Milano* 1979). However, a Maryland court came to an opposite conclusion (*Shaw vs. Glickman* 1980), holding that a therapist should respect the client's confidences except when the law expressly and explicitly prohibits maintaining confidentiality. Case law, it is apparent, is not always consistent.

Tarasoff and subsequent cases have thrown the whole question of privileged communication and appropriate protection into a kind of legal no-man's land. The therapist in the Tarasoff case was held liable for not warning Tarasoff's parents about the client's intentions. Had he taken the opposite course and warned the parents (and Tarasoff herself), the client could conceivably have sued him for breach of confidentiality. In either case, the therapist's decision could have been wrong.

So what can be done? Roth and Meisel (1977) list a number of possible steps to take when dealing with a violent or potentially violent client:

1. Ask the patient to warn the victim himself. (This has dangerous possibilities of a threatening confrontation escalating into the feared violence. The patient should be so informed.)
2. Get a consent from the patient to warn the intended victim.
3. Have a joint session with the patient and intended victim to disclose the threat and explore the factors leading up to it.
4. Have the patient turn in any weapons he possesses.
5. Increase the frequency of therapy sessions.

6. Consider medication as an adjunct.
7. Consider voluntary hospitalization.

Wexler (1981) cites literature on victimology to support his position that the therapist should work with both the client and his threatened victim (as in point 3 above). Not only are most victims part of an interpersonal system which includes the client, but they may also be behaving (either consciously or unconsciously) in ways that tend to trigger violence. Intervention at a system level may help both client and victim to change their behaviors and thus avert a tragedy.

Whatever course you take, whichever one or combination of possible interventions seem appropriate, there are two additional steps that are nearly always advisable. These are:

8. Consult with colleagues.
9. Get legal advice.

The first of these additions is protective of client, victim, and therapist; the second is primarily for your own benefit. Your own safety and protection are important and appropriate considerations.

The Tarasoff case not only illustrates the ambiguity of the law in dealing with cases where the rights of the client may conflict with the rights of other individuals, but also introduces the question of involuntary commitment. It is your absolute obligation as a professional care provider to know the laws regarding such commitment in the state in which you practice. Moreover, you must know the specific procedures for such commitment in your particular area. Whom do you call? What evidence do you need? What exactly will be done, how soon, and for how long? Many states have several kinds of involuntary restraint, from twenty-four-hour holds (usually for the purpose of psychiatric evaluation) to full commitment procedures. Know what they are; know what options are available.

Be aware that any such restraint necessarily involves violating your client's confidentiality. You can expect that the client will be angry with you; he may feel abandoned, betrayed, or even vindicated. ("See, you proved it; I knew you couldn't be trusted!") Should he continue in treatment, these will be issues which must be discussed; they will almost certainly take precedence over whatever else he has been dealing with.

Another area of confusion with regard to confidentiality has to do with minor clients, or clients who are otherwise considered legally incompetent. Again, the right of privileged communication varies from state to state, among professionals and among settings. A psychologist working for a school district, for example, may have different legal constraints than the same psychologist in private practice. Confidentiality is also dependent on the topic or issue; you may not be required to answer parents' questions about their daughter's pregnancy and subsequent abortion, for instance, but you might be absolutely required to answer questions about her use of marijuana or her school truancy.

The bottom line, of course, is that no one can compel you to talk if you are determined to keep silent. Would you go to jail rather than break what you consider to be an ethical or moral commitment to a client? Would you destroy records rather than allow them to be subpoenaed? The question may never arise for you, but it is one you should think about very clearly and carefully. Having thought through your own personal stance, your own values and commitment to them, at a time when you are not under pressure, will make it easier to make good decisions if and when a pressure situation does arise.

Most breaches of confidentiality do not occur in the drama of a court case or an involuntary commitment. They come in the offhand comment, the coffee break conversation, the seemingly innocuous passing on of an interesting therapeutic tidbit. "I have a client who...." "You'll never guess what a client told me today...." Therapists should make it a rule never to engage in this kind of chitchat, tempting as it may be. They should be equally careful never to discuss a client in the presence of another client, a colleague, a family member, a friend, or anyone else (Siegel 1979, p. 256).

One final word about confidentiality: do not promise it to a client unless you are sure you can follow through. Do not tell a client that you will never reveal what is said in a therapy hour; tell him that there may be circumstances under which you would have to break confidentiality and what those circumstances might be. Make sure that members of a therapy group agree to respect confidentiality, but make equally sure that each member understands that such an agreement, while it may be morally binding, has no legal status. Never offer to your client more than you are prepared to deliver; in the great majority of cases, he will respect your honesty, and the therapeutic relationship will be strengthened rather than weakened by your candor.

Extra-Therapeutic Relationships

"Deep down in his mind, no patient wants a nonprofessional relationship with his therapist, regardless of the fact that he may express himself to the contrary" (Fromm-Reichmann, p. 46). Clients will often ask for or maneuver to set up contacts with the therapist outside the therapeutic setting. Experts are divided as to the advisability of such contact; some see it as harmless or even beneficial, while others believe that it can interfere seriously with the course of treatment.

There is no question but that multiple relationships with a client do complicate the therapy situation. They are difficult to manage well and can easily get out of hand. It seems sensible, then, to avoid such relationships if possible, unless there is some very compelling reason for behaving otherwise. This rule is particularly valid for relative beginners, who may not yet be aware of all the tangles into which multiple roles can lead.

What is true for relationships during therapy is also true immediately following therapy. We have discussed this issue at some length in Chapter 6, so it need only be mentioned briefly here: the therapeutic relationship does not automatically end at official termination; the emotional attitudes of both client and therapist toward each other may linger for months or even years. There is no way that friendship with a former client can fail to be affected by the client-therapist relationship, any more than therapy with a friend as client can be immune from the attitudes and attachments of the friendship.

In summary: no matter what the issue, the ethical professional has three sets of guidelines. She must first know the law; she must secondly know the ethical standards adopted by her profession; she must finally know her own moral values and beliefs. She must be guided by all three in the practice of her profession. If they collide, she should certainly seek advice and consultation; ultimately, though, her own conscience must be her final resource. If I am to respect myself as a therapist, I must do what I know to be right. I must think, study, listen and then make my own decision.

THERAPIST SELF-CARE

Therapists are people, not machines. It may seem silly for me to emphasize that we need to take care of our physical and emotional needs. After all, anybody knows that. However, therapists, like physicians, tend to be notorious for neglecting to care for themselves. We often treat ourselves much worse than we would allow our clients to treat themselves. We neglect our bodies, and ride roughshod over our feelings. We can take it; we can be strong. Later, when there is time and we are not so busy, then we will take care of ourselves. How foolish! Cooks and carpenters know enough to keep their working tools well oiled and sharpened; surely we mental health workers should have the sense to do the same.

Physical Well-Being

A good therapist, who intends to continue to be effective in her work, must keep herself in good physical and emotional health, seeing to it that her life provides her with adequate satisfaction, making sure that her personal and social needs are being met outside her therapy office. Obviously, if your physical energies are depleted, you will have less to offer to your client. The task of the therapist is difficult and requires a great deal of energy and concentration. Although most of us recognize the mental/emotional effort needed to do good therapeutic work, it is easy to overlook the physical demands. After all, the therapist just sits and talks, doesn't she? No, she does not. The kind of focused concentration demanded of a therapist creates a physical energy drain as well as a mental one. Colby says it well: "To remain serene in the face of transference aggressions and to treat patients with a gentle benevolence requires that the therapist himself be in good physical and emotional condition. If you have a pain or feel sleepy or 'hung over,' then you should not see patients until your malaise has cleared....Like an athlete, the psychotherapist has to keep himself in an efficient working state" (1951, p. 24). The wise therapist is careful to get enough rest, to maintain a healthful diet, to exercise regularly, and to see his doctor and dentist for regular checkups as well as when anything goes wrong (1951, p. 24).

Taking good physical care of yourself also involves taking reasonable precautions to protect yourself physically. There is nothing noble about exposing yourself to unnecessary danger from a potentially violent client. Clients can and do become violent with therapists, although perhaps not as often as we fear. A recent survey of 453 therapists showed that while 60 percent feared being attacked, only 14 percent had actually been assaulted by a client (Bernstein 1981). Fourteen percent, though, is a lot; approximately one in seven of us, according to these data, can expect violence at the hands of a client.

The best defense against violence is preparedness: knowing your own limits, letting your client know that violence is unacceptable, and knowing what you would do to take care of yourself should it occur. "In the case of threatening or real violence in action, the psychiatrist is justified and required to firmly express his unwillingness to be its target. He should also see to it that adequate precautionary measures are taken" (Fromm-Reichmann 1950, p. 26). Some standard and common-sense precautions include: making sure that help is available, if needed, when meeting with a potentially violent client; refusing to give clients your home address or phone number; refusing to allow clients to bring weapons into the session; refusing to see a client who is under the influence of drugs or alcohol. Failing to take such elementary precautions is not only a discount of your own right to safety, but it also fails to provide the client with adequate protection from his destructive impulses.

Emotional Well-Being

Kovaks notes that Freud listed three essential elements of the good life: "to love fully and passionately, to work creatively at something which brought a fullness of purpose and joy, and to be able to play as children do." He then goes on to ask, "How many of us are able to do that? How many persons do we know who can? Shame, shame on us for settling for less" (1976, p. 325). It is all too easy for therapists to become so caught up in our work that we cannot really leave it, cannot love or play or work fully at anything else. That is sad for us and for our clients. Of course, we should enjoy our work, should take pleasure in doing it well; but it must not be our only or even our primary source of gratification. If the therapist comes to depend on her clients for emotional support and satisfaction, she will soon be taking from them rather than giving to them. The best way to avoid this state of affairs is to find and experience plenty of emotional closeness in our personal lives, to have interests and hobbies beyond our work as therapists, to care about people and things other than our clients.

Even if a therapist does a good job of balancing her interests and attachments, she will still find herself experiencing a great deal of emotional stress at times. Dealing with client issues, being a frequent spectator to and a participant in emotionally charged interactions will inevitably bring to the fore whatever unresolved problems the therapist herself has. Therapists do not have to be better or more stable than the average person, but they should certainly be more aware of their own issues. If I am not aware of my psychological games, I will inevitably play them out with my client with unfortunate consequences for us both. My issues are likely to be stirred up in my interactions with clients; his problems remind me of my own. Rollo May has commented on this phenomenon: "To speak frankly," he says, "I have never dealt with a counselee in whose difficulty I did not see myself, at least potentially. Every counselor, at least theoretically, will have this same experience" (1934, p. 39).

I know of only one way to deal with this problem, and that is to see to it that my own therapeutic needs are attended to. I believe that all therapists need to have experienced therapy as a client, not only to "know how it feels," but also because we simply cannot deal effectively with a client's problems until we have resolved or at least recognized our own. I also think that therapists need to return to therapy more than once during their career. It is more than preventive mental health for us; it is a matter of making sure that our tools are sharp, our vision clear. As a therapist, I offer myself to my client as an instrument for change. I am professionally obligated to maintain that self in as clear, uncluttered, and effective a state as possible.

Special Concerns

There are a number of situations that can create particular emotional strain for the therapist, things that arise so frequently that they need specific mention here. One of the foremost is lack of confidence. We fear that we will be mistaken or inadequate, that the client will not find us helpful, that we will say the wrong thing or at least fail to say the right thing. Wachtel's comment, which I quoted at the beginning of this chapter, bears repeating here: "Psychotherapy is no profession for the individual who likes certainty, predictability, or a fairly constant sense that one knows what one is doing. There are few professions in which feeling stupid or stymied is as likely to be a part of one's ordinary professional day."

There really is no way that we can avoid making mistakes; even when we have not been mistaken, we will often believe we were. "Thus conscience doth make cowards of us all," as Hamlet said. In our own anxiety and our need to conceal that anxiety from our clients, we close down and cover up, withholding what is often most needed. The therapist's anxiety makes the likelihood of error even greater; we protect ourselves and, in so doing, pull back from making good therapeutic contact with our clients. The last act in this sad little antitherapeutic drama comes when the client must switch roles and reassure the therapist, thus changing from care-receiver to care-giver, which is most assuredly not why he came for treatment. Again, either personal therapy or collegial consultation is the best way to deal with the problem of therapist anxiety. Talking it out with someone who has herself been there, discovering that you are not alone, and working on your underlying issues, will help you to meet your own needs outside of the session with your client.

Another common therapist pitfall is counter-transference: experiencing feelings toward the client that are more appropriately directed toward someone else in your past or present life. Counter-transference is not always a problem. It becomes a problem only when the therapist is not aware of it or when she begins acting on it. There will always be some counter-transference; the trick is to recognize it when it arises. Chessick gives a list of twenty therapist reactions or behaviors that can serve as warnings that unacknowledged counter-transference may be operating:

1. Inability to understand certain kinds of material that touch on the therapist's personal problems.
2. Depressed or uneasy feelings during or after sessions with certain patients.
3. Carelessness in regard to arrangements—forgetting the patient's appointment, being late for it, letting the patient's hours run overtime for no special reason.
4. Persistent drowsiness of the therapist during the session.
5. Over- or underassiduousness in financial arrangements with the patient.
6. Repeatedly experiencing erotic or affectionate feelings toward a patient.
7. Permitting or encouraging acting-out or acting-in.
8. Trying to impress the patient or colleagues with the importance of the therapist.
9. Cultivating the patient's dependency, praise, or affection.
10. Sadistic or unnecessary sharpness toward the patient in speech or behavior, or the reverse.
11. Feeling the patient must get well for the sake of the therapist's reputation and prestige.
12. Being too afraid of losing the patient.
13. Arguing with the patient, or becoming too disturbed by the patient's reproaches or arguments.
14. Finding oneself unable to gauge the point of optimum anxiety level for smooth operation of the therapeutic process.
15. Trying to help the patient in matters outside the sessions, such as in making financial arrangements or housing.
16. A compulsive tendency to "hammer away" at certain points.
17. Recurrent impulses to ask favors of the patient.
18. Sudden increase or decrease of interest in a certain case.
19. Dreaming about the patient.
20. Preoccupation with the patient or his problems during leisure time.

Attending these danger signals allows the therapist to "maintain neutrality," as Furrow (1980) puts it, by guarding against the possibility of unaware transference reactions to her clients. Knowing what I feel, and why I feel it, is the first and best deterrent of improper behavior.

A third kind of stressful situation occurs when one's client begins to act out in a potentially dangerous or damaging way. Even after having taken all of the legally required steps, doing everything we can think of to safeguard the client (and/or others), we are still prone to feel anxious and responsible for his behavior. Consultation helps, both emotionally and practically. Consultants are often able, because of their greater objectivity, to come up with options that the primary therapist has overlooked. But, as Schutz points out, "no amount of group collaboration can completely remove the therapist from his lonely position on the firing line when a client threatens suicide or some other form of destructive behavior. He simply has to learn to 'sweat it out,' recognizing that he may be impotent to effect any beneficial change" (1982, p. 47). Perhaps the best advice for the private practitioner, who is likely to feel even more isolated than her agency counterpart, is to limit the number of such crisis clients one takes on. At any one time, do not be treating more than two suicidal or violent or otherwise unusually needy clients. Two is enough; a therapist can handle only a finite amount of that kind of ongoing demand and drain.

In one sense, the therapist is in an emotional no-win situation. On the one hand, she must attempt to understand the client's world and experience from that client's point of view; she must enter into that subjective world in order to help the client to change it. On the other hand, she must maintain enough emotional detachment to keep herself healthy and in balance. Taking on the client's problems, becoming infected by his feelings and issues, is another pitfall for the unwary therapist. Hatton et al. talks of this danger in working with suicidal clients: " 'I've felt this miserable in the past,' reflects the care-giver. 'Was I suicidal? I feel terrible right now, myself. Will I become suicidal? Would I be able to cope with a similar situation?' " (1977, p. 35). Too much empathy becomes confluence, in which the therapist is no longer able to differentiate between her own feelings and those of the client. Again, there is no substitute for working with a professional colleague, becoming a client yourself, and sorting out your feelings. The alternative is ineffectiveness and therapeutic error, as well as needless personal discomfort.

Of course, no amount of personal work can make you immune to error. You will make mistakes, and sometimes your clients will suffer for them. Mistakes come with the territory. They cannot be avoided, but they can be recognized. The real mistake lies not in committing an error, but in failing to learn from it. Every mistake can be the signal for a new step toward therapeutic competence, if it is recognized, analyzed, and used for growth. Do not be complacent about your mistakes. They are not good, and nobody likes to make them. However, do not magnify them out of proportion, either. Like rocks in a stream, they can be used to trip and fall over or as a bridge to a new and better place.

Growth and Development

Most of what I shall say in this last section is a repeat and reemphasis of what I have said earlier. It revolves about a single theme: your competence as a therapist cannot exceed your competence as a human being. "I do not consider it possible to treat the therapeutic process as a purely technical one," says Strupp. "Unless these technical operations are undergirded by something else—call it love for one's work or whatever—therapy must remain a sterile, lifeless ritual" (1977, p. 87). If you are an enthusiastic, growing, open person, you may be an enthusiastic, growing, open therapist. If you lose your personal awareness, your zest for life, your curiosity, you will lose those qualities as a therapist as well.

I have already made my position clear regarding the need for therapists to tend to their own personal therapeutic needs. I shall content myself here with one last excerpt from Fromm-Reichmann:

> In order to be 'fully present' for the client, it is necessary to clear away the fears and preoccupations, the blind spots and the prejudices, with which beginning therapists, as well as more experienced ones, are heavily burdened. This cannot well be done by exhortation or by suppression or by purely cognitive learning. It can be done only through the light of increased self-awareness." (1950, p. 3)

Fromm-Reichman's logic speaks for itself.

Beyond personal therapy, the therapist stays alive and open through ongoing consultation, supervision, and education. We can never know everything; we will never know enough. There is always something around the corner—some new insight, some new way of listening to a client, some new theoretical perspective that will help us to work more effectively. Unless we are flexible and courageous enough to try new things—things we didn't learn in our training—our profession will never change or develop. And we will never grow as therapists. We have to be willing to try things that will seem strange, forced, even downright wrong, because new things seldom feel right the first time we do them. Like most other professionals, therapists and other mental health workers believe that ongoing education is an essential commitment. It is not only necessary, but it is fun! When it stops being fun, when you lose your capacity to be excited and intrigued by new ideas, then you are ready for a vacation from your clients; and they are in need of a vacation from you.

Above all, then, the professional therapist must be committed to growth: to personal and emotional growth, to professional growth, to constantly learning and experiencing and becoming. The only static thing about our profession is that we must never become static; the one thing we can expect is the unexpected. If you want a predictable, settle-down-and-be-comfortable job, do not become a therapist! At best, you will be run-of-the-mill and bored, and at worst you will make yourself and your clients miserable. Singer says:

> The question then is never how many or how much of life's problems the therapist has solved already but much more how much he continuously strives toward increased understanding and subtle solutions of issues in his life, how much he cherishes his own struggle for freedom and active involvement; or conversely, how much he has given up this effort, how defeated and resigned he is, how much he despairs about his own life and rejects the value of growth. (1965, p. 118)

The choice is clear: grow or give up, learn or decay, expand or stagnate. No other profession that I know of offers quite the same challenge. We know little that is certain, and we risk much that is unknown. We share the highest peaks and the lowest ebbs of our fellow-humans' existences. We climb, stumble, fall, and climb again. We get tired and have to rest; but we cannot stay away for long. The excitement of discovery, of exploring the ever-intricate patterns of human experience, calls us back. To you who would join this band or would renew your membership—welcome! May we support each other on our journeying, sharing the excitement and bearing the burdens together.

REFERENCES

ABLES, B. S. *Therapy for Couples*. San Francisco: Jossey-Bass, 1977.

ACKERMAN, E. H. *Short History of Psychiatry*. New York: Hafner, 1968.

American Psychological Association. "Ethical Principles of Psychologists." *Directory of the American Psychological Association*, pp. xxx–xxxiv. Washington, D.C.: American Psychological Association, 1981.

American Psychological Association. "Standard for Providers of Psychological Services." *Directory of the American Psychological Association*, pp. xxxv–xlii. Washington, D.C.: American Psychological Association, 1981.

ANASTASI, A. *Psychological Testing* (5th ed.), New York: Macmillan, 1982.

ARD, B. N. "Introduction." *Counseling and Psychotherapy: Classics on Theories and Issues*. In B. Ard (ed.), Palo Alto: Science & Behavior Books, 1975.

BALSAM, A. & BALSAM, R. *Becoming a Psychotherapist*. Boston: Little, Brown, 1974.

BANDLER, R. & GRINDER, J. *The Structure of Magic* (vol. 1). Palo Alto: Science & Behavior Books, 1975.

BERGIN, A. E. & LAMBERT, M. J. "The Evaluation of Therapeutic Outcomes." In A. E. Bergin & S. L. Garfield (eds.), *Handbook of Psychotherapy and Behavior Change* (2nd ed.). New York: John, Wiley, 1978.

BERNE, E. *Games People Play*. New York: Grove Press, 1964.

BERNE, E. *Principles of Group Treatment*. New York: Oxford University Press, 1966.

BERNSTEIN, H. A. "Survey of Threats and Assaults Directed Towards Psychotherapists." *American Journal of Psychotherapy*, vol. 35 (1981), pp. 542–549.

BERZON, B.; PIOUS, C.; & FARSON, R. "The Therapeutic Event in Group Psychotherapy: A Study of Subjective Reports by Group Members." *Journal of Individual Psychology*, vol. 19 (1963), pp. 204–212.

BIXLER, R. H. & BIXLER, V. "Clinical Counseling in Vocational Guidance." *Journal of Clinical Psychology*, vol. 1 (1945), pp. 145–155.

BLOCK, S., REIBSTEIN, J., & CROUCH, E. "A Method for the Study of Therapeutic Factors in Group Psychotherapy." *British Journal of Psychiatry*, vol. 134 (1979), pp. 257–263.

BORDIN, E. S. *Psychological Counseling* (2nd ed.). New York: Appleton-Century-Crofts, 1968.

BRAMMER, L. *The Helping Relationship: Process and Skills*. Englewood Cliffs, N.J.: Prentice-Hall, 1973.

BRAMMER, L. & SHOSTRUN, E. *Therapeutic Psychology*. Englewood Cliffs, N.J.: Prentice-Hall, 1968.

BRUCH, H. "Teaching and Learning of Psychotherapy." *Canadian Journal of Psychiatry*, vol. 26 (1981), pp. 86–92.

BUGENTAL, J. F. T. *The Art of the Psychotherapist*. New York: Norton, 1987.

BUROS, O. K. *Mental Measurements Yearbooks* (8 volumes). Lincoln: University of Nebraska Press, 1938–1978.

BUTCHER & MAUDAL. "Crisis Intervention." In *Clinical Methods in Psychology*. New York: John Wiley, 1976.

CAPLAN, G. *An Approach to Community Mental Health*. New York: Grune & Stratton, 1961.

CARKHUFF, R. R. *Helping and Human Relations*, vol. 1. "Selection and Training." New York: Holt, Rinehart & Winston, 1969.

CARKHUFF, R. R. & BERENSON, B. G. *Beyond Counseling and Therapy*. (2nd ed.). New York: Holt, Rinehart & Winston, 1977.

CASSIUS, J. & KOONCE, J. "Divorce as a Final Option in Family Psychotherapy." In R. Hardy & J. Cull (eds.), *Techniques and Approaches in Marital and Family Counseling*. Springfield, Ill.: Charles C. Thomas, 1974.

CATTELL, R. B.; EBER, H. W.; & TATSUOKA, M. M. *Handbook for the Sixteen Personality Factor Questionnaire*. Champaigne, Ill.: Institute for Personality and Ability Testing, 1970.

CHESSICK, R. D. *How Psychotherapy Heals*. New York: Science House, 1969.

COHEN, L. H.; CLAIBORN, W. L.; & SPECTER, G. A. *Crisis Intervention* (2nd ed.). New York: Human Sciences Press, 1983.

COLBY, K. *A Primer for Psychotherapists*. New York: Roland Press, 1951.

COREY, G. *Theory and Practice of Counseling and Psychotherapy* (3rd ed.). Belmont, Calif.: Brooks/Cole, 1986.

CORNIER, L. S. & HACKNEY, H. *The Professional Counselor*. Englewood Cliffs, N.J.: Prentice-Hall, 1987.

CORSINI, R. J. *Current Psychotherapies*. Itasca, Ill.: F. E. Peacock, 1979.

CORSINI, R. J. & ROSENBERG, B. "Mechanisms of Group Psychotherapy: Processes and Dynamics." *Journal of Abnormal and Social Psychology*, vol. 51 (1955), pp. 406–411.

CRITES, J. O. *Career Counseling*. New York: McGraw-Hill, 1981.

DAHLSTROM, W. G., WELSH, G. S., & DAHLSTROM, L. E. *An MMPI Handbook* (vols. 1 & 2). Minneapolis: University of Minnesota Press, 1972, 1975.

DESHAZER, S. *Brief Therapy: Two's Company*. New York: Norton, 1974.

DINKMEYER, D. C., & MURO, J. J. *Group Counseling* (2nd ed.). Itasca, Ill.: F. E. Peacock, 1979.

DIXON, D. N. & GLOVER, J. A. *Counseling*. New York: John Wiley, 1984.

EDDY, J. P.; LAWSON, D. M.; & STILSON, D. C. *Crisis Intervention* (2nd ed.). New York: Lanham, 1983.

EGAN, G. *Face to Face*. Monterey, Calif.: Brooks/Cole, 1973.

EGAN, G. *The Skilled Helper*. Monterey, Calif.: Brooks/Cole, 1975.

ENRIGHT, J. B. "Introduction to Gestalt Techniques." In J. Fagan & I. Shepherd (eds.), *Life Techniques in Gestalt Therapy*. New York: Harper & Row, 1970, pp. 40–67.

EWING, C. P. *Crisis Intervention as Psychotherapy*. New York: Oxford University Press, 1978.

EYSENCK, H. J. "The Effects of Psychotherapy: An Evaluation." *Journal of Consulting Psychology*, vol. 16 (1952), pp. 319–324.

FAIRCHILD, T. N. "Suicide Intervention." In T. N. Fairchild (ed.), *Crisis Intervention Strategies for School-Based Helpers*. Springfield, Ill.: Charles C. Thomas, 1986.

FILSTEAD, W. J. "Despair and Its Relationship to Self-Destructive Behavior." In N. Farberow (ed.), *The Many Faces of Suicide*. New York: McGraw-Hill, 1980.

FISHER, L.; ANDERSON, A.; & JONES, J. "Types of Paradoxical Intervention and Indications/Contraindications for Use in Clinical Practice." *Family Process*, (1981), p. 33.

FRANK, J. "Therapeutic Factors in Psychotherapy." *American Journal of Psychotherapy*, vol. 25 (1971), pp. 350–361.

FRANK, J.; HOEHN-SARIC, R.; IMBER, S.; LIBERMAN, B.; & STONE, A. *Effective Ingredients of Successful Psychotherapy*. New York: Brunner/Mazel, 1978.

FREEMAN, D. R. *Marital Crisis and Short-Term Counseling*. New York: The Free Press, 1982.

FREUD, S. "Analysis Terminable and Interminable." In S. Freud, *Standard Edition*, vol. 23. London: The Hogarth Press, 1953.

FRIED, E. "Basic Concepts in Group Psychotherapy." In H. Kaplan & B. Sadock (eds.), *Comprehensive Group Psychotherapy*. Baltimore: Williams & Wilkins, 1971.

FROMM-REICHMANN, F. *Principles of Intensive Psychotherapy*. Chicago: University of Chicago Press, 1950.

FURROW, B. R. *Malpractice in Psychotherapy*. Lexington, Mass.: Lexington Books, 1980.

GARFIELD, S. L. "Psychotherapy: A 40-Year Appraisal." *American Psychologist*, vol. 36 (1981), pp. 174–183.

GAZDA, G. M. (ed.). *Innovations to Group Psychotherapy*. Springfield, Ill.: Charles C. Thomas, 1968.

GAZDA, G. M. "Some Tentative Guidelines for Ethical Practice by Group Work Practitioners." In G. Gazda (ed.), *Basic Approaches to Group Psychotherapy*. Springfield, Ill.: Charles C. Thomas, 1982.

GIBSON, R. L. & MITCHELL, M. H. *Introduction to Counseling and Guidance*. New York: Macmillan, 1986.

GILMORE, S. *The Counselor-in-Training*. Englewood Cliffs, N.J.: Prentice-Hall, 1973.

GOLAN, N. *Treatment in Crisis Situations*. New York: The Free Press, 1978.

GOLDFRIED, M. R. "Toward the Delineation of Therapeutic Change Principles." *American Psychologist,* vol. 35 (1980), pp. 991–999.

GOLDMAN, J. *Becoming a Psychotherapist*. Springfield, Ill.: Charles C. Thomas, 1976.

GOODSTEIN, L. D. "Behavioral Views of Counseling." In B. Stefflre & W. H. Grant (eds.), *Theories of Counseling*. New York: McGraw-Hill, 1972.

GOTTMAN, J. & LEIBLUM, S. *Psychotherapy and How to Evaluate It*. New York: Holt, Rinehart & Winston, 1974.

GOULDING, R. L. "The Formation and Beginning Process of Transactional Analysis Groups." In G. Gazda (ed.), *Basic Approaches to Group Psychotherapy*. Springfield, Ill.: Charles C. Thomas, 1982.

GRINDER, J. & BANDLER, R. *The Structure of Magic* (vol. II). Palo Alto: Science & Behavior Books, 1976.

Group for the Advancement of Psychiatry. *Interactive Fit*. New York: Brunner/Mazel, 1987.

GURMAN, A. S. "The Patient's Perception of the Therapeutic Relationship." In A. S. Gurman & A. M. Razin (eds.), *Effective Psychotherapy*. New York: Pergamon Press, 1977.

HALE, W. D. "Responsibility and Psychotherapy." *Psychotherapy: Theory, Research and Practice,* vol. 13 (1976), pp. 298–302.

HALEY, J. *Strategies of Psychotherapy*. New York: Grune & Stratton, 1963.

HALEY, J. & HOFFMAN, L. *Techniques of Family Therapy*. New York: Basic Books, 1967.

HALPERIN, D. A. "Psychodynamic Strategies with Outpatients." In L. D. Hankoff & B. Einsidler (eds.), *Suicide: Theory and Clinical Aspects*. Littleton, Mass.: PSG, 1979.

HAMACHEK, D. *Encounters with Others*. New York: Holt, Rinehart & Winston, 1982.

HARDY, R. & CULL, J. "Marital Counseling: Goals and Dimensions." In R. Hardy & J. Cull (eds.), *Techniques and Approaches in Marital and Family Counseling*. Springfield, Ill.: Charles C. Thomas, 1974.

HARE-MUSTIN, R.; MARECEK, J.; KAPLAN, A.; & LISS-LEVINSON, N. "Rights of Clients, Responsibilities of Therapists." *American Psychologist,* vol. 34 (1979), pp. 3–16.

HARKNESS, C. A. *Career Counseling*. Springfield, Ill.: Charles C. Thomas, 1976.

HATTON, C. L.; VALENTE, S. M.; & RINK, A. *Suicide: Assessment and Intervention*. Englewood Cliffs: N.J.: Prentice-Hall, 1977.

HEALY, C. C. *Career Development*. Boston: Allyn & Bacon, 1982.

HIEBERT, W. & GILLESPIE, J. "The Initial Interview." In R. Stahmann & W. Hiebert (eds.), *Klemer's Counseling in Marital and Sexual Problems* (2nd ed.). Baltimore: Williams & Wilkins, 1977.

HIEBERT, W. & STAHMANN, R. "Commonly Recurring Couple Interaction Patterns." In R. Stahmann & W. Hiebert (eds.), *Klemer's Counseling in Marital and Sexual Problems* (2nd ed.). Baltimore: Williams & Wilkins, 1977.

HOFFMAN, LYNN. *Foundations of Family Therapy*. New York: Basic Books, 1981.

HOLMES, T. H. & RAHE, R. H. "The Social Readjustment Rating Scale." *Journal of Psychosomatic Research,* vol. 11, (1967), pp. 213–218.

HOWARD, G. S.; NANCE, D. W.; & MYERS, P. *Adaptive Counseling and Therapy*. San Francisco: Jossey-Bass, 1987.

HUTCHINS, D. E. & COLE, C. G. *Helping Relationships and Strategies*. Belmont, Calif.: Brooks/Cole, 1986.

HYNAN, M. T. "On the Advantage of Assuming That the Techniques of Psychotherapy Are Ineffective." *Psychotherapy Theory, Research and Practice,* vol. 18 (1981), pp. 11–13.

IVEY, A. E.; IVEY, M. B. & SIMEK-DOWNING, L. *Counseling and Psychotherapy* (2nd ed.). Englewood Cliffs, N.J.: Prentice-Hall, 1987.

JACKSON, D. "The Study of the Family." *Family Process,* vol. 4 (1965), pp. 1–20.

JAMES, M. *Techniques in Transactional Analysis*. Reading, Mass.: Addison-Wesley, 1977.

JOHNSON, D. W. & MATROSS, R. "Interpersonal Influence in Psychotherapy: A Social Psychological View." In A. Gurman & A. Razin (eds.), *Effective Psychotherapy*. New York: Pergamon Press, 1977.

KAZRIN, A; DURAC, J; & AGTEROS, T. "Meta-Meta Analysis: A New Method for Evaluating Therapy Outcome." *Behavior Research and Therapy,* vol. 17 (1979), pp. 397–399.

KOPP, S. *Back to One*. Palo Alto: Science & Behavior Books, 1977.

KOVAKS, A. L. "The Emotional Hazards of Teaching Psychotherapy." *Psychotherapy: Theory, Research and Practice,* vol. 13 (1976), pp. 321–334.

KRUMBOLTZ, J. D. "Promoting Adaptive Behavior: Behavioral Approach." In J. Krumboltz (ed.), *Revolution in Counseling.* Boston: Houghton-Mifflin, 1966.

KRUMBOLTZ, J. & SHEPPARD, L. "Vocational Problem-Solving Experiences." In J. Krumboltz & C. Thoreson (eds.), *Behavioral Counseling.* New York: Holt, Rinehart & Winston, 1969.

L'ABATE, L. "Beyond Paradox: Issues of Control." *American Journal of Family Therapy,* vol. 14 (1984), pp. 12–20.

MADANES, C. *Behind the One-Way Mirror.* San Francisco: Jossey-Bass, 1984.

MADANES, C. *Strategic Family Therapy.* San Francisco: Jossey-Bass, 1981.

MARTIN, P. *A Marital Therapy Manual.* New York: Brunner/Mazel, 1976.

MASSEY, R. "Passivity, Paradox, and Change in Family Systems." *Transactional Analysis Journal,* vol. 13 (1983), pp. 33–41.

MAY, R. *The Art of Counseling.* Nashville: Cokesbury Press, 1934.

MEAD, M. *Male and Female: A Study of the Sexes in a Changing World.* New York: William Morrow, 1949.

MEICHENBAUM, D. H. "Cognitive Modification of Test-Anxious College Students." *Journal of Consulting Psychology,* vol. 39 (1972), pp. 370–380.

MELTZOFF, J. & KORNREICH, M. *Research in Psychotherapy.* New York: Atherton Press, 1970.

MINUCHIN, S. *Families and Family Therapy.* Cambridge, Mass.: Harvard University Press, 1974.

MISHARA, B. & PATTERSON, R. *Consumer's Guide to Mental Health.* New York: Signet Books, 1979.

NADELSON, C. "Marital Therapy from a Psychoanalytic Perspective." In T. Paolino & B. McCrady (eds.), *Marriage and Marital Therapy.* New York: Brunner/Mazel, 1978.

PAPP, P. *The Process of Change.* New York: Guilford Press, 1983.

PARLOFF, M. "Shopping for the Right Therapy." *Saturday Review* (Feb. 21, 1976), pp. 14-16

PASCAL, G. R. *The Practical Art of Diagnostic Interviewing.* Homewood, Ill.: Dow Jones-Irwin, 1983.

PILETROFESA, J. J. & SPLETE, H. *Career Development.* New York: Grune & Stratton, 1975.

PITTMAN, F. S. *Turning Points.* New York: Norton, 1987.

POLSTER, E. & POLSTER, M. *Gestalt Therapy Integrated.* New York: Brunner/Mazel, 1973.

POPE, K. S.; TABACHNICK, B. G.; & KEITH-SPIEGEL, P. "Ethics of Practice." *American Psychologist,* vol. 42 (1987), pp. 993–1006.

PROCHASKA, J. D. *Systems of Psychotherapy: A Transtheoretical Analysis.* Homewood Ill.: Dorsey Press, 1979.

RAELIN, J. "Building a Career: The Effect of Initial Job Experiences and Related Work Attitudes on Later Employment." Boston: W. E. Upton Institute for Employment Research, 1980.

RIOCH, M.; COULTER, W.; & WEINBERGER, D. *Dialogues for Therapists.* San Francisco: Dorsey Press 1979.

ROGERS, CARL. *Client-Centered Therapy.* Cambridge, Mass.: Houghton-Mifflin, 1951.

ROSENBAUM, C. P. & BEEBE, J. E. Psychiatric Treatment: Crisis, Clinic, Consultation. New York: McGraw-Hill, 1975.

ROTH, L. H. & MEISEL, A. "Dangerousness, Confidentiality and the Duty to Warn." *American Journal of Psychiatry,* vol. 134 (1977), pp. 508–511.

SAGER, C. *Marriage Contracts and Couple Therapy.* New York: Brunner/Mazel, 1976.

SALVIA, J. & YSSELDYKE, J. *Assessment in Special and Remedial Education* (2nd ed.). New York: Houghton-Mifflin, 1981.

SATIR, V. *Conjoint Family Therapy.* Palo Alto: Science & Behavior Books, 1964.

SATIR, V.; STACHOWIAK, J.; & TASCHMAN, H. *Helping Families in Change.* New York: Jason Aronson, 1975.

SCHNEIDMAN, E. S. "An Overview: Personality, Motivation and Behavior Theories." In L. D. Hankoff & B. Einsidler (eds.), *Suicide: Theory and Clinical Aspects.* Littleton, Mass.: PSG, 1979.

SCHUTZ, B. *Legal Liability in Psychotherapy.* San Francisco: Jossey-Bass, 1982.

SCHUTZ, W. *The Interpersonal Underworld.* Palo Alto: Science & Behavior Books, 1966.

SELIGMAN, L. *Diagnosis and Treatment Planning in Counseling.* New York: Human Sciences Press, 1986.

SELVINI-PALAZZOLI, M. "Comments on Some Irreverent Thoughts on Paradox." *Family Process,* vol. 20 (1981), pp. 44–45.

SELVINI-PALAZZOLI, M.; BOSCOLO, L.; CECCHIN, G.; & PRATA, G. *Paradox and Counterparadox.* New York: Jason Aronson, 1978.

SHOLEVAR, G. P. "Assessment of Marital Disorders." In D. Golberg (ed.), *Contemporary Marriage.* Homewood, Ill.: Dorsey Press, 1985, pp. 290–311.

SIEGEL, MAX. "Privacy, Ethics, and Confidentiality." *Professional Psychology,* vol. 10 (1979), pp. 249–258.

SINGER, E. *Key Concepts in Psychotherapy.* New York: Random House, 1965.

SLUZKI, C. "Marital Therapy from a Systems Theory Perspective." In T. Paolino & B. McCrady (eds.), *Marriage and Marital Therapy.* New York: Brunner/Mazel, 1978.

SMITH, M. L. & GLASS, G. V. "Meta-Analysis of Psychotherapy Outcome Studies." *American Psychologist,* vol. 32 (1977), pp. 752–760.

SMITH, M. L.; GLASS, G. V.; & MILLER, T. I. *The Benefits of Psychotherapy.* Baltimore: Johns Hopkins University Press, 1980.

STEIN, C. *Practical Family and Marriage Counseling.* Springfield, Ill.: Charles C. Thomas, 1969.

STEINER, C. *Scripts People Live.* New York: Bantam, 1974.

STEINZOR, B. *The Healing Partnership.* New York: Harper & Row, 1967.

STEWART, N.; WINBORN, B.; JOHNSON, R.; BURKS, H.; & ENGELKES, J. *Systemic Counseling.* Englewood Cliffs, N.J.: Prentice-Hall, 1978.

STILES, W. B. "Psychotherapy Recapitulates Ontogeny: The Epigenesis of Intensive Interpersonal Relationships." *Psychotherapy: Theory, Research and Practice,* vol. 16 (1979), pp. 391–404.

STOLLER, F. "Marathon Group Therapy." In G. Gazda (ed.), *Innovations to Group Psychotherapy.* Springfield, Ill.: Charles C. Thomas, 1968.

STRUPP, H. "A Reformation of the Dynamics of the Therapist's Contribution." In A. Gurman & A. Razin (eds.), *Effective Psychotherapy.* New York: Pergamon Press, 1977.

STRUPP, H. *Psychotherapy: Clinical, Research, and Theoretical Issues.* New York: Jason Aronson, 1973.

STRUPP, H. "Psychotherapy: Research, Practice, and Public Policy." *American Psychologist,* vol. 41 (1986), pp. 120–130.

STUART, R. *Helping Couples Change.* New York: Guilford Press, 1980.

SUPER, D. E. "Perspectives on the Meaning and Value of Work." In N. Gysbers et al. (eds.), *Designing Careers.* San Francisco: Jossey-Bass, 1984, pp. 27–53.

SUPER, D. E. *The Psychology of Careers.* New York: Harper & Row, 1957.

TATE, G. T. *Strategy of Therapy.* New York: Springer, 1967.

THORNE, F. C. "Principles of Directive Counseling and Psychotherapy." In B. Ard (ed.), *Counseling and Psychotherapy: Classics on Theories and Issues.* Palo Alto: Science & Behavior Books, 1975.

TRUAX, C. B. & CARKHUFF, R. R. "Client and Therapist Transparency in the Psychotherapeutic Encounter." *Journal of Counseling Psychology,* vol. 12 (1965), pp. 3–9.

TRUAX, C. B. & CARKHUFF, R. R. *Toward Effective Counseling and Psychotherapy.* Chicago: Aldine, 1967.

TURNER, N. W. & STRINE, S. "Separation and Divorce: Clinical Implications for Parents and Children." In D. Goldberg (ed.), *Contemporary Marriage.* Homewood, Ill.: Dorsey Press, 1985, pp. 484–500.

WACHTEL, P. *Resistance.* New York: Plenum Press, 1982.

WATZLAWICK, P. *The Language of Change.* New York: Basic Books, 1978.

WATZLAWICK, P.; WEAKLAND, J.; & FISCH, R. *Change.* New York: Norton, 1974.

WEEKS, G. R. & L'ABATE, L. *Paradoxical Psychotherapy.* New York: Brunner/Mazel, 1982.

WELLS, R. A. *Planned Short-Term Treatment.* New York: Free Press, 1982.

WEXLER, D. *Mental Health Law.* New York: Plenum Press, 1981.

WILLIAMS, J. M. & WEEKS, G. R. "Use of Paradoxical Techniques in a School Setting." *American Journal of Family Therapy,* vol. 12 (1984), pp. 47–51.

WILLIAMSON, D. "Extramarital Involvements in Couple Interaction." In R. Stahmann & W. Hiebert (eds.), *Klemer's Counseling in Marital and Sexual Problems* (2nd ed.). Baltimore: Williams & Wilkins, 1977.

WOLBERG, L. *The Technique of Psychotherapy.* New York: Grune & Stratton, 1954.

YALOM, I. *Existential Psychotherapy.* New York: Basic Books, 1980.

YALOM, I. *The Theory and Practice of Group Psychotherapy.* New York: Basic Books, 1970, 1975, 1985.

ZARO, J.; BARACH, R.; NEDELMAN, D.; & BRIEBLATT, I. *A Guide for Beginning Psychotherapists.* Cambridge, England: Cambridge University Press, 1977.

ZUNKER, V. G. *Career Counseling.* Monterey, Calif.: Brooks/Cole, 1981.

INDEX